Homelessness in the United States— Data and Issues

Homelessness in the United States— Data and Issues

EDITED BY
JAMSHID A. MOMENI

FOREWORD BY
GERALD R. GARRETT

INTRODUCTION BY
BARRETT A. LEE

PRAEGER

New York
Westport, Connecticut
London

Library of Congress Cataloging-in-Publication Data

Homelessness in the United States—data and issues / edited by Jamshid
A. Momeni ; foreword by Gerald R. Garrett ; foreword by Barrett Lee.
   p. cm.
  Also published as v. 2: Data and issues of Homelessness in the
United States by Greenwood Press.
  Includes bibliographical references.
  ISBN 0–275–93632–5 (alk. paper)
   1. Homelessness—United States. I. Momeni, Jamshid A., 1938–
HV4505.H657 1990
362.5′0973—dc20   90–6758

A hardcover edition entitled *Homelessness in the United States: Volume II: Data and Issues* is
available from Greenwood Press (Contributions in Sociology, no. 87; ISBN 0–313–26792–8).

Library of Congress Catalog Card Number: 90–6758
ISBN: 0–275–93632–5

First published in 1990

Praeger Publishers, One Madison Avenue, New York, NY   10010
An imprint of Greenwood Publishing Group, Inc.

Printed in the United States of America

The paper used in this book complies with the
Permanent Paper Standard issued by the National
Information Standards Organization (Z39.48–1984).

10 9 8 7 6 5 4 3 2 1

To My Son Arash

Contents

Figure and Tables

Foreword

Volume I of *Homelessness in the United States* provides an unrivaled, in-depth picture of homelessness in America. No other book or study has taken such a methodical, state-by-state approach to examining contemporary homelessness. Taken collectively, these studies demonstrate that homelessness is a problem of national scope. They also help to answer basic, empirical questions for service providers and policymakers about the prevalence and extent, as well as the social and demographic characteristics, of homeless people.

In Volume II, Momeni assembles a collection of chapters focusing on specific issues about homelessness that go beyond the essentially descriptive groundwork and conceptual frameworks provided in Volume I. Rich with insights into different dimensions of homelessness, each of these chapters carries important implications for social action and policy reforms. For example, one of the hallmark features of the homeless population is an inordinately high rate of alcohol and drug addiction. In fact, recent studies suggest that as many as one-third to half of all homeless may suffer from alcohol and drug problems that make them a subpopulation with more complex, idiosyncratic service needs than other types of homeless. Similarly, since deinstitutionalization policies were implemented in the 1970s, the vast increase in the number of homeless with psychiatric disorders has dramatically changed the composition of homeless people. Yet, while it is important for researchers, practitioners, and policymakers to understand the nature and epidemiology of alcohol, drug, and psychiatric disorders among the homeless, it is also important to understand the social, political, and economic forces involved in developing policies and programs addressing these problems. In fact, one of the most appealing features of Momeni's organization of Volume II is that homelessness is understood not as a consequence of personal pathologies and failures of the homeless per se but as a constellation of socio-logical factors interacting simultaneously.

Similar to its companion Volume I, Volume II is not wedded to a single perspective on the nature and causes of homelessness. Instead, the themes of many of the chapters are eclectic and diverse. Among the most important of topics is the crisis in housing. However much personal and individual problems contribute to the genesis of homelessness, the United States' failure to develop and protect an affordable housing supply for low-income or impoverished people, including the homeless, is an integral aspect to understanding the causes of homelessness, not to mention developing viable solutions to the homeless prob-lem. Urban renewal of inner-city districts in the past two decades has brought about significant reductions in the supply of single-room occupancy hotels, which often served as a "bottom level" housing for many of today's homeless. These have not been replaced with suitable, low-income housing. Moreover, as some of the chapter authors in this book warn, shelters providing immediate, short-term housing offer no permanent solution to the housing problems faced by the homeless. Instead, shelters tend to institutionalize dependent, rather than inde-pendent, self-supporting life-styles. This lesson is an important one, especially for policymakers and program planners.

Finally, if there is a unifying message to the chapters in Volume II, it is that the complex nature of homelessness requires multiple approaches to its solution. Therapeutic recovery of the homeless with alcohol, drug, or psychiatric problems is short lived if there are no pathways to independent housing and self-support. "Give away" income programs, if possible at all, offer no long-term solutions to achieving stable, residential living for today's homeless. Job opportunities remain unobtainable goals unless new policies establish and adequately fund organized programs of retraining the homeless for occupations with incomes that make housing affordable. For many victims of homelessness, access to ongoing health care and support services will remain an enduring need; these services play a significant role in generating routes from homelessness and in sustaining independent living. In sum, *Homelessness in the United States* points to a con-clusion that in recent years has become a dominant theme in the politics of organizations and coalitions serving as advocates for the homeless: realistic solutions to the problem of homelessness rest not in establishing new and dramatic programs but in forging links between government and private agencies to create a systemwide responsiveness to the multiple needs of the homeless identified in these two volumes—housing, employment and income, family problems, edu-cation, substance abuse, psychiatric disorders, and health care.

—Gerald R. Garrett
College of Public and Community Service
University of Massachusetts, Boston

Preface

This is the second volume in the two-volume series, *Homelessness in the United States*. Volume I concentrates on the statewide distribution, variations, trends, and characteristics of the homeless population. The present volume, as its subtitle indicates, deals with the problem of data collection and specific causes and issues that relate to homelessness.

In Chapter 1, Appelbaum highlights the problems researchers will face in collecting data on homelessness. He discusses the difficulties in measuring the extent of homelessness accurately, and concludes that every effort to do so "is likely to produce an undercount." In Chapter 2, Burt and Cohen look at the socioeconomic and demographic correlates of homelessness based on interview data from a national sample of 1,704 homeless individuals using soup kitchens and shelters for the homeless in cities with a population of 100,000 or more. According to Burt and Cohen the solution to the problem requires devising a multifaceted approach yet to be designed by the policymakers. In Chapter 3, Cohen and Burt, employing the same set of interview data, examine the nutritional intake of the homeless population and conclude that hunger and lack of adequate nutritional intake is a major problem among homeless people. In Chapter 4, Milburn reviews research on drug abuse and homelessness. Many researchers, policymakers, and homeless individuals who have participated in the congressional hearings on homelessness have attested to the fact that the significant increase in the number of homeless people, especially homeless families, is primarily due to the decline in the government's commitment to public or low-cost housing for the poor. Hon. Charles E. Schumer, the congressman representing the 10th district in Brooklyn, N.Y., and the chairman of the Ad Hoc

Task Force on the Homeless and Housing, during a hearing held on December 20, 1988, stated that ''the problem of homelessness has grown in direct relationship to the decrease in the Federal commitment to housing, both nationally and in New York City.'' In Chapter 5, ''Homelessness as a Long-Term Housing Problem in America,'' Huttman documents the decline in the number of low-cost housing units and its relationship to increased homelessness in the United States. She suggests that since there are several distinctly different groups of homeless people with different housing needs and requirements (e.g., the elderly, families, mentally ill, etc.) ''the long term solutions are to provide housing of many types.''

The view that a significant number of homeless people are so as the result of mental illness and the deinstitutionalization of the mentally ill has been the subject of considerable discussion in all quarters concerned with the problem. And some researchers have disputed the myth of pervasive mental illness among the homeless population. In Chapter 6, Wilson and Kouzi, using the results from a Pittsburgh study, provide a social-psychiatric perspective on homelessness. Wiegand, in Chapter 7, deals with the question of day-to-day economic survival by the homeless. The plight of homelessness on children, and thus future adults, is examined in Chapter 8. A comparative analysis of homelessness and the methods of dealing with the problem in the United States, Canada, and Great Britain are provided in Chapter 9. In Chapter 10, Buss, the coauthor of *Responding to America's Homeless: Public Policy Alternatives,* (Praeger, 1986), briefly examines the proper course for public policy to deal with this social problem. In the last chapter, Momeni provides an overview of the problem.

With editing the present volume and its companion (Greenwood Press, 1989), the editor hopes to have provided readers with factual and empirical data as well as substantive discussions and analyses that help answer basic questions on homelessness and are useful to researchers, service providers, and policymakers.

—Jamshid A. Momeni

Acknowledgments

I wish to express my gratitude to Dr. James T. Sabin, executive vice-president of Greenwood Press/Praeger Publishers, who accepted the initial proposal for this two-volume project. The project's success will be due in part to Dr. Sabin's foresight and commitment. The trust placed in me acted as a major energizer for the completion of this work as scheduled. I must also thank the authors for their timely contributions and for their patience and cooperation in revising their manuscripts to meet the review and editorial requirements. Howard University's institutional support is appreciated.

Finally, I am greatly indebted to my wife, Dr. Mahvash Momeni, and my children, who provided most necessary moral support for this project.

Introduction

As I peruse the contents of the second volume of *Homelessness in the United States*, edited by Jamshid Momeni, another holiday season—and another surge of concern for America's homeless—is drawing to a close. Each November and December, with the onset of winter weather, service providers and advocacy groups direct our attention to the plight of those who are spending their time alone on the streets rather than in a warm house surrounded by family members and friends. In the spirit of the season, some of us rummage through our closets for clothing to donate, participate in our church's food drive, or help prepare a turkey dinner at the local rescue mission. Such gestures are reported by the media in glowing detail, and consciences are soothed for another year.

That this brief crescendo of public alarm over homelessness has become an annual event, as predictable a part of Christmas as exchanging gifts, attests to the ineffectual response to the problem in our society. One reason the problem remains unsolved is that opinions about homelessness outnumber empirically grounded facts by a wide margin, a situation this book and its predecessor (Volume I) seek to rectify. But more information alone will not do the trick. Several contributors to the present volume point out that most programs to aid the homeless have been piecemeal in design and sporadic in execution. They have also been concentrated disproportionately in the voluntary sector despite a desperate need for greater governmental involvement.

Until quite recently, when government has taken action, it has usually been at the state or municipal level where scarce resources are blamed for limiting what can be accomplished. In truth, ambivalent attitudes may have as much to do with government laxity on the issue as budgetary constraints do. Like their constituents, many public officials regard homelessness as a matter of personal choice or failure; hence, homeless people are believed to be undeserving of special assistance. Yet these same officials find it difficult not to pity the raggedly dressed "dumpster diver" or the young mother and her children huddled in a downtown doorway late at night. Indeed, in the context of an affluent society, the swelling ranks of citizens in such dire circumstances are rightfully viewed as a cause for national embarrassment.

The crucial point here is that homelessness makes us feel uncomfortable. Short of denying that a problem exists (the position favored by the federal government throughout a good portion of the 1980s), a common way of coping with our uneasiness is to define the homeless as "outsiders," to accentuate the differences between the deviant "them" and the normal "us." This strategy is employed in both academic and lay discussions that emphasize high rates of physical and mental illness, drug abuse, criminality, transience, and other stigmatizing traits among the homeless. Often based primarily on casual observations and hunches instead of evidence, extreme claims about the incidence of these characteristics have an unfortunate outcome: they lessen our sense of responsibility to do something about homelessness since those suffering from the condition are thought to have progressed so far beyond the bounds of normalcy that any "cure" seems unlikely to be effective or even wanted by the patient.

Perhaps the greatest service that Momeni and the scholars contributing to his two volumes have performed is to bring systematic data and analysis to bear on the presumed "outsider" status of the homeless. There are three important lessons to be learned from *Homelessness in the United States* in that regard. The first is that certain differences between homeless and settled persons have probably been exaggerated. In Volume I, for example, numerous chapters document the local origins and demographic diversity of urban homeless populations. Similarly, some of the chapters in Volume II suggest that drug use and mental illness—while obviously present in such populations—are less pervasive than popularly believed. Both demographically and behaviorally, then, homeless folk appear more like us than we may care to admit.

A second lesson concerns the everyday experiences of the homeless: getting enough to eat, finding and keeping a job, caring for one's children, obtaining adequate shelter, and so on. As Volume II underscores, it is in these relatively mundane realms of activity that the homeless depart most dramatically from the mainstream. The vast majority of Americans take the successful completion of such activities for granted, but to someone living on the street they constitute a set of problems that must be confronted anew each day in order to ensure survival. Given this daily struggle, the fact that any homeless people at all have managed to remain mentally and physically functional is truly remarkable.

The third lesson stresses the futility of current programs and policies designed to assist the homeless. According to the authors of Volume II, emergency responses like providing more shelter space or free meals—though well-intentioned—treat the symptoms of the problem to the neglect of its causes. As long as underlying nationwide trends in the economy, housing availability, mental health care, and welfare provision are ignored, homelessness can be expected to persist or intensify in severity. In the following pages, the authors offer a range of innovative proposals that address these structural roots.

Whether the proposals have any chance of receiving serious consideration from decisionmakers is unclear. Normally, some sort of endorsement must come from the disadvantaged target group itself, but the homeless are the ultimate "outsiders" politically. With the prospects for indigenous mobilization slim, it is up to advocates to lead the way. Many of the contributors to volumes I and II are excellent role models, using the results from their research to push for new ways of reintegrating the homeless into society. Books such as *Homelessness in the United States* play an important part as well, keeping the issue at the forefront of public awareness. One can only hope that enough consciences are pricked by the efforts of Momeni and his collaborators to spark real progress in eliminating homelessness before many more holiday seasons pass.

—Barrett A. Lee
Vanderbilt University

Homelessness in the United States— Data and Issues

1

Counting the Homeless

Richard P. Appelbaum

Few issues concerning the homeless have stirred up so much contentious debate
as the seemingly simple question, "How many are there?" On its face, the
question seems reasonable enough; after all, how can policymakers adequately
deal with a problem if they lack some accurate idea of its extent?

Efforts to estimate accurately the number of homeless are likely to prove
counterproductive. I have no doubt that if national security depended on getting
an exact count we could do it, but I also think the vast amount of money required
would be better spent elsewhere.

To get a better understanding of why I think the problem of measurement is
so difficult, I would like briefly to review three major studies.[1] Each relies on
a vastly different yet plausible methodology. Each was, I believe, fundamentally
sympathetic to the plight of the homeless. Each concluded that there are vastly
fewer homeless than was previously thought. Each, in my view, had a fatally
flawed estimation procedure. The three studies are the HUD Report (U.S. HUD,
1984), completed in April 1984 and by now the subject of two congressional
hearings and at least one lawsuit; Harvard economist Richard Freeman's (1986)
study of New York City's homeless; and Professor Rossi and colleagues' study
of Chicago's homeless (Rossi, Fisher, and Willis, 1986).

THE HUD STUDY

The HUD study was the first and, to my knowledge, the only study to attempt
a truly systematic *national* survey of homelessness. Because of its official status
and national scope, its low estimates have been particularly troubling to homeless

advocates. For that reason I shall review its limitations in somewhat greater detail than I will the other two studies. As with the others, a major objective was to identify the special problems and characteristics of people in shelters and on the streets. But along the way HUD decided that it first had to come up with a national estimate of the *extent* of homelessness. That turns out to have been a very bad decision. HUD's estimate of 250,000–350,000 persons was considerably fewer than the figure previously used. HUD used three methods to arrive at this figure, all of which suffered from similar problems. I will briefly discuss one of these approaches to illustrate what I believe to have been the principal error.

The research was based on interviews in 60 metropolitan areas, selected to constitute a national sample of three different-sized strata of places.[2] The interviews were conducted with shelter operators and other homeless activists through a "snowball" technique, whereby HUD hoped to identify all the experts in a given area, combining their various estimates in a sort of weighted average. The 60 metropolitan areas were in fact Ranally Metropolitan Areas, or RMAs— extremely large units developed by Rand McNally (1983) for use in their annual commercial marketing atlas.[3] The RMAs include central cities and outlying suburbs; they cut across city, county, and in some cases even state boundaries. This approach landed HUD in a methodological swamp, for they had apparently gathered estimates on homelessness for selected *cities,* and then proceeded as if those estimates applied to the much larger RMAs.

I say *apparently* because it was not immediately evident from HUD's published report that they had in fact made this error; it just struck me as highly improbable that they could have adequately covered all 60 RMAs, including some that are truly enormous in size. For example:

• The New York City RMA includes some 74 cities in 24 counties across three states; it has a total 1980 population of 16.6 million people, of which New York City itself accounts for only 43 percent.

• Los Angeles, the second largest RMA, is even more dispersed than New York, with 10.6 million people living in 88 cities in five counties; the Los Angeles City population is less than 33 percent of the total.

• The Chicago RMA has 7.8 million people in three states, 10 counties, and 46 cities, of which Chicago itself has only 40 percent.

Table 1.1 summarizes the population characteristics for the 20 RMAs with a population greater than 1 million. These 20 RMAs alone have a combined 1980 census population of 78.3 million—over one-third (34.5 percent) of the total national population of 227.2 million. One out of every three Americans lives in these 20 RMAs. By design, the HUD sample includes *all* six RMAs with over 4 million people: New York (16.6 million), Los Angeles (10.6 million), Chicago (7.8 million), Philadelphia (5.2 million), San Francisco (4.7 million), and Detroit (4.4 million).

Table 1.1
County and City Populations as a Percentage of RMA Population

City (RMA)	RMA Population	County: Population	% RMA	City: Population	% RMA
Baltimore	1,883,100	655,615	34.8	786,775	41.8
Boston	3,738,800	650,142	17.4	562,994	15.1
Chicago	7,803,800	5,253,655	67.3	3,005,072	38.5
Cincinnati	1,476,600	873,224	59.1	385,457	26.1
Cleveland	2,218,300	1,498,400	67.5	573,822	25.9
Detroit	4,399,000	2,337,891	53.1	1,203,339	27.4
Hartford	1,055,700	601,079	56.9	136,392	12.9
Houston	2,689,200	2,409,547	89.6	1,595,138	59.3
Kansas City, Mo.	1,254,600	629,266	50.2	448,159	35.7
L.A./Riverside	10,555,500	7,477,503	70.8	3,328,184	31.5
Miami	2,689,100	1,625,781	60.5	346,865	12.9
Minn./St. Paul	1,978,000	1,401,195	70.8	641,181	32.4
New York	16,573,600	7,071,639	42.7	7,071,639	42.7
Philadelphia	5,153,900	1,688,210	32.8	1,688,210	32.8
Phoenix	1,483,500	1,509,262	101.7	789,704	53.2
Pittsburgh	2,155,100	1,450,085	67.3	423,938	19.7
Portland	1,220,100	562,640	46.1	366,383	30.0
San Francisco	4,665,500	678,974	14.6	678,974	14.6
Seattle	2,077,100	1,269,749	61.1	493,846	23.8
Washington	3,220,700	638,432	19.8	638,432	19.8
Totals	**78,291,200**	**40,282,289**	**51.5**	**25,164,504**	**32.1**

The table also lists the county and city population for the chief city associated with each RMA.[4] The RMA is substantially larger than these other political units. For all 20 places, for example, the total county population is 52 percent of the total RMA population; cities make up only 32 percent of the RMA population. For the six largest RMAs, the figures for county and city populations as a percentage of RMA population are as follows:

RMA	County	City
New York	43%	43%
Los Angeles	71%	32%
Chicago	67%	39%
Philadelphia	102%	53%
San Francisco	15%	15%
Detroit	53%	27%

It is obviously of great importance to know whether the person interviewed believed himself or herself to be providing homeless estimates for the entire RMA, the county, or only the city.

Table 1.2
Number of Jurisdictions in Each RMA

RMA	States	Counties	Cities > 2,500
Baltimore	1	4	11
Boston	2	5	41
Chicago	2	10	46
Cincinnati	2	8	5
Cleveland	1	8	17
Detroit	1	5	23
Hartford	1	4	10
Houston	1	2	4
Kansas City, Mo.	2	6	10
Los Angeles/Riverside	1	5	88
Miami	1	3	24
Minn./St. Paul	1	6	10
New York	3	24	74
Philadelphia	4	12	16
Phoenix	1	1	7
Pittsburgh	1	6	8
Portland	2	7	5
San Francisco	1	9	31
Seatle	1	6	11
Washington	3	10	14
Totals	**32**	**141**	**455**

Table 1.2 indicates the number of jurisdictions within each RMA, including states, counties, and cities of over 25,000. The 20 largest RMAs encompass 455 cities in 141 counties across 32 states. This represents an average of approximately 7 counties and 23 cities per RMA. The 6 largest RMAs cover 65 counties and 278 cities—an average of 11 and 46, respectively. These figures are intended to illustrate the extremely large size of the RMAs and thereby suggest the corresponding difficulties associated with estimating their homeless population through a relatively small number of interviews.

I twice testified before congressional hearings concerning the HUD study. The first time I stated my suspicion—that HUD had by and large obtained homeless estimates for central cities only, and made their national projection on the assumption that these figures applied to the entire RMA. The second time, however, my testimony was considerably bolstered by access to HUD's raw interview protocols, obtained under the Freedom of Information Act (FOIA). These enabled me to confirm my earlier suspicions. Here is how HUD conducted their analysis and projections, as evidenced by the unreported information provided me under the FOIA.

HUD claimed to have conducted telephone interviews with "knowledgable observers" in the 60 metropolitan areas. Over 500 interviews, averaging one-half hour, were reportedly conducted, including 8–12 calls for each of the 20 largest RMAs. These estimates were then combined into a weighted average for each metropolitan area with the weights reflecting the reliability of each estimate.[5] Since, as we have seen, the 20 largest RMAs average 23 cities each, with the largest averaging 46, it seems doubtful on the surface that HUD's coverage could have been adequate.

The HUD questionnaire begins with the question, "1. How serious a problem is homelessness in city?" Note that no reference is made to RMA, or even to metropolitan area: the jurisdiction named is intended to be the city (or occasionally the surrounding county). Question 1 makes no attempt to define *city*, an omission that creates several problems. First, it is clear that the interviewee was not responding in terms of the RMA, since the term "RMA" was never mentioned.[6] Second, since question 1 refers to *city* rather than to *metropolitan area*, it is doubtful that the interviewee had the latter in mind when responding. The response, therefore, necessarily refers to a much smaller population base than either RMA or metropolitan area—the city itself.

Table 1.3 summarizes the number of estimates obtained for the 20 largest RMAs. They are based on my count of the questionnaires obtained under the FOIA.[7] While HUD obtained 285 completed questionnaires, only 205 of these— fewer than three-quarters—actually provided point-in-time estimates. This is an average of about 10 per RMA. There is substantial variation in response rate, with Cleveland and Baltimore providing only 4 estimates each at one extreme, and Los Angeles providing 35 at the other. Only 6 RMAs actually provided 10 or more estimates, again raising the question of how HUD could have covered the entire RMA population with so few interviews.

Let me use Chicago and Boston as examples. Chicago—the nation's third-largest RMA—has a population of 7.8 million in three states (Illinois, Indiana, and Wisconsin), 10 counties, and some 46 cities. It extends from Kenosha, Wisconsin, to Gary, Indiana, and as far west as Elgin, Aurora, and Joliet, Illinois. HUD attempted to cover this metropolitan area with 15 interviews, of which 9 eventually provided estimates (Table 1.4). For the City of Chicago itself, there are five estimates, four of which stem from a single study; the fifth is regarded as "very soft."[8] The five estimates vary from 12,000 to 28,000. None of the Chicago estimates is a primary source. HUD also obtained two estimates for suburban Cook County, one ranging from 700 to 1,200, the other for 2,000; the lower estimate bears the notation, "off the top of my head." HUD sought to get estimates in McHenry, DuPage, and Kane counties, but was refused. One estimate was obtained for Joliet (Will County), and one for Lake County (Illinois). Surprisingly, *no* estimates were obtained for the Indiana portion of the RMA—which includes such cities as Hammond, Gary, Portage, East Chicago, Highland, and Merrillville—nor for the Wisconsin portion.

In sum, it would appear that the homeless estimates for the Chicago RMA are based almost entirely on the City of Chicago, which contains only 39 percent of the total RMA population. Furthermore, these city estimates are not inde-

Table 1.3
Interviews and Point-in-Time Estimates, by Ranally Metropolitan Area

RMA	Number of Interviews	Estimates Obtained
Baltimore	9	4
Boston	8	8
Chicago	13	9
Cincinnati	10	9
Cleveland	14	4
Detroit	9	9
Hartford	6	6
Houston	8	6
Kansas City, Mo.	9	6
Los Angeles/Riverside	46	35
Miami	10	9
Minneapolis/St. Paul	7	7
New York	35	17
Philadelphia	17	14
Phoenix	10	10
Pittsburgh	13	11
Portland	7	7
San Francisco	36	23
Seattle	9	8
Washington	9	5
Totals	**285**	**207**

Source: HUD FOIA summary data and actual survey count.

pendently derived, but rather are largely based on the same study. The city estimates are augmented by two for suburban Cook County, one for Lake County, and one for the City of Joliet. These sources cannot be regarded as providing reliable primary coverage for the entire RMA.

In Boston, HUD derived its estimate largely from a half-dozen different sources—all of which, in turn, got *their* estimates from the same place, an Emergency Shelter Commission census that found 2,800 homeless persons on the streets and in the shelters in October 1983 (City of Boston, Emergency Shelter Commission, 1983).[9] HUD then used this number as if it applied to the greater metropolitan area, which includes virtually the entire urbanized eastern

Table 1.4
Summary of Chicago RMA Interviews

City/County	Surveys	Estimates	Low	High
City of Chicago	6	5	12,000	28,000
Suburban Cook County	2	2	700	2,000
City of Joliet (Will County)	1	1	12	12
Lake County	1	1	100	100
McHenry County	1	0		
DuPage County	1	0		
Kane County	1	0		
Totals	**13**	**9**	**12,812**	**30,112**

Note: No estimates were sought from Indiana portion of the RMA.

seaboard—some 3.7 million people in 41 cities, five counties, and two states (Massachusetts and New Hampshire). HUD completely ignored the homeless outside of Boston, even though the city itself contains only 15 percent of the total RMA population.

HUD made the same error in most of the cities it surveyed: it interviewed a handful of people in each city who offered "guesstimates" of the number of homeless, and then applied those figures to the surrounding RMA. When you look over the protocols it is evident that the majority of respondents were talking about their immediate area: occasionally their city, often their neighborhood, but *never* the RMA. (Who has ever heard of an RMA anyway?)

In hopes of "hardening" these obviously soft data, HUD subcontracted to Westat—a highly respected survey research firm—to conduct a scientific sampling of shelter operators in the three-size strata of RMAs. Presumably the greater expertise of shelter operators would provide a cross check on the method just described. The Westat survey unfortunately did not provide reliable data, which is probably why the HUD Report itself does not summarize the Westat results by RMA—it simply indicates the total number of homeless estimated by Westat (353,000), providing HUD with its upper "reliable" bound. But HUD (under the FOIA) released to me a summary computer printout of the Westat RMA results that is extremely revealing.[10]

Table 1.5 and Table 1.6 summarize these results. Since HUD has not indicated how the separate estimates for each RMA are combined into a single figure (are they added? averaged?), I have simply reported the range of estimates in Table 1.5, and Westat's raw data in Table 1.6. Several conclusions can be drawn:

First, the response rate is *extremely* low. In all, 64 responses were obtained for the 20 RMAs—an average of only 3 for each RMA. Apart from New York, which had 11 responses, no RMA had more than 5. Six RMAs had only 2

Table 1.5
Westat Estimates compared with HUD Survey Estimates

RMA	No. Ints.	No. Ests.	WESTAT Range Low	WESTAT Range High	"Reliable" Range Low	"Reliable" Range High
Baltimore	3	2	10,500	20,000	630	750
Boston	4	2	3,000	5,000	3,100	3,300
Chicago	6	2	2,000	30,000	19,400	20,300
Cincinnati	3	3	1,000	5,000	800	950
Cleveland	2	2	500	600	400	420
Detroit	2	2	300	4,500	7,200	7,800
Hartford	2	1	250	250	600	1,800
Houston	6	4	200	9,000	5,200	7,500
Kansas City	4	2	40	500	340	400
L. A./Riverside	7	3	25,000	40,000	31,300	33,800
Miami	1	1	1,500	1,500	5,100	6,800
Minn./St. Paul	4	3	599	2,000	870	1,150
New York	15	11	998	40,000	28,000	30,000
Philadelphia	5	5	100	10,000	2,200	5,000
Phoenix	4	4	2,000	3,000	750	1,400
Pittsburgh	1	1	1,500	1,500	600	1,175
Portland	5	3	2,500	20,000	1,400	1,700
San Francisco	4	4	1,000	2,000	7,700	8,800
Seattle	6	4	1,500	10,000	3,100	3,250
Washington	7	5	2,000	10,000	3,000	6,400

Source: WESTAT computer summary, and HUD Report, table 2.

responses each, including Chicago, Boston, Baltimore, Cleveland, Detroit, and Kansas City. Three RMAs produced only a single response each—Pittsburgh, Miami, and Hartford. The Los Angeles estimate is based on only three estimates. There is simply no way that *any* useful RMA totals could be obtained with so few responses. It is inconceivable that a single shelter operator in Miami, for example, could provide an accurate figure for the entire Miami RMA, with its 2.7 million people in 24 cities, or that two shelter operators could do the same for Chicago, the second-largest metropolitan area in the United States.

Second, there is enormous variability among even the few estimates that were obtained for each RMA. The two Baltimore estimates are 10,500 and 20,000. The two Chicago estimates are 2,000 and 20,000. The three Los Angeles estimates are 25,000, 26,000, and 40,000. The list could be extended, but the point is that Westat could not possibly have combined such diverse estimates into a single reliable figure for each RMA.

Finally, the Westat figures for each RMA differ greatly from HUD's other

Table 1.6
Estimates of Homeless for 20 Metropolitan Areas: Westat Survey of Shelter Operators

New York.............		Houston.............		Kansas City.............	
	998		200		40
	6,000		500		500
	6,000		2,000		nr = 2
	10,000		9,000		
	15,000		nr = 2	Los Angeles.............	
	20,000	Miami.............			25,000
	20,000		1,500		26,000
	30,000		nr = 0		40,000
	36,000				nr = 4
	40,000	Baltimore.............		San Francisco.............	
	40,000		10,500		75
	nr = 4		20,000		1,000
Philadelphia.............			nr = 1		1,200
	100	Chicago.............			2,000
	2,700		2,000		nr = 0
	2,700		20,000	Seattle.............	
	2,700		nr = 4		1,500
	10,000	Detroit.............			2,000
	nr = 0		300		5,000
Boston.............			4,500		10,000
	3,000		nr = 0		nr = 2
	5,000			Phoenix.............	
	nr = 2	Cleveland.............			950
Pittsburgh.............			500		950
	1,500		600		2,000
	nr = 0		nr = 0		3,000
Hartford.............		Minneapolis.............			nr = 0
	250		599	Portland.............	
	nr = 1		1,300		2,500
Washington.............			2,000		4,500
	2,000		nr = 1		20,000
	2,500	Cincinnati.............			nr = 2
	3,000		1,000		
	4,500		1,800		
	20,000		5,000		
	nr = 2		nr = 0		

nr: Nonresponse.

Source: WESTAT computer summary.

estimates. For example, HUD's "reliable" range for Baltimore is 630–750 (HUD Report, Table 2); yet the Westat survey indicates 10,500–20,000. Significant discrepancies are also found for Cincinnati, Detroit, Hartford, Miami, Philadelphia, Phoenix, Portland, San Francisco, and Seattle.

I do not know if HUD's undercount was intentional—a part of a Reagan administration conspiracy to deemphasize the problem of homelessness, as others have argued. But I will say this: HUD's research is sloppy and poorly executed, producing hidden errors that HUD revealed only when forced to do so under the FOIA, and has subsequently never acknowledged.[11]

There is one other major flaw in the HUD study that bears mention because it is endemic to all studies of homelessness: the difficulty (if not impossibility) of defining "homelessness" in a way that does not do a disservice to those who lack shelter. HUD limits its definition to people sleeping on the streets or in emergency shelters. It explicitly excludes residents of halfway houses, congregate living facilities, long-term detoxification centers, single-room occupancy (SRO) hotels, and people forced to sleep temporarily in someone else's residence because they have no alternative. Even within HUD's restricted definition, it is obviously difficult to locate people who avoid authorities or who have lost their housing and wind up sleeping in cars, abandoned buildings, or on friends' sofas.

THE FREEMAN STUDY

Freeman used an altogether different approach from HUD—a survey of 516 homeless people in a single place, Manhattan, which was then projected to a national estimate of approximately a third of a million homeless.[12] I must admit that I was intrigued by the thought of projecting homelessness in a single city to a national figure, even if that city is New York. Here is how it was done.

Each homeless person surveyed on the streets or in a shelter was asked: "What percentage of last year did you spend on the street, in a shelter, or at home?" The response enabled Freeman to compute the chances that a person on the street tonight will wind up in a shelter tomorrow and to compare this with the chances that a person in a shelter tonight will remain there tomorrow. It is then supposed to be possible to calculate the number of homeless people on New York City's streets as a mathematical function of the number of people in its shelters—a number we can easily obtain. The calculation reveals that there are 3.23 homeless people in New York City for every person in a shelter.[13] This ratio is applied to HUD's previous estimate of the national number of people in shelters to derive the national homeless figure.

This approach appears to be mathematically sophisticated. Unfortunately, it also violates common sense. It makes as least three highly implausible assumptions.[14]

1. It assumes that the number of homeless is somehow determined by the number of shelter beds in the ratio of 3.23 to 1. According to this faulty logic, the most effective solution for homelessness is to do away with shelters altogether: no beds, no homeless people. In fact, of course, the number of beds reflects local funding and policy and unfortunately not the number of homeless.

2. New York City is not typical of the rest of the United States. It is under court order to provide shelter, and in fact has one of the most extensive shelter programs in the country. New York last year spent more money on emergency shelter than the entire national FEMA Program over the past three years combined. Even if it were true that one out of every three homeless persons in New York was sheltered, this would hardly be true of other places with less aggressive shelter programs. But I don't believe the ratio is true even for New York, and this is the third problem—one we saw also with the HUD study:

3. The study's sample does not adequately represent the homeless population of New York City, resulting in an underestimation of the homeless/shelter ratio even there. Freeman surveyed only the "visible" homeless—people in shelters, soup kitchens, and scruffy looking individuals on the street. But as I noted before, there are many homeless who are not visible, who shun the streets, the soup kitchens, and the shelters. Such "invisible homeless" simply don't figure into the estimates. Yet they may well constitute the majority of the homeless population.

THE ROSSI-FISHER-WILLIS STUDY

Rossi's study is the most systematic effort to date to conduct a sample census of the homeless in a single city. Using trained interviewers from the National Opinion Research Center (NORC), homeless people on the streets and in shelters of Chicago were surveyed on two occasions—fall 1985 and winter 1986. These surveys yielded an estimate of 2,000–3,000 homeless in Chicago—considerably lower than even HUD's conservative estimate of about 20,000.[15] I shall not concern myself with the shelter component of this study, since I believe the sampling of shelter residents to be relatively nonproblematic. But the street census is a different matter.

Using a sophisticated sampling methodology, the NORC interviewers—accompanied by off-duty Chicago police officers for protection—attempted an exhaustive census of every individual on sampled blocks between the hours of 1:00 A.M. and 6:00 A.M.[16] Every nook and cranny on the sampled blocks was searched out—hallways and doorways, alleys, cars, roofs, and open basements. When people were encountered, they were offered a dollar and asked a series of questions to determine if they were homeless. If so, they were offered an additional four dollars and asked to complete a detailed questionnaire.

In the fall survey, for example, 318 people were encountered, of whom about three-quarters were willing to talk to the interviewers; 23 of these admitted to being homeless. The winter survey produced 30 homeless, out of slightly fewer encounters.[17] The two separate surveys produced 23 and 30 self-identified homeless people, respectively—out of a total of some 600 people encountered on the streets in the early morning hours. It is this handful of homeless who provided the basis for the fall and winter projections of homelessness in Chicago.

To project to a citywide estimate, the researchers divided the number of self-identified homeless people they found by the number of blocks surveyed, producing an estimate of the average number of homeless people per block. This figure was then multiplied by the number of blocks in the city to come up with a citywide total.[18] According to this method, in the fall of 1985 there were 42 homeless people on the 300-odd blocks where Chicago's homeless are most likely to congregate, and 1,400 street people throughout the city. The following winter this total had dropped to only 500.

I believe there are two major flaws with this approach. First is the assumption that people interviewed were forthcoming in telling whether or not they were homeless. It should be recalled that only about 1 in 10 of those who were at all willing to talk admitted to being homeless. What were the other 9 doing on the street between 1:00 A.M. and 6:00 A.M.? Is it not possible that at least a few of them were also homeless but understandably reluctant to admit it to their early-morning interrogators? And what of the people who refused to be screened at all?[19] Isn't it likely that most if not all of these were homeless?

These questions are important, since when you are projecting from a base of only 20–30 people, another 20–30 who somehow escaped your net will double your total projection. When the number of respondents is miniscule both in absolute terms and relative to the sample size, *response bias* becomes a potentially serious issue. In this case, I believe it may have proven catastrophic to the study's projection. For example, if we assume that half of those who refused to be interviewed were homeless and that half of those who claimed they were *not* homeless were lying to the interviewers, then the fall projection nearly triples—from 2,300 to 6,300. If we assume that 90 percent of those encountered were in fact homeless, regardless of what they said or didn't say to the interviewers, then the total more than quadruples to 10,000.[20] The point is that given the miniscule number of people making up the baseline for the projection, it becomes essential to determine with exact precision the accuracy of the questionnaire's determination of homelessness. Tiny fluctuations in the number of self-identified homeless—either through avoiding the interviewers altogether, refusing to respond to the screening questions, or giving false answers—will produce enormous differences in the citywide total.

This raises the second problem with the study, by now familiar to us: the definition of homeless. The Chicago study's definition excluded people in rooming houses, SROs, jails, halfway houses, and detoxification centers. It did not survey people riding the buses and trains, an important haven for homeless people in Chicago, especially in the winter. It could not account for those who saw the interview team approaching and left the block. And it declined to define as homeless those who were temporarily sleeping in other people's homes.

CONCLUSION

I am not simply trying to nit-pick; after all, you can't do everything. But that is just the point. I believe that the problem of counting the homeless is, in a practical sense, intractable. Every effort is likely to produce an undercount, and every undercount fuels the Reagan administration's zeal for further slashing of funds.

I am not against gathering useful data for policy purposes. But if you must count, I have four brief suggestions I think are useful:

1. Be very careful to distinguish between *visible homeless* and *homeless*. The people who can be seen are, I believe, only the tip of the iceberg, and the results of counts should emphasize this fact. I would suspect that homeless families are especially likely to be undercounted, along with undocumented workers and others who for whatever reason shun people with clipboards.

2. *Never* make a national projection out of a local survey. I would not even mention this if one well-respected economist had not already tried it.

3. Do not spend a lot of money on highly sophisticated efforts to gain precise estimates, since—in my view—the marginal returns on such efforts do not warrant the expense. Use the money to build a shelter or fund a soup kitchen. Street counts with volunteers, such as the recent Boston study, produce numbers that are more than adequate for policy-making.

4. Take all results with a grain of salt: the stronger the claims of the study, the more grains of salt.

NOTES

1. This chapter draws on Appelbaum (1984, 1985, and 1986). A number of other studies have been done that attempted accurate local counts of homeless. These include censuses in Washington, D.C. (Robinson, 1984), Phoenix, Arizona (Brown et al., 1983), Nashville, Tennessee (Wiegand, 1985; Nashville Coalition for the Homeless, 1986), and Boston (City of Boston, Emergency Shelter Commission, 1983 and 1986).

2. The three strata are 50,000–250,000; 250,000–1,000,000; and over 1,000,000.

3. Rand McNally (1983) defines RMAs as including "(1) a central city or cities; (2) any adjacent continuously built-up areas; and (3) other communities not connected to the city by a continuously built-up area if the bulk of their population [8 percent of the population or 20 percent of the labor force] is supported by commuters to the central city and its adjacent built-up areas." Rand McNally has identified 394 RMAs in the United States.

4. The largest metropolitan division customarily used by the U.S. Census—the Standard Metropolitan Statistical Area (SMSA)—is also typically smaller than the RMA; for the 20 largest RMAs, the corresponding SMSA population is 62.7 million, or 80 percent of the RMA population.

5. HUD Report, pp. 4, 13. See Appendix table A–4 for the weights. HUD nowhere indicates how the weights were in fact applied to produce a single estimate.

6. In fact, of course, the acronym *RMA* would not have been meaningful to interviewees, and so could not have been used.

7. These figures differ slightly from those provided to me in summary materials prepared by HUD, which indicated that 206 point-in-time estimates were obtained from 276 completed surveys.

8. The study referred to is the Task Force on Emergency Shelter, Social Services Task Force of the Department of Human Services, "Homelessness in Chicago," October 1983.

9. The study excluded abandoned buildings, dumpsters, parking garages, MBTA bus and train yards, most parked cars, and dead-end alleys—as well as the Charlestown and West Roxbury areas. The commission told HUD interviewers that their own figure was a "gross underestimate," with 5,000–10,000 as a more accurate number; HUD chose to ignore this revised figure.

10. Partially shown in Table 1.6.

11. In this regard the HUD study differs from the other two studies reviewed below, which—following the customary canons of scholarly research—provide sufficiently detailed information for the reader to determine whether or not significant flaws are likely to exist. HUD, on the contrary, was not open concerning its methodology or probable sources of error.

12. Three hundred and eleven persons were interviewed in shelters and 205 on the streets. Freeman estimated 279,000 homeless in 1983 (when the survey was conducted), projected to 350,000 in 1985.

13. These estimates actually apply to single people only; individuals in families are estimated separately (see n. 14 following).

14. Another problem is with the assumption that the people interviewed were capable of giving a reliable response to the question in the first place ("What percentage of last year did you spend on the street, in a shelter, or at home?")—which required them mentally to compute the percentage of nights during the past year they had been in each location. Try it yourself. With samples this size the margin of error due to sampling alone is as great as 7 percent—for example, if the street people reported an average of 50 percent of their nights were spent in shelters, the actual figure could be anywhere between 43 percent and 57 percent. Finally, the estimate for homeless families is based on the faulty assumption that *all* homeless families are sheltered, and that therefore the number is never greater than the number of available beds for family members.

15. It should be noted that HUD's estimate is for the Chicago RMA, whereas Rossi's is for the city alone. As previously noted, Chicago contains 39 percent of the RMA population.

16. To construct their sample of blocks, the researchers divided Chicago's 19,409 blocks into three different strata based on the likelihood of homeless people being found (low, medium, and high density). 49 blocks each were sampled from the high- and medium-density strata, with 70 blocks sampled from the low-density strata in the fall survey and 147 sampled in the winter survey. Thus, a total of 168 blocks were sampled in the fall and 244 in the winter.

17. The exact figures were: for the fall survey, 318 people were encountered, of whom 232 granted screening interviews producing 23 self-identified homeless. For the winter survey, 289 people were encountered, of whom 238 granted screening interviews, producing 30 self-identified homeless.

18. These calculations were made separately for each of the three strata. The number

of self-identified homeless was adjusted slightly upwards for undercounting, under the assumption that the people who refused to talk at all were homeless in the same proportion as those who responded to the initial screening interview. Thus, for example, in the fall survey 5 homeless people were identified on the 49 sampled "high density" blocks, yielding a ratio of .102 homeless per block. When multiplied by the 295 high-density blocks in the city (and adjusted for those who refused to be screened), a figure of 42 homeless results.

19. There were 86 people in the fall survey who refused to be screened—over four times the number of self-identified homeless. In the winter survey 51 people refused to be screened, almost twice the number of self-identified homeless.

20. These figures are derived from a recomputation of Rossi et al.'s (1986) Table A–2, increasing the number of homeless for each strata by allocating first 50 and then 90 percent of all refusals and self-identified nonhomeless to the homeless category. Since under this model the correct identity of every individual on the street is assumed to be known, the remaining nonhomeless figure is no longer inflated by a multiplier.

Even within the study's reported data, there are tremendous fluctuations in the number of homeless encountered at different times and places. In medium-density blocks, for example, 15 homeless were encountered in the fall and none in the winter. In high-density blocks, the reverse was true: 5 were found in the fall and 28 in the winter.

REFERENCES

Appelbaum, Richard P. 1984. Analysis of HUD Report on Homelessness in America. *Congressional Record*. May 24, Banking Committee Serial No. 98–91 (oral and written testimony before congressional hearings).
———. 1985. Further Analysis of HUD Report on Homelessness in America. *Congressional Record*. December 4, Banking Committee Serial No. 99–56 (oral and written testimony before congressional hearings).
———. 1986. Comments on the Freeman Estimates of Homelessness. University of California at Santa Barbara, Sociology Department (unpublished xerox of statement given at press conference in Boston, September 5).
Boston, City of, Emergency Shelter Commission. 1983. The October Project: Seeing the Obvious Problem. Boston: ESC (October).
———. 1986. Census of Boston's Homeless. Boston: ESC (October).
Brown, Carl, Steve MacFarlane et al. 1983. *The Homeless of Phoenix: Who Are They and What Should Be Done?* Phoenix: South Community Mental Health Center (report prepared for the Consortium for the Homeless).
Freeman, Richard. 1986. *Permanent Homelessness in America?* Cambridge, Mass.: National Bureau of Economic Research.
Nashville Coalition for the Homeless. 1986. Coalition Enumeration Brings Questions. *Newsletter* 1: 3.
Rand McNally. 1983. *Commercial Atlas and Marketing Guide*. Chicago: Rand McNally.
Robinson, Frederic G. 1984. *Homeless People in the Nation's Capital*. Washington, D.C.: University of the District of Columbia, Center for Applied Research and Social Policy.
Rossi, Peter, Gene A. Fisher, and Georgianna Willis. 1986. *The Condition of the Homeless*

in Chicago. Amherst and Chicago: Social and Demographic Research Institute and NORC.

U.S. HUD. 1984. *Report to the Secretary on the Homeless and Emergency Shelters*. Washington, D.C.: U.S. Department of Housing and Urban Development.

Wiegand, R. Bruce. 1985. Counting the Homeless. *American Demographics* 7: 34–37.

2

A Sociodemographic Profile of the Service-Using Homeless: Findings from a National Survey

Martha R. Burt and Barbara E. Cohen

During the past decade, homeless people have become increasingly visible on the streets of many U.S. cities. Local studies of the homeless have mushroomed in the past few years, and Congress has only recently supported the first significant federal legislation directed toward homeless people (the Stewart B. McKinney Homeless Assistance Act of 1987). To develop appropriate policies to address the problems of the homeless and to prevent homelessness, information is needed about the characteristics of homeless individuals. Since many of the most important of these characteristics (such as the proportion that are families, or the proportion who have a major mental illness) vary substantially from locality to locality, local studies can only go so far in assisting policymakers to design appropriate programs at the national or state level. The data reported here partially fill this information gap, giving for the first time a national profile of the homeless.

This chapter presents basic descriptive data from a nationally representative sample of 1,704 homeless individuals and places these findings in the context of other studies that have obtained data from samples of homeless individuals.[1] The study was designed to yield detailed interview data on homeless individuals who use soup kitchens and shelters for the homeless in U.S. cities of 100,000 or more. A nationally representative sample of 20 cities was drawn in which 400 providers were randomly selected—representing soup kitchens, shelters without meals, and shelters with meals. Then, 1,800 homeless individuals were randomly selected from among the homeless using the services of the providers in the sample. Final sample sizes were 381 providers and 1,704 homeless service users. In addition, a nonrandom sample of 142 persons who had *not* used meal or shelter services during the week before the interview was identified by asking local providers and police in the 20 sample cities to help locate sites where homeless people congregated—parks, train or bus stations, certain street corners, culverts, or day shelters that did not offer meals—and then interviewing homeless persons at these sites. The interviews were conducted with homeless users and nonusers of shelter and meal services in March 1987.

This study is the only one based on nationally representative sample data to interview individual homeless persons, and the only study ever to collect detailed information from the homeless on their eating patterns.[2] Two limitations should be mentioned. Although nationally representative, the data do not apply to homeless individuals in cities under 100,000 population. And since the in-person interview data were collected during March 1987, they do not necessarily reflect the situation during other months in the year.

One of the difficulties in establishing exactly how many of the homeless share particular characteristics has been the local nature of existing studies. In addition to the inherent differences in the populations of different localities, local studies have drawn their samples from different universes—some going only to shelters, some going to streets and shelters, some including soup kitchens but not shelters, and so on. Since, as will be seen below, the characteristics of homeless people differ significantly from location to location, these inconsistencies make generalizations from local studies difficult.

Yet knowing with some confidence who the homeless are is important, since policies to help people out of homelessness or to prevent homelessness in the first place will depend to some extent on the personal characteristics, histories, and experiences of homeless people. This chapter presents important descriptive data from a national study and also compares the results on key variables to parallel data from 14 local studies that interviewed homeless individuals.

DEMOGRAPHIC PROFILE

The data presented below come from 1,704 homeless adults 18 and older. Throughout, the data have been weighted to be representative of all service-using homeless adults in the United States in cities of 100,000 or more. Individuals were located and interviewed in soup kitchens and in two types of shelters, those that served meals and those that did not (the former predominate). Initially, individuals were grouped by their pattern of service use to see whether homeless people who used particular types of services differed from those who used other services. Analysis of these data revealed that 29 percent of homeless service-users use only soup kitchens, 32 percent use only shelters, and 38 percent use both soup kitchens and shelters. Because virtually every characteristic of homeless people varied by their pattern of service use, data are presented showing this pattern.

Basic demographic information about the homeless is given in Table 2.1, which shows distributions for sex, race, and age for the homeless population by pattern of service use. The adult homeless population is predominantly male (81

Table 2.1
Sex, Race, and Age of Homeless Service Users (Weighted Percentages)

	Homeless Individuals Who:			
Characteristic	Use Only Soup Kitchens (N = 223)	Use Only Shelters (N = 670)	Use Both Shelters & Soup Kitchens (N = 811)	Total Sample (N = 1704)
Total	24	36	40	100
Sex				
Male	93	68	84	81
Female	7	32	16	19
Race				
Black	40	35	47	41
White*	43	51	43	46
Hispanic	13	12	7	10
Other	0	2	3	3
Age				
18 - 30	20	32	35	30
31 - 50	65	47	48	51
51 - 65	11	17	17	16
66+	4	3	0	3

N: Refers to unweighted data. All percentages are based on weighted data.
* White non-Hispanic.

percent in the total sample); the major deviation from this pattern occurs among those individuals who use only shelters. More than half of the service-using homeless adult population is nonwhite, with blacks making up 41 percent and Hispanics 10 percent. The skewness of the racial distribution of the homeless population can be seen by comparing it to that of the U.S. population as a whole and to the U.S. population in poverty. Blacks are 12 percent of the U.S. population as a whole, 13 percent of the U.S. population in Metropolitan Statistical Areas (MSAs), and 27 percent of the U.S. population in poverty;[3] their presence among the homeless is thus three to four times their presence in the entire United States and MSA populations and about one-third more than their presence in the poverty population. Hispanics constitute 7 percent of the entire U.S. population, 7 percent of the MSA population, and 16 percent of the U.S. population in poverty,[4] but 10 percent among homeless service-users. Their numbers among the homeless are thus slightly higher than their representation in the population as a whole and the MSA population but lower than their representation among persons in poverty.

The modal age category among homeless service-users is 31–50; the next most frequent category is 18–30. The deviation from this pattern occurs among those homeless who use only soup kitchens. These people are more likely to be middle aged (31 to 50 years old—65%) than are users of shelters only (47%) or homeless who use both soup kitchens and shelters (48%).

HOUSEHOLD COMPOSITION, MARITAL STATUS, EDUCATION, AND SOURCES OF INCOME

Table 2.2 presents household composition, marital status, and education information. The household composition for shelter-only users stands out. The proportion of single females among those who use only shelters was two to four times higher than for other service-use patterns, while the proportion of families (any household with children) is clearly much greater among those with this service-use pattern than among those who use only soup kitchens or who use both shelters and soup kitchens.

As data in Table 2.2 indicate, only 10 percent of service-using homeless households are families (defined as a multiperson household with at least one child present), whereas 83 percent are single-person households. This finding contrasts sharply with popular reports that as high as one-third of the homeless are families. The difference probably can be attributed to different ways of counting the homeless. Corroboration for the statistics presented here comes from the only other available study with national data on the homeless (Wright and Weber, 1987) derived from individuals who used special health services for the homeless in 19 American cities. Wright and Weber (1987) report data from which one can calculate that the percentage of homeless adults who have children with them is 9 percent.

A provider, looking at who occupies the available beds on any given night, makes an estimate that more than half of the homeless are families—because more than half of the shelter's beds are occupied by members of families, including children. However, family households are larger than single-person households, so a count of *households* will result in a lower proportion of families. It is also true that families tend to stay in shelters longer, so that any assessment based on a single night will overestimate the number of families. Our calculation uses a seven-day period and is based on households. The average number of children per family household was 2.2; 86 percent of the homeless family households in our data were headed by a single adult (of which 93 percent were single females).

Looking at the data from this study in the same way that a provider might, we can estimate the proportion of persons among the homeless, including children, who are attached to homeless families (those with at least one child) and who are attached to households with relatives or spouse but without children. If children are included in the total count, 23 percent of homeless persons are members of homeless families. Of these, two-thirds are children (15 percent of the 23 percent). An additional 4 percent of homeless persons are attached to

Table 2.2

Household Composition, Marital Status, and Education of the Service-Using Homeless, by Their Pattern of Service Use (Weighted Percentages)

	Homeless Individuals Who:			
	Use Only Soup Kitchens N = 223	Use Only Shelters N = 670	Use Both Shelters & Soup Kitchens N = 811	Total Sample N = 1704
Household Composition				
Single Persons				
Males	83	64	79	75
Females	3	12	6	8
Families (Children Present)				
Female Headed	1	15	5	8
Other (2-Parent, Male Headed)	1	3	0	2
Other Household Types [a]	12	2	1	6
Total	**100**	**100**	**100**	**100**
Marital Status				
Never Married	55	54	56	55
Currently Married	18	7	9	10
Divorced/Separated	25	29	32	29
Widowed	3	10	3	5
Total	**100**	**100**	**100**	**100**
Education				
Elementary (0 - 7)	16	9	5	9
Some High School (8 - 11)	49	32	40	39
High School Graduate	23	31	39	32
Some Post High School	8	19	13	14
College Graduate	3	9	2	5
Some Post College	0	1	1	1
Total	**100**	**100**	**100**	**100**

N: Referes to unweighted data. All percentages are based on weighted data. [a] Includes married couples without children, unmarried couples without children, and persons with other relatives, but not with children or spouse.

multiperson homeless households without children but with a spouse or other adult relative present, and 4 percent are unmarried couples without children.

Marital status differs substantially among users of different facilities. The soup kitchen-only population contains the highest proportion of currently married individuals—soup kitchen-only users are twice as likely to be currently married as are those who use shelters only, or those who use both soup kitchens and shelters. Homeless persons with different service-use patterns do not differ much among the other categories of marital status.

Slightly fewer than half of the total sample did not graduate from high school (48%), but 32 percent do have a high school diploma or equivalent, and 20 percent have some post-high school education. Individuals who use only soup kitchens have somewhat lower levels of educational achievement overall, with 65 percent reporting less than a high school education; users of shelters only are the best educated, with only 41 percent reporting less than a high school education. Nevertheless, these levels of educational attainment are lower than levels for the United States as a whole, among whom only 19 percent of adults aged 18–59 and over had not completed high school in 1986. They are much closer to the educational attainment for persons 18–59 years of age below the poverty level in 1986, among whom 43 percent were not high school graduates.[5]

The data already presented reveal a homeless population that is predominantly male, more heavily minority, and less well educated than the general U.S. population in MSAs or than the U.S. poverty population. It is younger than the U.S. adult population in MSAs, with many more of its members in the 24–44 age group and significantly fewer elderly persons. The homeless population is also overwhelmingly more single; 83 percent of homeless households are single individuals, compared to only 25 percent of households in MSAs. Furthermore, among homeless families with children present, 88 percent are headed by women compared to 15 percent in family households in MSAs.[6] Thus even more than the poor in general, homeless individuals and homeless family heads have certain characteristics that are associated with poor earning power—a direct contributor to their homeless state.

INCOME LEVELS AND INCOME SOURCES

Respondents reported receiving very little cash income within the 30 days prior to the interview. Seventeen percent reported no cash income during this period. The median income per household is $58, meaning that half of our respondents received less that $58 from all sources during the month preceding the interview (including those who received nothing). Seventy-five percent of respondents received $119 or less during the past month.

The average income per person for the preceding 30 days was $137, which is 28 percent of the federal poverty level for a one-person household in 1987.[7] It is also interesting to compare $137 per person to the median monthly U.S. per-capita income for 1986, recently reported in the *Washington Post*. That figure is $1,217, almost nine times the income reported by homeless persons in our survey.

Homeless persons who use only soup kitchens have substantially lower mean incomes at $94 per month; users of shelters only are highest at $158 per month, while users of both types of facilities are very close to the shelter-only users at $145 per month. These disparities in income by service-use pattern are due at least in part to differential participation in welfare programs. Those using only shelters are three times as likely as those using only soup kitchens to receive income maintenance (AFDC, General Assistance, or SSI), while people who use both soup kitchens and shelters are twice as likely as soup kitchen-only users to get income maintenance. Families are more likely to be receiving income maintenance, and since families are also more likely to use shelters than to limit themselves to soup kitchens, the differences in income by pattern of service use are to some extent attributable to the presence of families in shelters. However, some part of the difference is also probably due to the greater service intensity of shelters compared to soup kitchens. Shelters are more likely to have staff who help the shelter clients apply for benefits than are soup kitchens; their clients benefit by being more often the recipients of public programs.

Despite their histories of joblessness and homelessness and their lack of regular income, our sample respondents are not heavy users of welfare services. Table 2.3 presents respondents' sources of cash income during the 30 days preceding the interview, for the sample as a whole (first row) and broken out by selected demographic characteristics.

Females are less likely to report cash income during the past 30 days resulting from working or from handouts, and more likely to report cash income from means-tested benefits than males or than the sample as a whole. Blacks and Hispanics are more likely to report income from General Assistance and from food stamps than are whites, who report more income from "other" sources. Blacks report less income from working than either whites or Hispanics.

Younger respondents (18–50) report more cash income from working, from AFDC and GA, from handouts, and from other sources; older respondents (51 and older) are more likely to receive SSI and other benefits. Those homeless in a household with a child report more receipt of AFDC and GA and less from handouts and from "other" than respondents who do not have a child with them. Sources of cash income do not vary by whether or not the respondent has completed at least a high school education.

DURATION OF CURRENT PERIOD OF HOMELESSNESS AND JOBLESSNESS

Table 2.4 reports the duration of the respondents' current period of home-lessness and joblessness. The measure of the duration of homelessness is the respondent's answer to the question, "When was the last time you had a home or other permanent place to stay?" This question asked the length of the present

Table 2.3

Current Sources of Income among the Service-Using Homeless, by Selected Characteristics (Weighted Percentages; N = 1704)

Percent Who Received Income From

Characteristics	Working	AFDC	GA	SSI	Food Stamps	Other Benefits[a]	Hand-outs	Other[b]
Total Sample	25	5	12	4	18	7	17	31
Sex								
Male	25	2	9	3	13	7	18	43
Female	18	17	28	8	37	6	9	32
Race								
Black	19	7	16	3	20	6	15	34
White	28	2	7	5	14	9	15	50
Hispanic	30	7	20	3	23	4	17	32
Age								
30 or less	33	9	15	2	18	3	21	46
31-50	25	4	11	4	18	4	17	46
51-65	9	1	14	5	19	17	10	24
66+	12	0	0	19	3	65	1	2
Homeless with Children								
Yes	23	33	33	2	48	4	4	26
No	24	1	10	4	14	7	18	43
Education								
Less than 12 Yrs.	22	5	12	4	16	7	20	39
12 Yrs. or More	26	4	12	3	19	7	16	45

N: Refers to unweighted data. All percentages are based on weighted data.
[a]: SSDI, Social Security, veteran's benefits, worker's compensation, unemployment insurance.
[b]: Received money from relatives, friends, trading or swapping things, gifts, selling blood, other.

episode of homelessness in months and years. By this definition the median length of time homeless for the entire sample is 10 months, but the mean is 39 months. This difference is due to a relatively small part of the sample who have been homeless for a very long time (7 percent have been homeless for 10 years or more). Users of both soup kitchens and shelters tend to be homeless the longest with a mean number of months homeless of 44 and a median of 12.

Respondents report even longer time periods during which they have not held a steady job (defined as employment at the same job for three months or more) than they do for duration of homelessness. The median number of months since the last steady job for the entire sample is 21 months, with a mean of 47 months. Soup-kitchen-only users are at the very high end of this distribution, with a mean

Table 2.4
History of Homelessness and Work among the Service-Using Homeless, by
Pattern of Service Use (Weighted Percentages)

	Homeless Individuals Who:			
	Use only Soup Kitchens N = 223	Use Only Shelters N = 670	Use Both Shelters & Soup Kitchens N = 811	Total Sample N = 1704
Length of Current Period of Homelessness				
Under 2 months	5	14	4	08
2 - 3 months	10	16	12	13
4 - 6 months	30	16	14	19
7 - 12 months	7	16	16	14
13 - 24 months	9	19	17	16
25 - 48 months	21	8	10	12
Over 4 years	18	12	26	19
Total	**100**	**100**	**100**	**100**
Mean (in months)	37	33	44	39
Median (in months)	14	7	12	10
Months Since Last Steady Job				
Under 2 months	0	4	1	2
2 - 3 months	4	12	7	8
4 - 6 months	12	15	15	14
7 - 12 months	12	15	19	16
13 - 24 months	13	16	14	14
25 - 48 months	13	7	18	13
Over 4 years	45	32	26	33
Total	**100**	**100**	**100**	**100**
Mean (in months)	67	42	40	48
Median (in months)	26	17	21	21

N: Refers to unweighted data. All percentages are based on weighted data.

number of months of 67 since last steady job and a median of 26 months; homeless persons who use only shelters and those who use both shelters and soup kitchens have fairly similar histories of job holding with means of 42 and 40 months and medians of 17 and 21 months, respectively, since their last steady job. These data indicate that the average service-using homeless person has not held a steady job for four years, and that half of the service-using homeless have not held a steady job for almost two years.

A common rule of thumb among service providers is to use the length of time someone has been homeless as a rough indicator of how difficult it will be to help that person resume a stable, homed life in the community. From this perspective, the shorter the period of homelessness, the easier it will probably be to help someone. Homeless people who use only soup kitchens are clearly bimodal in this respect, with almost half (46%) reporting periods of homelessness of six months or less, but an almost equal number (39%) reporting homelessness of two or more years duration. Users of shelters only are the shortest term homeless, on average.

All other things being equal, it has been assumed that the shorter-term homeless are easier to help toward self-sufficiency. However, the data on work experience are sobering. It is clear from comparing the two distributions that many homeless people have not worked for a lot longer than they have been homeless, and that the differences among service-use patterns noted for the length of homelessness almost disappear when looking at the length of time since the respondent last held a steady job.

Lack of education and lack of job skills among many homeless persons probably hinder their efforts to get back in the mainstream. The higher the educational attainment of homeless people in this study, the more likely they are to have worked for pay during the past month and the higher their reported income per person in their household. Women are less likely to have worked during the past 30 days, as are those homeless households with children (mostly female-headed) and those receiving income maintenance. Respondents with more health problems and respondents who have a history of different types of trouble (mental hospitalization, chemical dependency treatment, and state or federal imprisonment) are less likely to have worked during the last 30 days. Income per person is affected by participation in public income maintenance programs and in public programs that compensate people for disabilities (such as SSDI, veterans' benefits, and workers' compensation). Participation in these programs raises the average monthly income per person that homeless people report.

Certain homeless people are more likely than others to receive public benefits. Those with histories of mental hospitalization or chemical dependency treatment are more likely to get these benefits (mostly SSI and GA), as are households with children (mostly AFDC and GA). It is quite likely that many people with chronic health and mental health problems will continue to be less able to work and that family heads with long histories of welfare dependency will need special assistance before they are able to become self-supporting. Thus the circumstances of large segments of the homeless population demand careful attention as policy is made. Many homeless persons are unlikely to become completely self-sufficient even with substantial help. Therefore an important policy issue is whether and how they are to be maintained in decent surroundings.

COMPARISON TO OTHER STUDIES OF THE HOMELESS

Having presented some of the basic characteristics of our sample of homeless service users, we now turn to a presentation of how our sample compares on these variables with samples described in other research on the homeless. For these comparisons we used only studies that interviewed homeless persons. Excluded were those reports that relied on the estimates of providers to describe the homeless population. Table 2.5 presents these comparisons. The first column of Table 2.5 gives data from the present study; the subsequent 14 columns show the findings from 14 other studies undertaken in particular communities. The bottom row of the table gives the sample size (*N*) for each study reported; the three rows immediately above give the locations from which respondents were sought—soup kitchens, shelters, and the streets.

Descriptive data from our sample confirm some generalizations that might be made on the basis of the descriptive statistics obtained from previous studies of local populations. In the other studies, between 52–100 percent of the respondents were male (excluding one study that only interviewed women), compared to our 81 percent. The proportion of nonwhite persons ranged from 23–74 percent compared to our 54 percent; this is the largest range seen on Table 2.5, and appears to be influenced more by the geographical location of the study than by other variables. Age and marital status distrubutions appear very similar across studies, as does the proportion who were high school graduates. The proportion of our sample receiving income maintenance is on the low end, and the proportion who worked for pay within the last month is on the high end of the ranges from other studies, but both are still well within those ranges.

The most difficult comparisons to make are for length of time homeless, because the studies report the data in noncomparable ways. Nevertheless, as near as can be determined, the present sample is well within the range from other studies. The proportion homeless for 12 months or more is on the high end, but this is most likely the result of the inclusion in our study of homeless persons who used only soup kitchens. Such persons were excluded from most other studies but, as the data just reported in Table 2.4 indicate, homeless persons who used only soup kitchens had been homeless for longer on average than those who used shelters only or both shelters and soup kitchens.

CURRENT RESIDENCY, SLEEP, AND SHELTER PATTERNS

Length of Residency in City

A very considerable proportion of the homeless are long-term residents of the cities they inhabit despite the general feeling in many localities that "our city attracts the homeless; they are not natives of here." A large proportion (43%) had lived in their city for 11 years or more, 7 percent had lived there for 6 to 10 years, and 16 percent for 1 to 5 years. Fewer than one-third (29%) of the homeless in our sample had lived for less than 6 months in the city where we found them; 19 percent had lived there for less than 1 month. Five percent had lived there for 6 to 12 months. This question was asked with regard to continuous

Table 2.5
Comparisons of Descriptive Data from Other Studies

	Urban Institute (87)	Chicago (85-86)	Minneapolis (85-86)	L.A. DMH (84-85)	L.A. UCLA (84)	Multnomah Co., Or. (84)	Baltimore (83)	Cincinnati (86)	Massachusetts (85)	Ohio (84)	Detroit (84-85)	Milwaukee (84-85)	Multnomah Co., Or. (85)	Chicago (83)	Seattle (86)
Sex: %Male	81	76	85	96	100	85	92	65	81	81	71	87	00	67	52
Race: %nonwhite	54	69	54	73	53	23	72	39	30	33	74	40	27	59	49
Age:															
% < 30	30	25	63[b]	36	22	29	na	29	48[b]	35	(x=	31	67[b]	43[b]	49[k]
%31 - 50	51	55[c]	37[c]	45	55	48	na	27[d]	38[ae]	44	35)	47	29[e]	49[c]	23[l]
Marital Status															
% never married	55	57	53	59	57	40	60	na	61	45	52	36	29	na	na
Education															
% H.S. Graduate or more	52	55	47	51	60	47	42	na	52	44	43	na	52	na	na
Length of Time Homeless															
% ≤ 3 months	21	32	na	55[f]	36[f]	33	na	na	na	49[g]	na	32[g]	33	37[g]	na
% > 12 months	47	39	na	30	49	41	na	13	na	27	na	28	41	28	na
% > 4 years	19	13	na	na	17[h]	na	na	na	na	na	na	8[i]	na	16[i]	na
Income Maintenance[j]															
% yes, now	20	35	na	15	16	13	na	24	37	24	na	32	19	22	na
Worked for Pay Last Month:															
% yes	25	39	36	32	20	18	na	na	25	25	12	na	na	na	na
Respondents from:															
SK	x	-	x	x	-	x	x	-	-	x	-	-	x	-	-
SH	x	x	x	x	x	x	-	x	x	x	x	x	x	-	x
Street	-	x	x	x	-	x	-	-	x	x	-	x	x	x	-
N =	1,704	722	339	379	107	131	271	801	282	979	75	237	190	80	351

[a]: only 33% homeless; [b]: 17 - 34; [c]: 31 - 54; [d]: 31 - 45; [e]: 35 - 54; [f]: ≤ 6 month; [g]: ≤ 2 months; [h]: ≥ 5 years; [i]: > 3 years;

[j]: AFDC, GA or SSI; [k]: 18-44; [l]: 45 - 59

residency, and respondents were asked to ignore temporary absences from the city if they had considered it their home for some time. These residency patterns are important since they suggest that the problems of homelessness are home grown and must be solved in each community rather than attributed to poor conditions elsewhere.

Sleep Patterns during the 24 Hours Preceding the Interview

Fifty-three percent of respondents had slept or rested in a shelter for the homeless during the 24 hours preceding the interview. Thirteen percent had spent the night on the streets, in parks, or in other open places. Five percent used public indoor spaces for sleeping or resting, such as bus stations, train stations, subways, bars, all-night movies, laundromats, and others. Eight percent spent the night in someone's room, apartment, or house; 9 percent used abandoned buildings; 4 percent used vehicles; and 10 percent reported other sleep or resting places. These other places included places where they paid (e.g., flophouses) and institutions (e.g., hospital, jail, detoxification centers).

Seven-day Shelter Patterns

We obtained from every respondent a description of where they sought shelter for sleep or rest during the seven days preceding the interview. The data indicate that only one-third of the sample (34%) slept in shelters continuously throughout the week, and that more than half of our respondents (58%) used shelters three nights a week or less. The data also indicate that about one-fourth of the sample (22%) had access to someone else's home or apartment for some number of days during the week. Four percent reported the use of such places for every night of the week in question; however, this pattern did not involve a regular arrangement at a single place.

Only 18 percent of our respondents reported using *only* the streets, parks and other public places for sleep or rest during the week preceding the interview, and 63 percent of respondents did not sleep in public places on any of the previous seven nights. However, 46 percent of the homeless respondents who used only soup kitchens reported continuous use of public places for sleeping during the week before the interview. One possible explanation that has been proposed for the behavior of individuals who use only soup kitchens is that they do not need to use shelters because they have other resources such as family or friends who can take them in for the night, or money to rent an SRO room. Our data indicate that this is not the case, and that those homeless who use only soup kitchens receive very little shelter from any source.

Finally, 14 percent of respondents reported spending at least one night "elsewhere" during the week in question—most often, in a car, bus, van, or other vehicle. Institutions (jails, hospitals, detoxification centers) were the next most frequently mentioned "other" location for sleeping and resting.

Characteristics of Last Stable Living Situation

Forty-one percent of respondents indicated that their last stable living situation was an apartment; for 20 percent it was a room, and for 31 percent it was a house. Eight percent reported some other kind of place—usually an institution. While living in this prior residence, 32 percent of respondents lived alone, and 68 percent lived with others. Of those sharing their last stable residence, 17 percent shared with a spouse, 21 percent with children, 24 percent with parents, 12 percent with siblings, 9 percent with grandparents or other relatives, and 29 percent with friends. Ten percent mentioned other persons. Many people shared living space with people from more than one of these categories.

When asked why they left their last stable living situation, 13 percent said they were evicted, 9 percent were asked to leave, 13 percent did not get along with the people there, and 5 percent had to leave a condemned building. Fully 62 percent of the sample also gave "other" responses. Approximately one third of these reflect difficulties with finances—"could not afford," "rent went up," "lost my job and couldn't pay the rent," and other such responses. Other reasons for leaving included "left town to look for work," "too crowded," "I was drinking, doing drugs," "left for treatment program, went into hospital or other institution," "went to jail or prison," and the end of a relationship, either through death or break up, with someone who paid the rent (parent, spouse, or partner). It is also quite possible that people had several reasons for leaving their last residence, although most gave only one answer. For example, someone could have lost a job because of drinking and then not been able to pay the rent. Some of the "other" responses also suggested that drinking and drug taking disrupted relationships, and overcrowding may often have had the same effect.

HEALTH AND MENTAL HEALTH PROBLEMS

Health

Sixty-five percent of the homeless people in our survey indicated that they had seen a doctor or visited a clinic or hospital emergency room at least once during the past year. Parallel statistics from Rossi et al. (1986) and Farr et al. (1986) show that 71 percent of Chicago's homeless population and 75 percent of the Los Angeles skid-row population had seen a doctor at least once during the past year. National data from the 1985 National Health Interview Survey (NCHS, 1987a) indicate that 89 percent of the entire U.S. population and 90 percent of those with incomes less than $10,000 had seen a doctor during the preceding 12 months.

Respondents were asked whether they experienced any of 11 serious health problems that often affect the homeless, and also to list other health problems they had. Forty-four percent of respondents indicated that they had *no* health problems; 31 percent reported one problem; 11 percent reported two problems,

8 percent reported three, and 7 percent reported four or more problems. The most commonly reported medical conditions were upper respiratory tract infections (colds, coughs, bronchitis, chest infection), 21 percent; arthritis, rheumatism, joint problems, 15 percent; and high blood pressure, 15 percent. Heart disease/stroke, problems with the liver, and problems walking, lost limbs, and other physical handicaps each were reported by 7–10 percent of respondents. Between 2 and 6 percent reported each of: diabetes (sugar in the blood); anemia (poor blood); pneumonia; and tuberculosis (spitting up blood). Nineteen percent of respondents reported a wide variety of other medical conditions.

These data indicate that 56 percent of the homeless in our sample were afflicted by a variety of relatively serious medical conditions that could impair their ability to become self-sufficient through work even if they were not disadvantaged in other ways.

The final general health question asked of homeless respondents is identical to a standard question asked on the National Health Interview Survey (NCHS, 1987b)—"Would you say your health, in general, now is excellent, very good, good, fair, or poor?" The most common way to look at these health data for the homeless is to focus on the proportion that perceive their health as *fair or poor*. Among our respondents the proportion is 38 percent. This proportion is similar to the findings of Rossi et al. (1986) for Chicago, which were 36 percent. They are lower than the proportion reported for Los Angeles skid-row homeless, of 48 percent fair or poor (Farr et al., 1986). Five other studies of the homeless report a range of 30–60 percent rating their health as fair or poor (Burt and Cohen, 1988b). All studies of the homeless report proportions with fair or poor responses that are much higher than these responses among the U.S. adult population as a whole. Data from the 1986 National Health Interview Survey (NCHS, 1987b) indicate that only 10 percent of adults between 18–64 reported their health as either fair or poor. Data from the 1985 National Health Interview Survey (NCHS, 1987a) for the low-income population show that 20 percent rate their health as fair or poor. The elderly, who give their health lower ratings than adults under 65, are included in these low-income statistics; even so, the ratings of the homeless are lower in all studies.[8] These comparisons indicate the relatively impaired health status of the homeless.

Mental Health

Nineteen percent of the sample reported spending at least one night in a mental hospital at some time in their lives, suggesting that at least this proportion of the homeless have experienced serious mental distress. Our figure compares to a range of 17–30 percent in 11 other studies that interviewed the homeless, with two outliers of 13 percent (Vernez et al., 1988) and 45 percent (Mulkern et al., 1985).[9] No statistics are available for comparison with the U.S. population.

Two other indicators of mental distress revealed high levels. In answer to our question about suicide, "Was there ever a time in your life when you felt so bad that you tried to kill yourself, that is, tried to commit suicide?'' 21 percent of our respondents said yes. This is a startlingly high proportion compared to the U.S. population as a whole (2.9%), the lowest fourth of the U.S. population on an education/income/occupation index (3.9%), and even compared to individuals who have ever in their lifetime received any of 21 diagnosis of major psychiatric disorders (7.4%).[10]

These suicide data reflect lifetime suicide attempts. We do not know whether they occurred before or after the respondent became homeless. More direct evidence for the current degree of depression and demoralization felt by homeless people comes from a scale designed to measure these constructs directly—Center for Epidemiological Studies Depression scale, or CES-D.[11]

On the CES-D, research has indicated that a score of 16 or higher indicates psychological distress of sufficient magnitude to require immediate treatment and assistance (Eaton and Kessler, 1981; Radloff, 1977). In our sample, 43 percent of respondents had an adjusted CES-D score of 16 or higher, indicating that these homeless persons are indeed seriously psychologically distressed. The median CES-D score was 15.0, and the mean was 16.7. These statistics from the present study compare with a mean of 19.2 among Chicago's homeless (Rossi et al., 1986), and a mean of 8.5 for the adult U.S. population based on data from the National Health and Nutrition Examination Survey.

Indicators of mental distress bore a significant relationship to the amounts and varieties of food eaten. Higher levels of mental distress as measured by the CES-D were predictive of lower dietary intake, lower frequency of eating meals, and a higher likelihood of going without food for a whole day. Also, perceptions of diet adequacy and interest in food were both lower the higher the CES-D score.[12] These findings have implications for efforts to improve the nutrition of the homeless. They point to specific parts of the homeless population who may experience greater dietary deficiencies than the average homeless person.

Institutionalization Experiences

We have already reported the frequency of mental hospitalization among our sample. Respondents were also asked about other institutionalization experiences, although they were not asked whether these occurred before or after becoming homeless. Thirty-three percent of the sample reported having been a patient in a detoxification or treatment center for alcohol or drug abuse. Fifty-two percent had spent more than 3–4 days at a time in a city or county jail, and 24 percent had committed crimes of sufficient seriousness and repetitiveness to result in state or federal imprisonment. We distinguished state or federal prison experience from county jail experience because many homeless get arrested by police while on the streets and taken to jail for a few days. The level of serious criminal involvement indicated by state or federal imprisonment reported by our sample is thus quite high, especially when one considers current court procedures that routinely opt for probation or confinement in county facilities for first offenses and for lesser offenses.[13]

We combined the data about drug or alcohol treatment, imprisonment, and mental hospitalization in a variety of ways to summarize individual experiences with institutionalization. Looking first at jail/prison experiences, 20 percent of the sample had been in both, 36 percent in one or the other, and 44 percent had never served time in either a jail or a prison.

Combining information from drug or alcohol treatment and mental hospitalization, 9 percent of the sample had experienced both, 34 percent had experienced one or the other, and 57 percent had never experienced either. When we combined all four types of institutionalization—jail, prison, drug/alcohol treatment, mental hospitalization—two-thirds (66%) of the sample had experienced at least one of these four, and 18 percent of the sample had experienced three of them or all four. Twenty-seven percent had experienced only one, and 21 percent had experienced two.

The Homeless Who Do Not Use Services

To achieve comparison data for the homeless who do not use services, as noted above, we interviewed homeless persons at congregating sites (bus stations, culverts, etc.) who had not used any kind of shelter or soup kitchen for the past week. Of the 455 people identified as homeless at these sites, only 32 percent, or 142 people, had *not* used a soup kitchen or a shelter during the past week. Since this was a small and not necessarily representative sample, statistically rigorous comparisons between them and the service-using homeless cannot be made. Nevertheless, the general picture is relatively clear.

An argument has been made that homeless people who do not use soup kitchens and shelters are better off and more able to take care of themselves than those who use services. This argument runs that these people do not have to use services because they have more resources of their own, both material and "street smarts." The data from this study totally refute this argument. On virtually every measure, the homeless who do not use services appear to be more disabled, with fewer resources, and with a less-promising history on which to build a future.

Nonusers are somewhat more likely to be male than service users (89% vs. 81%), to be nonwhite (66% vs. 54%), to be poorly educated (45% vs. 52% with less than a high school education), and to be middle aged (76% vs. 67% who are between 31 and 65).

A whole variety of comparisons indicates that the homeless who do not use services fare less well than those who do. The homeless who do not use services reported being homeless longer (median number of months was 22 vs. 10 for service users) and having been without a steady job for longer (median number of months was 34 vs. 21 for service users). They made substantially less use of public benefits (AFDC, GA and SSI), with only 9 percent receiving any of these benefits compared to 20 percent of service users. Food-stamp receipt was similar

(9 percent for nonusers compared to 18 percent for service users). Median income per person for the last month was also lower ($38 for nonusers vs. $58 for service users), partly as a result of not participating in public-benefit programs.

Nonusers also reported being less healthy and having more mental problems. Fifty-seven percent said their health was fair or poor compared to 38 percent for service users. Twenty-seven percent (compared to 19 percent) had a history of mental hospitalization, 31 percent (compared to 21 percent) had attempted suicide, and 70 percent (compared to 49 percent) had depression/demoralization scores that indicated the need for immediate clinical treatment.

Nonusers were equally likely to have served time in state or federal prison but were more likely to have been in jail for more than 3–4 days (63% vs. 52%). They were also more likely to have received inpatient chemical dependency treatment than service users (42% vs. 33%). Combining all of these institutionalization experiences (mental hospitalization, chemical dependency treatment, jail, and prison), somewhat more of the unusers than the users had experienced at least one (72% vs. 66%).

The homeless who do not use services also had poorer eating patterns than the service-using homeless on every measure, as described in Cohen and Burt's chapter in this volume.

These comparisons point up the relatively more severe plight of the homeless nonservice users, and disprove the argument that these people stay away from services because they do not need them. They also suggest that outreach efforts are needed to encourage nonusers to seek the help that is available through soup kitchens, shelters, and other services.

CONCLUSIONS AND IMPLICATIONS

The clear message of these data is that the homeless are very poor and that substantial numbers of them have problems that will prevent them, at least in part, from becoming completely self-sufficient even with substantial help from programs and services. One-third have histories of chemical dependency, one-fifth have histories of mental hospitalization, and almost 1 in 10 have both. One-fourth have serious criminal records (state or federal imprisonment). Almost half have not graduated from high school, and many have not worked for very long periods of time. The types of assistance needed to increase their incomes and the stability of their living situation are not so different from the types of assistance that have long been recommended to help people with these difficulties— the need is only more intense and more immediate.

In addressing both ameliorative approaches for those already homeless and preventive approaches to keep people from becoming homeless, a key question for policymakers is "Why now?" People with the problems found among the homeless have always been here—but why have they been on the streets during this decade in increasing numbers? Shelters are not the ultimate solution, although they are a humane and essential first response. Rather, policymakers have to look at the complex of shifts and changes that have occurred during the decade of the 1980s in the housing market, in the job market, in the buying power of income support and housing support programs, in eligibility for public support programs, in the buying power of the minimum wage, and in the skill levels of the labor force. There is obviously an increasing "affordable housing gap" in many communities in this country such that very poor people, including those with disabilities, are increasingly unable to afford housing. No single, simple approach will address this complex of factors, just as the homeless population itself includes people who have become homeless through different patterns of interaction among these factors. Policymakers must take a judicious look at the causes of homelessness and then design a multifaceted, sophisticated approach to closing the affordable housing gap.

NOTES

1. The full study report may be obtained from The Urban Institute library, 2100 M Street N.W., Washington, DC 20037. Martha R. Burt and Barbara E. Cohen, *Feeding the Homeless: Does the Prepared Meals Provision Help? Volume I: Report to Congress; Volume II: Supporting Tables and Documentation.* The study was supported by Contracts No. 53–3198–6–41 and 53–3198–7–101 with the U.S. Department of Agriculture, Food and Nutrition Service, Office of Analysis and Evaluation.

2. See Cohen and Burt's chapter in this volume for the study's findings related to eating patterns.

3. Bureau of the Census, *Statistical Abstracts of the United States: 1987*, Tables 17 and 745 (estimated data for 1985); *State and metropolitan Area Data Book, 1986*, Table A (for 1980 MSA data—the census data most parallel to the jurisdictions from which we drew the homeless sample for this study).

4. Bureau of the Census, *Statistical Abstracts of the United States: 1987*, Tables 19 and 745 (estimated data for 1985); *State and Metropolitan Area Data Book, 1986*, Table A (for 1980 MSA data). The Census Bureau notes that "Hispanic-origin people may be of any race," reflecting the fact that "Hispanic" is not considered a race by the Census, and Hispanics may be included as black, white or "other" in the Census Bureau's statistics on race.

5. U.S. Department of Commerce, Bureau of the Census, *Current Population Reports: Consumer Income*, Series P–60, No. 158. Statistics calculated from information given in Table 9.

6. Bureau of the Census, *State and Metropolitan Area Data Book, 1986*, Table A. The MSA population was selected for comparison because it is the best available source of national data for the urban population surveyed in the present study.

7. Our figure—average income per person—was derived by dividing the total reported household income by the number of persons in the household. Thus if a person reported income of $56 and was a single-person household, "average income per person" for his household would be $56. If a person reported income of $300 and was head of a three-person household, "average income per person" for the household would be $100. The standard deviation was $199. Federal poverty figures were taken from the U.S. House of Representatives Committee on Ways and Means, *Background Material and Data on*

Programs within the Jurisdiction of the Committee on Ways and Means, 1988 Edition, Committee Print 100–29, 100th Congress, 2d Session, March 24, 1988. Table 1, Appendix I, p. 711. Tripling $137 per person for a three-person household yields a monthly income of 54 percent of the poverty level for a family of three.

8. NCHS, 1987b, Series 10, #164 for 1986 national data from the National Health Interview Survey, adults aged 18–64; NCHS, 1987a, "Health United States 1986," Table 39 for low-income population data from the 1985 National Health Interview Survey covering all persons 4–86 + . We used the 18–64 U.S. adult population as the appropriate comparison because 98 percent of our service-using homeless sample were in this age range. Unfortunately, simultaneous breaks by age and income level were not available, so the low-income statistics reflect responses of individuals aged 4–86 + .

9. As discussed in Burt and Cohen, 1988b.

10. Unpublished data obtained from the National Institute of Mental Health were used to make these comparisons. Data supplied by Eve Moscicki, NIMH, Center for Epidemiological Studies, personal communication, 1987, citing a background paper for the Secretary's Task Force on Youth Suicide. Data come from Epidemiological Catchment Area (ECA) studies in five major cities, generalized to the U.S. population as a whole.

11. The CES-D (Radloff, 1977) is a scale developed by the Center for Epidemiological Studies (CES) of NIMH to measure depression (hence, CES-D). The original version used on the National Health and Nutrition Examination Survey has 20 items. The Chicago study (Rossi et al., 1986) followed a New York Psychiatric Institute practice and used six of the items selected to measure both depression and demoralization. We used these same six items in the present study, and followed Rossi et al.'s methodology to adjust the results into a score equivalent to the 20-item CES-D. The six items, which used a three-point scale of "never," "some of the time," and "most of the time," were:

Was your appetite so poor that you did not feel like eating?
Did you feel so tired and worn out that you could not enjoy anything?
Did you feel depressed?
Did you feel unhappy about the way your life is going?
Did you feel discouraged and worried about your future?
Did you feel lonely?

12. See Cohen and Burt's chapter in this volume for further discussion of eating patterns and the factors that affect them among the homeless.

13. No national comparison statistics are available to indicate the proportion of the adult U.S. population who have experienced at least one imprisonment in a state or federal facility in their lifetime. National Criminal Justice Reference Service, personal communication.

REFERENCES

Burt, Martha R., and Barbara E. Cohen. 1988a. *Feeding the Homeless: Does the Prepared Meals Provision Work? Volume I: Report to Congress; Volume II: Supporting Tables and Documentation.* Washington, D.C.: Urban Institute.
———. 1988b. *Review of Research on Homeless Persons.* Washington, D.C.: Urban Institute.
Chaiklin, Harris, and M. Lipton. 1984. *Family Status and Soup Kitchen Use: Some Policy*

Considerations. Baltimore: University of Maryland, School of Social Work. Paper presented at National Conference on Family Relations, October 24, 1984.

Eaton, W. W., and L. G. Kessler. 1981. Rates of Symptoms of Depression in a National Sample. *American Journal of Epidemiology* 114 (4): 528–538.

Farr, Rodger K., P. Koegel, and A. Burnam. 1986. *A Study of Homelessness and Mental Illness in the Skid Row Area of Los Angeles*. Los Angeles: Los Angeles County Department of Mental Health.

King County Department of Planning and Community Development. 1986. *Homelessness Revisited: 1986 Seattle-King County Emergency Shelter Study Update*. Seattle, Wash.: King County Department of Planning and Community Development, Housing and Community Development Division.

Mowbray, Carolyn T., V. S. Johnson, A. Solarz, and C. J. Combs. 1985. *Mental Health and Homelessness in Detroit: A Research Study*. East Lansing, Mich.: Michigan Department of Mental Health.

Mulkern, Virginia, V. J. Bradley, R. Spence, S. Allein, and J. E. Oldham. 1985. *Homelessness Needs Assessment Study: Findings and Recommendations for the Massachusetts Department of Mental Health*. Boston, Mass.: Human Services Research Institute.

Multnomah County Social Service Division. 1984. *The Homeless Poor*. Multnomah County (Portland), Oreg.

———. 1985. *Homeless Women*. Multnomah County (Portland), Oreg.

National Center for Health Statistics. 1987a. *Health United States: 1986*. Washington, D.C.: U.S. Government Printing Office.

———. 1987b. *Current Estimates from the National Health Interview Survey: United States 1986*. Washington, D.C.: NCHS, Series 10, #164.

Piliavin, Irving, M. Sosin, and H. Westerfelt. 1987. Tracking the Homeless. *Focus* 10 (4): 20–25. Madison, Wisc.: University of Wisconsin-Madison Institute for Research on Poverty.

Radloff, Lenore S. 1977. The CES-D Scale: A Self-report Depression Scale for Research in the General Population. *Applied Psychological Measurement* 1: 385–401.

Ropers, Richard, and M. Robertson. 1984. *Basic Shelter Research Project*. Los Angeles, Calif.: UCLA School of Public Health.

Rosnow, Mark J., T. Shaw, and C. S. Concord. 1985. *A Study of Homeless Mentally Ill Persons in Milwaukee*. Milwaukee, Wisc.: Human Services Triangle, Inc.

Rossi, Peter H., G. A. Fisher, and G. Willis. 1986. *The Condition of the Homeless in Chicago*. Amherst, Mass.: Social and Demographic Research Institute, University of Massachusetts; Chicago, Ill.: National Opinion Research Center (NORC).

Roth, Dee, J. Bean, N. Just, and T. Saveanu. 1985. *Homelessness in Ohio: A Study of People in Need*. Columbus: Ohio Department of Mental Health, Office of Program Evaluation and Research.

Task Force on Emergency Shelter. 1983. *Homelessness in Chicago*. Chicago, Ill.: Task Force on Emergency Shelter, Social Services Task Force, Department of Human Services, City of Chicago.

Vernez, Georges, M. A. Burnam, E. A. McGlynn, S. Trude, and B. S. Mittman. 1988. *Review of California's Program for the Homeless Mentally Disabled*. Santa Monica, Calif.: The Rand Corporation, February 1988.

Woods, William K., and E. L. Burdell. 1987. *Homelessness in Cincinnati*. Cincinnati, Ohio: Applied Information Resources.
Wright, James D., and E. Weber. 1987. *Homelessness and Health*. Washington, D.C.: McGraw-Hill.

3

Food Sources and Intake of Homeless Persons

Barbara E. Cohen and Martha R. Burt

In the past few years both homelessness and hunger have become the focus of much public attention. Studies have been completed focusing on the characteristics of the homeless; others have documented hunger among the general population in various regions of the nation. However, none has focused on hunger among the homeless. Given the magnitude of public and private efforts to supply those in need with food at emergency feeding sites, it might be assumed that homeless people do not have a problem getting adequate amounts of food. Results from a nationally representative sample of 1,704 homeless individuals show that for many homeless individuals hunger is indeed a problem.[1] In this study we had the opportunity to collect both information on the food being provided to the homeless at soup kitchens and shelters and information on the food intake of the homeless population. This chapter focuses on the food intake of the service-using homeless individuals interviewed for the study.

The study was designed to yield detailed interview data on a nationally representative sample of service-using homeless individuals who used soup kitchens and shelters for the homeless in U.S. cities of 100,000 or more. A nationally representative sample of 20 cities was drawn in which 400 providers were randomly selected—representing soup kitchens, shelters without meals, and shelters with meals. Then, 1,800 homeless individuals were systematically selected from among the homeless using the services of the providers in the sample. Final sample sizes were 381 providers and 1,704 homeless service users. In addition, a nonrandom sample of 142 persons who had *not* used meal or shelter services during the week before the interview was identified by asking local providers and police in the 20 sample cities to help locate sites where homeless people congregated—parks, train or bus stations, certain street corners, culverts, or day shelters that did not offer meals—and then interviewing homeless persons at these sites. The interviews were conducted with homeless users and nonusers of shelter and meal services in March 1987.

This study is the only one based on nationally representative sample data to interview individual homeless persons, and the only study ever to collect detailed information from the homeless on their eating patterns.[2] Two limitations should be mentioned. Although nationally representative, the data do not apply to homeless individuals in cities under 100,000 population. And since the in-person interview data were collected during March 1987, they do not necessarily reflect the situation during other months in the year.

The data presented below come from 1,704 homeless adults 18 and older. Throughout, the data have been weighted to be representative of all service-using homeless adults in the United States in cities of 100,000 or more. Individuals were located and interviewed in soup kitchens and in two types of shelters: those that served meals and those that did not (the former predominate). Initially, individuals were grouped by their pattern of service use to see whether homeless people who used particular types of services differed from those who used other services. Analysis of these data revealed that 29 percent of homeless individuals use only soup kitchens, 32 percent use only shelters, and 38 percent use both soup kitchens and shelters. Because virtually every characteristic of homeless people varied by their pattern of service use, data are presented showing this pattern.

This chapter begins with a description of how the homeless perceive their diets, how often they eat, and where they get food. It then presents an analysis of the foods they reported eating during the day immediately preceding the interview and ends with an analysis of factors affecting food consumption.

PERCEPTION OF FOOD SUFFICIENCY

Although our research enabled us to measure the specific food intake of homeless individuals, it was equally important to measure the perceptions that homeless people have about the adequacy of their diets. Responses to a question about the healthfulness of their diet indicated that more than half saw their diets as either fair or poor, with 28 percent reporting "fair" diets and 23 percent reporting "poor" diets. Thirty-one percent described their diets as good, while only 18 percent described them as either excellent or very good.

Perceptions of Diet

Respondents described the sufficiency of their diet by indicating whether they got enough of the kinds of food they wanted, enough but not what they wanted, or sometimes or often not enough to eat. Among the homeless respondents, 38 percent indicated that their diets were insufficient with respect to the total amount of food eaten, 43 percent indicated an insufficient amount of foods they most desire, and 19 percent indicated sufficient amounts of the food they most desired. Table 3.1 presents their responses as well as the responses to a similar question asked of a nationally representative sample of women 19–50 years old on the Continuing Survey of Food Intake by Individuals (CSFII 1985; Mathematica Policy Research, 1987). It is clear that the homeless respondents were much less satisfied with their diets than respondents from households of all incomes and somewhat less satisfied than respondents whose incomes were less than 76 percent of the official poverty line.

If our homeless respondents answered that they sometimes or often did not get enough to eat, they were also asked to indicate how often this happened. Among those who stated that they did not always have enough to eat, most indicated that this situation prevailed either every day (38%) or every other day (31%). These figures (reported in the lower panel of Table 3.1) correspond to 15 percent and 11 percent of the entire homeless sample, respectively. Thirty-one percent (12 percent of the entire sample) indicated that this situation occurred for them twice a week or less often. Among those saying they did not have enough to eat, significant reasons cited for this circumstance were "no money to buy food"—77 percent (29 percent of total sample); "can't get to place serving food"—26 percent (10 percent of total); "no place to cook food"—21 percent (8 percent of total); "no place to get food"—25 percent (9 percent of total).

FREQUENCY OF EATING

Asking more specifically about the number of times they usually ate during a day, homeless people reported that they ate 1.9 times per day on average (with a median of 1.4 times). This compares for the average American adult to 3 meals per day or more—a pattern reported by only 25 percent of homeless respondents. Table 3.2 presents the responses to this question and questions on the number of days on which they may have gone without any food. The responses are presented as weighted percentages of the total sample and weighted percentages of the sample using only soup kitchens, using only shelters, or using both soup kitchens and shelters. Soup-kitchen-only users reported eating least frequently, and shelter-only users reported eating most frequently. (This question did not define "eating"; therefore it can not be assumed that each "time" reported refers to a meal.)

When questioned about the past week's intake, 36 percent of the homeless individuals in this study said that they had gone for at least one whole day without any food during the past seven days. Again we see the pattern of soup-kitchen-only users reporting the most number of days without food, and shelter-only users reporting the fewest such days. "Having no money for food" was the most commonly cited reason for going without food (58 percent—21 percent of total sample). "No place to get food" was cited next often (30 percent—11

Table 3.1

Service-Using Homeless Persons' Perceptions of Food Sufficiency (Weighted Percentages; N = 1704)

| | | Respondents from: | |
| | UIS* Service Using Homeless | CSFII | |
		Households of All Incomes	Household <76% of Poverty
"Which of the following best describes your situation in terms of food you eat?"			
Get enough of the kinds of food you want to eat	19*	70	31
Get enough, but not always what you want to eat	43	27	49
Sometimes do not get enough to eat	19	3	15
Often do not get enough to eat	19	1	5
	100	100	100

| | Homeless Respondents (UI Study): | |
	All Respondents	Respondents Saying Sometimes or Often Not Enough to Eat
"How often do you find that you do not have enough to eat?"		
Every day	15*	38*
Every other day	11	31
Two times a week	6	17
Once a week	4	9
Several times a month	2	4
Less often than several times a month	0	1
	38	100

UIS: Urban Institute Study.

N: Refers to unweighted N's from this study. All percentages in columns marked by an * are based on weighted data from the present study.

Source: For Continuity Survey of Food Intake of Individuals (CSFII) data, Mathematica Policy Research, 1987, Tables 3.1.1 and 3.1.3.

Table 3.2

Reported Frequency of Eating among Homeless Service Users, by Pattern of Service Use (Weighted Percentages)

	Homeless Individuals Who:			
Question	Use Only Soup Kitchens (N = 223)	Use Only Shelters (N = 670)	Use Both Shelters and Soup Kitchens (N = 811)	Total Sample (N=1704)
"How many times do you usually eat in a day?				
Less than once	21	1	3	7
Once	27	23	37	30
Twice	40	36	39	38
Three Times	8	31	18	20
Four Times	2	8	2	4
> four times	2	1	1	1
	100	100	100	100
"During the last 7 days, did you go a whole day without eating? How often?"				
None	41	77	68	64
one	40	14	12	19
Two	13	4	10	9
Three	5	1	8	5
Four or more	1	4	2	3
	100	100	100	100
"Ever go without anything to eat for two or more days at a time? How often?"				
Never	51	72	62	63
Few times a year	10	7	8	8
Once a month	3	5	9	6
Twice a month	9	4	6	6
Once a week	27	12	15	17
	100	100	100	100

N: Refers to unweighted data. All percentages are based on weighted data.

percent of total sample), followed by "missed meal time" (22 percent—8 percent of total sample), "no way to get to place with food" (11 percent—4 percent of total sample), "was sick" (10 percent—4 percent of total sample), and "not hungry" (10 percent—4 percent of total sample).

Respondents were also asked whether they sometimes went for two or more days without eating, and if so, how often that occurred. For all respondents this distribution was bimodal, with many (63%) never going for two days or more without eating, but a meaningful proportion (17%) saying that this happens to them once a week. Respondents who did not use shelters at all but used only soup kitchens revealed a significantly higher frequency of sometimes going without food for two days or more, with 27 percent saying this happened to them once a week, compared to 15 percent for whom this was true among those who used both soup kitchens and shelters, and 12 percent who reported this level of not eating among those who used only shelters.

It is evident that homeless persons who use only soup kitchens indicated lower frequencies of eating and more dissatisfaction with their diet than did persons who use shelters. Personal characteristics of soup-kitchen-only users may help explain this finding.[3] Users of soup kitchens only are older, less educated, homeless longer, jobless longer, and have fewer current resources and less income than homeless persons who use shelters.

Factors Associated with Frequency of Eating

Regression analyses were done on respondents' answers to the three questions reported in Table 3.2 to determine some of the factors associated with their reported frequency of eating. Included in the regressions as independent variables were five variables either directly associated with food or with the presence of income to make obtaining food possible: number of days during the week that the respondent eats at a shelter, receiving income maintenance now (AFDC, GA, SSI), the amount of food-stamp benefits being received, cash income during the last 30 days, and having a place to cook food. Six demographic descriptors were also included: age, education, being a member of a minority group, gender, being a one-person household, and being in a homeless household with a child. Finally, seven variables were included that describe certain problems associated with homelessness: number of health problems, having been a patient in a mental hospital, having been a patient in a drug or alcohol rehabilitation program, number of servings of alcohol the day before the interview, score on a measure of current depression/demoralization (CES-D), the number of months since the respondent last held a steady job (defined as a job lasting three months or more), and the number of months that the respondent had been homeless. Table 3.3 presents the results of these regressions for the three dependent variables:

- "daily"—number of times the respondent reported "usually eating in a day" (high values represent *more* frequent eating);

Table 3.3
Factors Associated with Frequency of Eating Reported by Service-Using Homeless Individuals (Standardized Regression Coefficients; N = 1704)

Independent Variables	Dependent Variable		
	Daily	No Eat	Two Days
Current depression/demoralization (CES-D - high = more)	-.135**	.240****	.139*
Gender (1=female 0=male)	-.171*	-.312***	.311**
Homeless household includes child	.507***	.003	-.258*
Reported number of health problems	-.226***	-.187**	-.029
Days/week eat at shelter	.151**	-.052	-.068
Drug/alcohol trtmt. (1=yes; 0=no)	-.110	.280****	.068
Single (1=yes; 0=no)	-.060	-.405****	.143
Food stamp benefit received- $ per person/month (range=$0 - $81)	.162**	.048	.064
Months of homelessness	.117*	-.097	.022
Months since last steady job	-.003	.015	.132*
Education	.063	-.118*	-.035
Age	-.061	.111	-.168*
Reported income/last 30 days	.075	-.055	-.101
Minority status (1=yes; 0=no)	.061	.037	.030
Has a place to cook food	-.087	-.015	.014
Receives income maintenance now	-.033	-.093	-.012
Mental hospitaliza. (1=yes; 0=no)	.085	.030	-.083
Number of servings of alcohol	.019	-.043	-.111
Adjusted R^2	.373	.282	.143

N: Refers to unweighted data. Regressions are based on weighted data.
* $p < .05$; ** $p < .01$; *** $p < .001$; **** $p < .0001$

- "no eat"—number of days out of the seven days immediately preceding the interview that respondent reported going without eating (high values represent *less* frequent eating);

- "two days"—how often the respondent reported "ever going without eating for two days or more at a time" (high values represent *less* frequent eating);

giving the standardized regression coefficients for the effects of each predictor variable on the three dependent variables. The larger the coefficient, whether positive or negative, the more important it is in explaining the value of the dependent variable. Predictor variables have been arranged in the table to reflect their relative importance in affecting the dependent variables.

As can be seen in Table 3.3, many factors were significantly associated with the frequency of eating reported by the service-using homeless persons in this study. Together they explained 37 percent of the variance in the number of times homeless persons ate daily ($R^2 = .373$), 28 percent of the variance in the number of days without food during the last week ($R^2 = .282$), and 15 percent of the variance in the frequency of going two days or more without eating ($R^2 = .148$).

Among the income and food-related variables, the two significant ones were the number of days the respondent ate at a shelter during the past 7 days and the amount of the food-stamp benefit being received. Both were consistently associated with reports of more frequent eating on a daily basis.

Among the demographic variables, being female was associated with less-frequent eating daily and on a long-term basis (''two days''), but with a lower frequency of having gone for whole days without food during the past week. The presence of a child in a household was strongly associated with a greater frequency of eating daily and with a lower frequency of going without food on a long-term basis. Being single, whether male or female, was associated with a greater frequency of having gone without food during the past week, as was having a higher level of education. Being older was associated with less of a likelihood of having gone without food for two days or longer.

Turning to those variables that may characterize certain segments of the homeless population, the two having the strongest effects were current depression/demoralization and the number of health problems. A depression scale developed by the Center for Epidemiological Studies at the National Institute of Mental Health (known as the CES-D) was used to measure respondents' current levels of depression/demoralization. This variable proved to be the strongest predictor in the model; the higher one's depression/demoralization, the less frequently one ate on all measures. The number of reported health problems was associated with less-frequent eating on a daily basis, but with a lower frequency of having gone without food in the past week.

The regression results also indicated that having a history of treatment for drug or alcohol abuse was associated with less-frequent eating during the past week. For the final two variables in the equation, the longer one had been homeless, the more frequently one reported eating daily; and the longer the time since one held a steady job, the more often one went without food for two days or more.

WHERE THE HOMELESS EAT

We inquired about their sources of food during the seven-day period preceding the interview. The question asked ''On how many days during the past week did you get food from . . . ?'' Therefore a respondent could indicate that he or she had gotten food at soup kitchens on 6 days, at restaurants on 4 days, and at grocery stores on 3 days, meaning that they got food at more than one place per day.

Sixty-four percent of the homeless respondents in this study reported eating at soup kitchens at least once during the 7 days preceding the interview. Eighteen percent ate at soup kitchens only once a week, 9 percent ate there twice, 20 percent ate there on 3 to 6 days of the week, and 18 percent ate at soup kitchens on 7 days of the week. Homeless individuals who used soup kitchens at all ate at soup kitchens 3.6 days per week on average.

Fifty-one percent of homeless service-users had eaten at shelters during the past week. Most of these ate at shelters throughout the entire week (58 percent— 30 percent of total sample). Twelve percent of those eating at shelters ate there only once, and the remainder (30%) ate there on 2 to 6 days during the past week. Homeless individuals who ate at shelters where they also lived ate there on 5 out of the past 7 days, on average.

Twenty-nine percent of the sample cited restaurants where they paid for food as an eating place during the past 7 days. Eight percent of the sample ate in restaurants on 1 day during the week, 10 percent ate there on 2 days, and 7 percent ate there on 3 to 6 days. Four percent reported eating at restaurants on 7 days of the week preceding the interview.

No other source was mentioned by more than 19 percent of the sample; most were mentioned by only 5–10 percent. Grocery stores were mentioned by 19 percent, a relative or friend's home by 18 percent, trash cans by 9 percent, and handouts from the back door of a restaurant were mentioned as a source by 8 percent. Food wagons and food pantries were each cited by 5 percent of respondents.

Since there were numerous types of places where the homeless got food, we created four combined categories of food sources. These were:

• service providers (soup kitchens or shelters);

• stores or restaurants where they purchased raw or prepared food;

• meals obtained from friends, relatives, or handouts at the back doors of restaurants; and

• trash cans.

Respondents reported to us the number of days during the past seven days on which they got food from the different sources; therefore the base variables must be interpreted as *how often* someone got food from a source. Based on these data, we created variables reflecting the "number of times a source was used as a proportion of all times that all food sources were used." These variables can be summarized by their means and interpreted as the mean proportion of time that a particular source was used.

Table 3.4 summarizes the information about food sources and includes data to illuminate the effects on food sources of some of the same variables used in

Table 3.4
Average Percentage of Time during Past Seven Days That Homeless Service Users Obtained Food from Four Combined Sources, by Selected Variables (Weighted Percentages; N = 1704)

Selected Variables	Source of Food			
	Service Providers	Restaurant or Grocery, For Cash	Friends, Relatives, Handouts	Trash Cans
All Respondents	65	17	9	3
Gender				
Male	66	16	8	3
Female	61	20	11	1
Race				
Minority	63	14	11	3
Nonminority	67	21	5	2
Household with Child	51	29	10	1
Household without Child	66	16	8	3
Income Maintenance				
Yes	63	18	8	3
No	65	17	8	3
Food Stamps				
Yes	58	23	9	4
No	66	16	9	3
Drug/Alcohol Treatment				
Yes	65	19	8	4
No	65	16	9	2
Mental Hospitalization				
Yes	72	10	10	3
No	63	19	8	3
Current Depression/Demoralization				
Yes (High CES-D)	64	13	11	3
No (Low CES-D)	65	21	6	2

N: Refers to unweighted data. All percentages are based on weighted data.

the regressions presented above. The data in Table 3.4 are mean, or average, percents. The first row of Table 3.4 shows that on average all respondents got food from service providers 65 percent of the time, from restaurants or grocery stores 17 percent of the time, from friends and relatives 9 percent of the time, and from trash cans 3 percent of the time. All data in the table refer to the reports of food sources during the last seven days.

Table 3.4 does not reveal any extreme deviations from the overall pattern for all respondents as a result of status on the descriptive variables whose effects were explored. However, some differences did occur that are worth pointing out. Minority homeless persons were somewhat less likely to use service providers and to pay for food at restaurants and grocery stores than were nonminority homeless persons in this survey; they were also more likely to get food from friends and relatives. Homeless households with at least one child were less likely to eat at service providers and were slightly more likely to eat with relatives or friends or to buy food from grocery stores or restaurants than were homeless households without children.

Homeless persons receiving food stamps used service providers less and paid more often than those who did not get food stamps. Receipt of income maintenance did not affect reported sources of food. Persons with a history of mental hospitalization used services more often and paid for food less often than those who had never been hospitalized. A drug or alcohol treatment history or scores reflecting current depression or demoralizatin did not affect reported sources of food.

Data collected on the meals available to homeless people through soup kitchens and shelters showed that they are of relatively good variety and nutrient content (Burt and Cohen, 1988). The data available from individuals do not allow us to determine where people ate all of their meals. However, data indicate that 321,000 provider meals are available each day in cities of 100,000 or more, and we estimate these could supply only 1.4 provider meals daily for each homeless person, including children, in these cities. Homeless individuals may eat meals elsewhere that are either more or less adequate than provider meals. However, data on homeless individuals' eating patterns, presented below, suggest that their diet is less than adequate.

INDIVIDUAL FOOD INTAKE

The data on food intake were collected from individuals in the form of a one-day food list. Interviewers asked individuals to try to remember everything that they had eaten on the previous day. The method used to collect these data took approximately 7–8 minutes (out of a total interview time of 15 minutes), and was never intended to approach the level of detail and completeness possible for a 24-hour recall procedure, which may take as long as 20–60 minutes. Despite the time constraints, the information reported is more detailed than previously obtained for the homeless and provides insight into the quantities and varieties of food consumed by the service-using homeless population.

The recorded data were coded into food groups, and the estimated number of portions eaten were also recorded. Systematic procedures were used to translate amounts of food into numbers of servings. Since we knew we could not collect exact information on food preparation methods or on the sizes of each portion, a nutrient analysis was never planned. Aside from lack of a nutrient analysis however, the analysis of individual one-day food lists paralleled the analysis of provider meals. We analyzed the one-day food lists for the total number of servings consumed, for the number of food groups represented among the five core groups and five additional groups, and for the number of portions consumed within each food group.

Number of Servings

We looked first at the total number of servings that homeless individuals reported consuming on the day prior to the interview. Eight percent of the sample reported that they did not eat anything during the day before the interview. The median number of servings reported on the one-day food lists used in this study was 9, meaning that half of the respondents ate more servings than this and half ate fewer. The mean was 9.1 servings. The cutoff for the lowest quartile was 5 servings (25 percent of respondents ate fewer than 5 servings overall during the preceding day), and the third quartile cutoff was 13 servings (25 percent of respondents ate more than 13 servings). Users of soup kitchens only reported the lowest number of servings; although users of shelters only reported the highest number, their figures are not greatly different from those who use both soup kitchens and shelters.

Number of Different Food Groups

We also characterized the diets of the homeless by counting the number of food groups represented on the one-day food list. The 10 food groups used for this purpose are:

Core	Additional
1. Milk and Milk Products	6. Fats and Oils
2. Grain Products	7. Baked Goods
3. Fruits and Fruit Juices	8. Sweets
4. Vegetables	9. Sweetened Beverages
5. Meats and Meat Alternates	10. Salty Snacks

The analysis created two different variables using these 10 food groups. These variables are intended to show the *variety* of foods eaten by homeless people. The first 5 food groups (milk and milk products, grain products, fruits and fruit juices, vegetables, and meat and meal alternates) are considered the core of an adequate diet. One variable therefore indicates how many of the first 5 food groups were in the respondent's food intake for the day before the interview. The second variable indicates how many of the 5 additional food groups (fats and oils, baked goods, sweets, sweetened beverages, and salty snacks) were in the respondent's diet for the previous day. Although less nutritious, foods from these food groups nevertheless can contribute calories to a person's diet. When levels of daily food intake are low, calories are important, and a complete analysis should indicate the amounts available of even these foods.[4]

Table 3.5

Percentage of Service-Using Homeless Respondents Who Report Eating Foods from Different Food Groups, by Pattern of Service Use (Weighted Percentages)

Homeless Individuals Who:

	Use Only Soup Kitchens (N= 223)	Use Only Shelters (N = 670)	Use Both Shelters & Soup Kitchens (N = 811)	Total Sample (N = 1704)
Number of Food Groups Reported Present in Diet From:				
5 Core Groups[a]				
No groups	8	12	12	11
1 group	9	6	8	8
2 groups	28	17	22	21
3 groups	41	27	31	32
4 groups	12	20	22	19
All 5 groups	2	18	5	9
Median No. of Core Groups	3	3	3	3
Additional 5 Groups[b]				
No groups	42	25	25	29
1 group	38	29	33	33
2 groups	17	26	28	24
3 groups	3	17	9	11
4 groups	0	3	5	3
All 5 groups	0	0	0	0
Median No. of Additonal Groups	1	1	1	1

N: Refers to unweighted data. All percentages are based on weighted data.
        Due to rounding errors, all percentages do not add up to 100%.
[a]:   Milk and milk products, grain products, fruit and fruit juices, vegetables, and
        meats and meat products.
[b]:   Fats and oils, baked goods, sweets, sweetened beverages and salty snaks.

Table 3.5 reports the results. Among the 5 core food groups, the number of different food groups mentioned in any one-day food list ranged from 0 to 5, with a mean of 2.7 (not shown) and a median of three food groups. For the remaining 5 food groups, the range was 0 to 4, with a mean of 1.3 (not shown) and a median of 1. Eight percent reported eating nothing the previous day.

As the distributions in Table 3.5 indicate, homeless persons who used only

Table 3.6
Average Number of Servings per Food Group in One-Day Food Lists Reported by Service-Using Homeless Persons (N = 1704)

Food Group	Average Number of Servings	
	Homeless Service Users	USDA Recommendations
Milk and Milk Products	.8	2
Grain Products	1.7	6 - 11
Fruits and Fruit Juices	.5	2 - 4
Vegetables	1.1	3 - 5
Meat and Meat Alternates	2.3	2 - 3
Fats and Oils	.4	N/A
Baked Goods	.5	N/A
Candy	.5	N/A
Sweetened Drinks	1.2	N/A
Salty Snaks	.1	N/A
USDA Recommendation*		15 - 25

N: Refers to unweighted data. All figures in Table 6 taken from interviews with homeless individuals are based on weighted data.

*Source: Human Nutrition Information Service, USDA (1986). ''Nutrition and Your Health, Dietary Guidelines for Americans: Eat a Variety of Foods.'' **Home and Garden Bulletin #** 232 (No. 1, April 1986: 3).

soup kitchens reported eating the fewest different food groups from among both the 5 core food groups and the remaining 5 food groups.

Average Number of Servings per Food Group

In addition to looking at the total number of servings of any food and at the number of different food groups represented in the one-day food lists reported by homeless individuals, we also looked at the number of servings within each food group. An adequate diet (based on USDA recommendations presented in USDA Home and Garden Bulletin #232–1, April 1986) would have 2 servings from the milk group, 6–11 servings from grains, 2–4 servings from fruits, 3–5 from vegetables, and 2–3 servings from the meat group. Table 3.6 presents the data from the one-day food lists of our sample, which can be compared to these recommendations. Looking at the average number of servings per food group in Table 3.6 shows that homeless individuals in our sample reported eating more meat or meat alternates than food from the other groups. However, regardless of which food group one considers, the average diet of the homeless in our sample as recorded on the one-day food lists was extremely low in the fruit group and fats group and quite low in vegetables and milk. In addition, con-

Table 3.7
Average Percentage of Homeless Individuals' Daily Intake from Grains, Meats, Vegetables and Fruits, Milk, and Miscellaneous Food (Weighted Percentages; N = 1704)

Food Group	Average Percentage of Total Daily Intake
Grain Products	20
Meat and Meat Alternates	28
Vegetables and Fruits	17
Milk and Milk Products	8
Miscellaneous Food	24

N: Refers to unweighted data. Percentages are based on weighted data.

sumption of all groups was low compared to USDA daily intake recommendations for an adequate diet. Compared to the 15–25 servings recommended from the milk, meat, fruit, vegetable, and grains groups, the average number of servings from all of these groups eaten by the homeless is 6.4. The average number of servings from all food groups in their diets was 9.1.

We can look at the patterns of consumption from the different food groups in two other ways—consumption from each group as a proportion of total consumption, and the proportion of individuals reporting no consumption of foods from a particular group.

Percentage of Total Intake from Specific Food Groups

To get a better understanding of the individuals' diets, we calculated the percentage of total number of servings recorded as daily intake that came from grain products, fruits and vegetables, meat and meat alternates, milk, and miscellaneous food. This division of the food groups was established after reviewing the frequencies and means of the number of servings in each group. Since vegetables had an extremely low intake rate, they were combined with fruits. The similarities in the nutritional makeup of these foods makes this combination a logical one. The miscellaneous food category combines salty snacks, baked goods, sweets, and sweetened beverages. The food group not included is fats and oils because it had such a low intake rate. The results, presented in Table 3.7, show that meats and meat alternates contributed the greatest proportion of intake reported on the one-day food lists at 28 percent. The miscellaneous food group represented 24 percent of intake; while adding calories, these foods do not add to the quality of the overall diet. The lowest intake from a single food group (except for fats, which were not included in this breakdown) was from milk, at 8 percent of total intake.

Food Groups Lacking from the Diet

The diets of homeless people are relatively lacking in the five food groups considered the core of an adequate diet. Calculations based on descriptions of what homeless people said they ate the day before the interview reveal that 65 percent had not consumed any milk or milk products during that day, 43 percent had eaten no fruits or vegetables, 30 percent had eaten no grain products, and 20 percent had eaten no meat or meat alternates such as dry beans, peas, and peanut butter. Persons who used only soup kitchens were more likely to have eaten no grain products or meats/meat alternates than persons using shelters, but did not differ much on intake of the other food groups. National comparisons for a one-day period from the Nationwide Food Consumption Survey conducted in 1977–1978 showed these foods to be present much more often in the diets of the average American. That survey found that 19 percent of Americans had eaten no milk or milk products, 14 percent had eaten no vegetables, 46 percent had eaten no fruits, 4 percent had eaten no grain products, and 7 percent had eaten no meat or meat alternates (Human Nutrition Information Service, 1980).

Intake Score

The intake score provides us with a way to rate the number of servings from each food group with significant nutrient value against the recommended number of servings. The scores in this study are based on the availability of 5 of the 10 food groups used in our analysis (milk and milk products, fruit, vegetables, grain products, and meat and meat alternates). Scoring was done as follows: (1) the number of servings of each of the five major food groups was recorded; (2) this number was truncated to equal no more than the EFNEP recommended number of servings from each group; and (3) the truncated number of servings from each group was totaled. The maximum intake score was 12. Table 3.8 reports intake scores for the service-using homeless population by pattern of service use.

The mean intake score of the service-using homeless population was 4.9 out of a possible 12; the median was 4.1. The scores ranged was from 0 to 12, with 60 percent of respondents scoring between 0 and 5. As we have seen in other data on eating patterns reported in this chapter, homeless individuals who used only soup kitchens reported lower intake, on average, than individuals who used shelters or who used both soup kitchens and shelters. Regardless of pattern of service use, however, the intake scores reported by our sample of homeless individuals reveal a relatively poor level of daily intake compared to the optimal score of 12. Their intake scores suggest that they ate less than half of the food groups and numbers of servings considered adequate daily intake for adults. The intake scores reported imply that the diets of the homeless in this study lacked adequate amounts of food from several food groups.

These data raise some interesting questions, especially when they are compared

Table 3.8
Intake Score, by Pattern of Service Use

Homeless Individuals Who:

Intake Score	Use Only Soup Kitchens (N = 223)	Use Only Shelters (N = 670)	Use Both Shelters & Soup Kitchens (N=811)	Total Sample (N=1704)
0	8	12	12	11
1	3	3	6	4
2	11	8	7	8
3	17	5	11	10
4	10	14	19	15
5	11	8	9	9
6	13	13	7	11
7	2	8	7	6
8	19	9	8	11
9	3	8	8	6
10	1	7	5	5
11	1	2	1	1
12	0	2	1	1
Mean	4.7	5.4	4.6	4.9
Median	4.0	5.0	4.4	4.1

N: Refers to unweighted data. All figures are based on weighted data.

to the information collected about the nutritional content of the meals available from providers. For total number of servings reported, the mean for provider meals was 6.8 servings compared to a mean of 7.9 (median of 7.2) servings reported by individuals as their entire intake for the preceding 24 hours. For the number of the 5 core food groups represented, the mean for provider meals was 3.5 groups; for individuals it was 2.7 groups for their daily intake (the medians were 3 groups for both provider meals and individual daily intake). For the remaining 5 food groups, the mean for provider meals was 1.4 groups compared to 1.3 groups as reported by individuals for their entire day's intake. Only in the case of total number of servings did the reports of individuals exceed what was available in *one* average provider meal. For the number of the 5 core food groups represented, individual reports were significantly lower than the parallel index for provider meals.

These results raise the issue of whether homeless individuals underreport their daily food intake or whether the pattern of results means that many of the homeless are not eating all of the foods available at provider meals or are not eating at providers all the time. First, even on full-scale 24-hour recalls, certain subgroups of U.S. adults underreport their food intake, so it would not be surprising if the homeless also underreported. Both the general tendency to underreport and the greatly shortened and less detailed method of data collection would push the results in the direction of underreporting intake. Second, homeless persons may not eat all that is available at provider meals, even when they take food on their plates. Our observations of provider meals focused on what was served, not on what was actually consumed and what was thrown away. Nor did we take into account second helpings when these were available. It may also be that our observations misestimated the quantities of ingredients from different food groups present in mixed dishes. Third, as we saw earlier in this chapter, homeless persons reported low frequencies of daily eating, with the average respondent eating less than twice a day (mean = 1.9). It may be that some of the "times" they reported eating during a usual day did not represent full meals, and therefore we would expect that their intake would be less.

To assess whether the one-day food list responses of homeless individuals were consistent with other responses about their eating patterns, correlations were calculated among two measures of dietary intake (number of servings, and number of 5 core food groups) and:

- perceived healthfulness and adequacy of diet;
- number of times they eat daily, days without eating during last seven days, and frequency of going two or more days without eating;
- current receipt of food stamps;
- number of nights out of the past seven that the respondent spent in a shelter; number of days during the past seven that the respondent got food from soup kitchens and from shelters; and
- current depression/demoralization (CES-D) and responses to "During the last week, was your appetite so poor that you did not feel like eating . . . never, some of the time, most of the time?" (one item on the CES-D).

The correlations show quite strong associations among the various indicators of diet adequacy and eating patterns obtained through interviews with homeless individuals. They also indicate some of the factors associated with more adequate diets. The three measures of dietary intake derived from the one-day food lists are all highly correlated and are also associated with reported frequency of eating. They are also associated with perceptions of the healthfulness of the diet and less strongly associated with perceptions of diet adequacy.

Food-stamp receipt was associated with more frequent eating and better perceptions of diet healthfulness and adequacy.

Scoring higher on the CES-D, a measure of current depression/demoralization, was strongly associated with poorer dietary intake, lower frequency of eating, and less-frequent use of shelters. A single item from the CES-D measuring poor appetite during the past week showed most of the same patterns of association. The consumption of alcohol was marginally associated with a lower number of the five core food groups in the one-day food list and more strongly associated with a lower number of the remaining five food groups. Alcohol consumption was also associated with less-frequent use of shelters (for either sleeping or eating) and with more-frequent use of soup kitchens.

Finally, the number of nights out of the previous seven that a homeless individual reported sleeping at a shelter and the number of days during the previous seven that someone ate at a shelter were strongly positively associated with all of the dietary intake, eating frequency, and perceptions of diet variables. However, the number of days the respondent reported eating at soup kitchens during the seven days prior to the interview was negatively associated with dietary intake and with perceptions of diet. It was *not* associated with frequency of eating. This association probably reflects the fact that 35 percent of shelters serving meals served two meals per day, and 54 percent served three meals per day, whereas 72 percent of soup kitchens served only one meal per day. Thus for a homeless person, living in a shelter that serves meals appears to be a critical factor in getting enough to eat, whereas exclusive use of soup kitchens is not as reliable a source of nutrition.

On the basis of this correlational analysis, we conclude that there is great consistency in the information given by the homeless about their food intake, frequency of eating, and perceived adequacy of their diets. Although the absolute level of dietary intake as measured by the one-day food list is most likely to be an underreporting of actual intake, the same conclusion could be reached for every method of obtaining dietary information, even the most elaborate. Regardless of the confidence one can place in these data as absolute figures, one must read them as indicating a *relatively* low level of food intake, and one considerably below a diet supplying all necessary nutrients.

Factors Affecting Dietary Intake

To gain a better understanding of what factors affect dietary intake we ran regression analyses similar to those presented earlier (Table 3.3). Table 3.9 presents the standardized regression coefficients for the equations involving the measures of dietary intake derived from the one-day food lists—number of servings, number of five core food groups, and number of remaining food groups. The size of these coefficients indicates the degree of influence the predictor variables have on the dependent variables. Larger absolute size of a coefficient corresponds to greater influence.

The predictor with the strongest impact on variables measuring dietary intake is the number of days one eats at a shelter; the more days, the greater the number of servings from each food group and from the five core food groups. Other variables having a similar effect are the amount of food-stamp benefits received and the length of time for which one was homeless. The receipt of income maintenance was associated with eating more in general as well as having a greater number of servings from the additional food groups.

While being a member of a minority group, being older, and not having a

Table 3.9
Factors Associated with Dietary Intake Reported by Service-Using Homeless Individuals (Standardized Regression Coefficients; N = 1704)

Dependent Variable:

Independent Variables	Number of Servings Range = (0 - 68)	Number of Five Core Food Groups (0 - 5)	Number of Additional Food Groups (0 - 4)
Number of days ate at shelter	.144*	.145*	.113
Receives income maintenance	.154*	.081	.230**
Food stamp benefit received-			
$ per person/month (range =$0-$81)	.208**	.213**	.084
Months of homelessness	.145*	.252***	.067
Minority status (1=yes; 0=no)	-.156**	-.093	-.130*
Gender (1=female; 0=male)	.170	-.081	-.296**
Age	-.219**	-.074	-.014
Has no place to cook food	-.162*	-.109	-.070
Months since last steady job	.041	.022	-.148*
Number of reported health problems-	.095	-.149*	.082
Current depression/demoralization			
(CES-D - High = more)	-.063	-.040	-.028
Mental hospitaliza. (1=yes; 0=no)	-.014	-.031	-.015
Number of servings of alcohol	-.041	-.064	-.102
Education	-.109	-.061	.006
Reported income/last 30 days	.043	.039	-.010
Single (1=yes; 0=no)	.046	-.070	.191
Homeless household includes child	.034	.067	-.003
Drug/alcohol trtmt. (1=yes; 0=no)	.041	-.090	-.018
Adjusted R^2	.228	.258	.200

N: Refers to unweighted data. Regressions are based on weighted data.
* $p<.05$; **$p<.01$; ***$p<.001$

place to cook food were all associated with having consumed a smaller number of total servings, only having minority status was associated with a lower number of servings from the additional food groups. Being female was associated with eating more additional foods, a longer period of time since working steadily was associated with eating less additional foods, and a greater number of health problems reported was associated with having a smaller number of servings of the core food groups.

The Homeless Who Do Not Use Services

To achieve comparison data for the homeless who do not use services we interviewed homeless persons at congregating sites (bus stations, culverts, etc.)

who had not used any kind of shelter or soup kitchen for the previous week. Since this was a small and not necessarily representative sample, statistically rigorous comparisons between them and the service-using homeless cannot be made. Nevertheless, the general picture is relatively clear.

The homeless who do not use services had poorer eating patterns than the service-using homeless on every measure. They relied much more heavily on trash and on handouts as sources of food. They ate fewer meals per day, averaging only one meal per day (mean = 1.36) compared to the almost two meals of the service users (mean = 1.92). They were much more likely to have gone one or more days without eating during the seven days prior to the interview, with a mean of somewhat over one day (1.35) in comparison to a mean of under one day for service users (0.66).

The homeless who do not use services were less likely to report getting enough to eat and were quite unlikely to get what they wanted to eat. More nonusers than users described the quality of their diet as fair or poor and appeared less likely to have eaten foods from the five core food groups.

SUMMARY AND CONCLUSIONS

Data collected show that the meals available to homeless people through soup kitchens and shelters are of relatively good variety and nutrient content. However, data indicate that 321,000 provider meals are available each day in cities of 100,000 or more; we estimate that these meals supply only 1.4 provider meals for each homeless person on any given day. Homeless individuals may eat less-adequate meals elsewhere, so we can draw no firm conclusions about whether all the meals they eat are as adequate as the average provider meal. However, data on homeless individuals' eating patterns suggest that their diet is less than adequate.

Those who used only soup kitchens but never went to shelters ate less well than those who used shelters as well or shelters only. Soup-kitchen-only users reported fewer meals per day, more days in the week without eating, more periods of going two or more days without eating, and poorer outcomes on other indicators of eating patterns. The more often homeless people ate at a shelter during the week, the better their diet and eating patterns.

The information presented in this chapter clearly states that hunger is a problem for the homeless population. Hunger, particularly in the United States, is usually a function of inadequate economic resources with which to purchase food. While the private, nonprofit sector has made great efforts to provide food for the homeless population, we have seen that even this is not enough to avoid the problem of hunger. Legislation was passed in August 1988 expanding the Food Stamp Program and other federal nutrition programs as a response to documented evidence of increased hunger. Although some of these changes may affect hunger among the homeless population, more government action will be necessary to ensure that all homeless individuals are adequately fed.

Specific suggestions for increased action include increasing the availability of surplus food, providing more cash directly to meal providers, including soup kitchens and shelters in the food distribution system that now serves the school lunch/breakfast program (to ensure that they not only get the basic commodities available through USDA, but also the expanded list of foods available to school feeding sites), and expanding funding for the central kitchens that prepare home-delivered meals for the elderly and disabled so that they can prepare additional meals for the homeless to be distributed through the use of mobile "food wagons." This last suggestion would help bring food to those shown in our study to have the lowest and least nutritious food consumption, those homeless on the streets who do not use any meal or shelter facilities.

NOTES

1. The full study report may be obtained from The Urban Institute library, 2100 M Street N.W., Washington, DC 20037. Martha R. Burt and Barbara E. Cohen, *Feeding the Homeless: Does the Prepared Meals Provision Help? Volume I: Report to Congress; Volume II: Supporting Tables and Documentation*. The study was supported by Contracts No. 53–3198–6–41 and 53–3198–7–101 with the U.S. Department of Agriculture, Food and Nutrition Service, Office of Analysis and Evaluation.

2. See Burt and Cohen's chapter in this volume for the study's findings related to the sociodemographic characteristics of the homeless.

3. See Burt and Cohen's chapter in this volume.

4. Because the interviewers only had 7–8 minutes to complete all food-related questions, the recording of foods eaten during the previous day is necessarily less precise than with a standard 24-hour recall procedure. Results cannot therefore be interpreted as precise measures of diet quality, since no assessment was possible of nutrient quantities. However, examining the *variety of foods* eaten by the homeless is informative, especially when looking at the proportion of the homeless whose daily intake does or does not include foods from each of the five core food groups.

REFERENCES

Burt, Martha R., and Barbara E. Cohen. 1988. *Feeding the Homeless: Does the Prepared Meals Provision Help? Volume I: Report to Congress; Volume II: Supporting Tables and Documentation*. Washington, D.C.: The Urban Institute.

Human Nutrition Information Service, USDA. 1980. *Food Intakes and Nutrients, Individuals in One Day in the U.S., Spring 1977*. Preliminary Report #2. Hyattsville, Md: HNIS-USDA.

4

Drug Abuse among Homeless People

Norweeta G. Milburn

This chapter reviews the sparse research literature on drug abuse among homeless people in the United States, discusses the limitations of previous research, and identifies analytical questions that should be considered in future research. Drug abuse is viewed as a problem behavior that deviates from the norm of socially accepted behaviors. In this context, the use of any illicit drug, such as marijuana; the excessive use of any licit drug, such as alcohol; and the misuse of any prescribed medication will be defined as drug abuse. The chapter builds upon a previous review by Mulkern and Spence (1984) that examined the prevalence of drug abuse, characteristics of drug abusers, and the level of drug abuse among homeless people. The chapter focuses primarily on drugs other than alcohol, even though studies on homeless people do not always make a distinction between substances that are abused.[1] Because so little has been written on drugs other than alcohol, the chapter includes relevant conference presentations and reports from state and city governments in addition to published articles on the topic.

UNDERLYING ASSUMPTIONS ABOUT HOMELESSNESS

Several underlying assumptions about homelessness guide this review—assumptions pertaining to how it has been studied, its "newness" as a social problem, how it is defined, its causes, its temporal nature, and its relation to drug abuse.

The first assumption is that the methods used in the study of homeless people have been seriously flawed. More than 25 years ago Levinson (1963) noted a number of significant methodological problems in the research on homeless

people, including (1) inadequate sampling, with samples of convenience being
the norm; (2) the lack of meaningful typologies of homeless people—typically
homeless people were all placed in the same category; and (3) inadequate measures of the behavior of homeless people.

Recently, Milburn and Watts (1985) and Bachrach (1984) described some of
these same flaws in the methods of current research on the homeless population.
They observed that many studies of homeless people had sampling deficiencies
and lacked a clear conceptual framework. In addition, they noted that researchers
studying the homeless looked simultaneously at widely varying subgroups, including skid-row alcoholics, shelter users, and young vagrants, which made it
difficult to generalize about the homeless population.

Consequently, research findings on homeless people must be interpreted with
caution. Before any generalizations may be made about the homeless population,
critical issues related to the sampling and study/site setting must be taken into
account (Bachrach, 1984). Research on homeless people requires an unusual
degree of creativity and resourcefulness on the part of investigators. Such research
is inherently difficult to develop and implement due to the high mobility and
inaccessibility of the target population as well as the often debilitating effects
of the environmental and psychological circumstances of the homeless. These
considerations are particularly important to bear in mind when considering the
scant research literature on drug abuse among homeless people.

The second underlying assumption is that homelessness is not a new phenomenon, despite our current heightened awareness of the problem. Accounts of
homelessness date back to the 1800s (Milburn and Watts, 1985). However, its
definition and relative importance as a "social problem" have changed over
time. The homeless population has become increasingly more heterogeneous
(Morrissey and Dennis, 1986). During the Great Depression, this population
consisted primarily of hobos, tramps, vagrants, and migrant laborers (Caplow,
1940; Cross and Cross, 1937; Culver, 1933; Gray, 1931; Kerr, 1930; Locke,
1935; Outland, 1939). From the 1950s through the early 1970s, the homeless
population included occupants of skid row—primarily male, chronic alcoholics
(for example see Bahr, 1969a, 1969b; Blumberg et al., 1970; Levinson, 1957;
Spradley, 1970; Wiseman, 1970; Wood, 1979). After the widespread deinstitutionalization of mental patients during the late 1960s, the population was
considered to include the seriously mentally ill (for example see Lazare et al.,
1972; Priest, 1976; Segal et al., 1977). More recently, those who are economically disadvantaged—such as single women and their children; young, single,
unemployed men, and runaway youth—have also been included in this population
(Hope and Young, 1986). Despite the expanded character of the homeless population, demographic trends suggest that the current homeless population in the
United States is predominantly male, single, usually under age 40, and slightly
more likely to be a member of an ethnic minority group (Arce et al., 1983; Roth
et al., 1985; Morse and Calsyn, 1985; Levine and Stockdill, 1986; Martin,
1986).

Thus, the present homeless population in the United States does not comprise a single group or particular type of individual. Instead, this population has various subgroups with different characteristics and needs. Over time, the composition of the homeless population has shifted, reflecting major social, political, and economic changes in the United States. These varying characteristics of the target population must be considered when a specific problem behavior such as drug abuse is examined.

The third assumption that guides this chapter is that social scientists do not have a consistent definition of homelessness. This is due in part to the diversity of the homeless population. For the purpose of this chapter, homelessness is defined as the lack of adequate permanent shelter *and* resources—such as money, family, and friends—to acquire permanent shelter. Specifically, homelessness is the "inability to acquire and maintain adequate permanent housing" (Watts and Milburn, 1987).

Some researchers and advocates have challenged this definition. They argue that homelessness should simply be defined as not being housed, sheltered, or domiciled, because defining it otherwise places the blame for homelessness upon the individual and does not attribute responsibility to the role that societal forces play (Baxter and Hopper, 1982; Morse, 1986). I believe, however, that homelessness must be attributed to both societal and individual dynamics. Homelessness is a circumstance (Hopper, 1987) that reflects both an individual's inability to meet his or her needs *and* society's failure to provide suitable mechanisms that enable all citizens to meet their needs.

It is important to remember, nevertheless, that people who are homeless do, in fact, lack adequate housing. The lack of housing is central to the whole notion of homelessness and must not be overlooked or underestimated.

The fourth underlying assumption is related to the third: lack of resources causes homelessness. The resources that an individual needs to acquire and maintain housing include:

- *Personal* resources such as stable mental and physical health, independent living skills, job skills, and literacy;

- *Environmental* resources such as accessible, caring, service-oriented health and mental health systems that provide outreach services and engage in active case management, a public education system that provides adequate learning experiences, and a system that provides affordable, appropriate, and available housing;

- *Economic* resources such as employment in a job that pays sufficient wages to maintain a decent (e.g., self-sufficient) standard of living, and access to Supplemental Security Income (SSI) and public assistance when necessary; and

- *Social* resources such as family and friends that can provide emotional, instrumental, and informational social support (Watts and Milburn, 1987).

Drug abuse can impact upon these resources in a number of ways. For example, drug abuse can be deleterious to an individual's physical and mental health.

Drug abuse can also make an individual unable to work, and behaviors associated with drug abuse can alienate friends and relatives. Several studies have cited drug abuse as a cause of homelessness. For example, in studies of homeless people in Ohio and Massachusetts, 7 percent and 14 percent of the samples, respectively, cited drug and/or alcohol abuse as a reason for their circumstance (Mulkern et al., 1985; Roth et al., 1985).

The fifth assumption is that homelessness also has a temporal component that modifies its impact upon individuals. The temporal quality of an individual's homeless state is related to his or her personal, environmental, economic, and social resources. Simply put, individuals with more resources are less likely to become homeless. Moreover, if they do become homeless, it is less probable that they will become *prolonged homeless people*. Through its impact upon an individual's resources, drug abuse can contribute to the temporal quality of an individual's homeless state. In this regard, categories of homeless people include the:

- *Displaced homeless*—usually individuals who are forced out of housing because of economic or situational hardships such as an eviction or fire;
- *Episodic homeless*—individuals who are in a cycle of having or not having housing depending upon the availability of funds; and
- *Prolonged homeless*—individuals who have been without permanent housing for a protracted period of time (Hoffman et al., 1982; Rooney, 1980; Arce et al., 1983; Watts and Milburn, 1987).

With these five assumptions in mind, what follows is a review of what is known about the significance of drug abuse among homeless people.

THE SIGNIFICANCE OF DRUG ABUSE AS A PROBLEM AMONG HOMELESS PEOPLE

Alcoholism has always been a serious problem among the homeless population, particularly when the group under study consisted of an older, male, skid-row subgroup (for example, see Bahr, 1969a; 1969b). However, with the declining age of the homeless population, other forms of drug abuse seem to be increasingly more prevalent (Jones et al., 1984; Lamb, 1982; Siegal and Inciardi, 1982; Stark, 1985). Some researchers estimate that between 10 to 15 percent of the homeless population nationwide have drug abuse problems (Levine, 1984). Drug abuse has also been found to be more prevalent among homeless people than among non homeless people (Fischer et al., 1986). Nonetheless, there is very little empirical data on just how much the abuse of drugs other than alcohol occurs among homeless people, and whether it is truly more prevalent in this population than it is among the general population. Unfortunately, the homeless population is not included in the large survey studies conducted by the National Institute on Drug Abuse such as the "Monitoring the Future" project (Johnston et al., 1979) and the Household Survey (Abelson et al., 1977). These are surveys of respondents with fixed addresses (Miller et al., 1983).

Recent studies suggest that drug abuse does occur with some degree of frequency among homeless people (Arce et al., 1983; Bassuk et al., 1984; Roth et al., 1985; Hoffman et al., 1982). However, because drug abuse has not been consistently defined across these studies, measures of drug abuse vary, ranging from psychiatric assessments (Bassuk et al., 1984) to self-reports of having a "drug abuse" problem (Hoffman et al., 1982).

A number of theoretical explanations on why individuals use and become dependent upon drugs have been developed. Unfortunately, these theories do not offer much insight into why drug abuse occurs among homeless people and may be more prevalent among this group than it is among the general population. For example, Merton's structural model (1968), which describes behavioral strategies that individuals can use to adapt to the constraints and pressures of society to achieve goals, suggests that homelessness and drug abuse are forms of retreatism. According to this model, homeless people have engaged in one form of retreatism by being, for the most part, disengaged from the achievement-oriented goals of the broader society such as providing for one's basic needs (e.g., food, shelter, and clothing). Thus, one would expect such people to be engaged in another form of retreatism, that is, drug abuse. However, this model assumes the notion of freedom of choice—that an individual is free to choose how to function in society—as well as the notion of equal opportunity for all—that each individual is afforded the same opportunities.

In reality, individuals do not make choices in a vacuum about how they will live their lives. Societal roles and expectations dictated by various characteristics—such as their economic, physical, racial, or ethnic status—often play a very critical role in the range of choices that are available to individuals. Merton's model (1968) does not take these factors into account. The cause of disengagement, whether it is an individual choice or the result of societal forces often cannot be determined. Consequently, this model does not provide an axiomatic explanation. One can argue that people are homeless and use drugs because they choose to disengage from societal norms. One can also argue that homelessness and drug abuse are reactions to economic and other societal forces that are beyond individuals' control and that prevent them from maintaining a normal lifestyle.

A second model by Jessor and Jessor (1977) takes into account the role societal forces play as well as the vicissitudes of homelessness that can contribute to drug abuse. Their model suggests that drug abuse may be more prevalent among homeless people than it is among the general population, because in addition to its being a way to reject conventional norms, drug abuse is also a way of coping with stress and/or failure. A somewhat related finding is the observation that some homeless people, particularly those who have symptoms of mental illness, use drugs as a form of self-medication (Rosnow et al., 1985). Taking drugs appears to alleviate some of their psychiatric symptoms.

Neither model provides a satisfactory explanation of why drug abuse may be more prevalent among homeless people than it is among the general population. Better theoretical explanations clearly need to be developed.

RESEARCH ON DRUG ABUSE AMONG HOMELESS PEOPLE

Mulkern and Spence's Review of Studies on Drug Abuse

Mulkern and Spence (1984) reviewed current research on homeless people to determine the prevalence estimates of drug abuse and the level of drug use among homeless individuals, and to delineate the characteristics of homeless individuals who used drugs. They identified eight studies that represented the "best available" data on drug abuse among homeless people. Table 4.1 provides a summary of their findings on these studies.

Prevalence of drug abuse and level of drug use. Overall, it is difficult to generate accurate prevalence estimates from these studies because of the varied research methods that were employed, particularly with respect to the sampling strategies and measurement instruments. The prevalence estimates for lifetime drug use (whether an individual had ever used drugs) ranged from 3 to 55 percent. Prevalence estimates for annual drug use (whether an individual had used drugs within the past year) ranged from 44 to 55 percent. For daily drug use, the range was 3 to 4 percent.

The reported data do not lend themselves to a reasonable breakdown for the prevalence of current drug abuse. However, Mulkern and Spence (1984) attempted to provide reasonable estimates by defining it as "regular and frequent" drug use. Based on this definition, they noted prevalence estimates of 3 to 20 percent for current drug abuse among homeless people who were shelter users and prevalence estimates of 25 percent for current drug abuse among homeless people who lived on the streets.

Levels of drug use were not identifiable because the definitions of drug use varied across these studies.

Characteristics of drug users. Only two studies reported detailed demographic information on homeless drug users. In a study of 236 homeless people in single-room occupancy (SRO) hotels in New York City conducted by the city's Division of Substance Abuse Services (1983), 40 percent of the women and 27 percent of the men had "substantial" drug problems. Minorities (Blacks and Hispanics) used drugs more than nonminorities did. Higher-income homeless people used drugs more than did those who had lower incomes.[2]

The other study was conducted by Mulkern and Spence (1984) on 250 homeless people in the shelters and streets of Boston. They found 9 percent of the women and 36 percent of the men in the shelter subsample and 25 percent of the women and 39 percent of the men in the street subsample used drugs. In addition, 35 percent of the minorities and 27 percent of the nonminorities in the shelter subsample and 44 percent of the minorities and 35 percent of the nonminorities in the street subsample used drugs.

From these two studies, sex differences in drug use among homeless people are inconclusive. In the first study, more women than men had drug problems; whereas in the other study, more men than women used drugs. This inconsistency may be partly attributed to differences in the operational definition of drug abuse used in the two studies.

Methodological limitations. While the eight studies reviewed by Mulkern and Spence (1984) represented the best studies on drug abuse among homeless people, they are not truly comparable for several reasons. Samples of homeless people were selected from various types of settings, including food programs, shelters, streets, parks, and SRO hotels, with shelters used most frequently. Other settings such as jails and hospital emergency rooms, places where homeless people can also be found, were not considered.

The samples also varied in composition. Some studies referred to the respondents as adults, whereas other studies referred to them simply as "people," leaving open the possibility that some of the respondents may have been adolescents or children.

Drug use was not consistently defined across studies. For example, the notion of "regular" drug use varied considerably from study to study. Moreover, differences in occasional use, regular or frequent use, and dependence had not been examined in homeless people. The types of drugs that were used were often unknown because many of the studies used terms like "street" or "illicit" drugs to define drug categories rather than a recognized pharmacological typology. When specific drugs were delineated, the use of marijuana was noted most frequently, followed by the use of cocaine, minor tranquilizers, hallucinogens, and stimulants, as well as sedatives and narcotics.

The review by Mulkern and Spence (1984) also provided very little data on demographic characteristics of drug users who were homeless. In addition, data relating the duration of homelessness and drug use among respondents were not reported. Finally, most of the studies were done in the northeast and western sections of the United States, making generalizations to populations in other parts of the nation difficult.

Other Studies on Drug Abuse

Like the studies reviewed by Mulkern and Spence (1984), other studies of homeless people and drug abuse provide inconclusive results. For example, varying prevalence rates of drug abuse among the homeless are reported. Various methodological issues also make comparability across these studies problematic. Table 4.2 provides an overview of these findings.

Prevalence of drug abuse. As can been seen in Table 4.2, the prevalence estimates for drug abuse varied across these studies in part because drug abuse was defined in a number of different ways. The assessment of drug abuse also

Table 4.1

Studies with Data on Drug Abuse Reviewed by Mulkern and Spence (1984)

Investigator(s)	Location	Date of Study	Study Site	Sample (N)
1. C. Brown S. McFarlane R. Paredes L. Stark	Phoenix, AZ	June-July, 1982	Food Programs	150 adults
2. S. Crystal	New York, NY	May, 1982	Shelter	128 men (long-term residence)
3. L. Stark	Phoenix, AZ	March, 1983	Shelter & Urban Camps	195 adults
4. Div. of Substance Abuse Services Albany, NY	New York, NY	June , 1983	SRO Hotels	236 people
5. P. Robinson	Boston, MA	May-June, 1984	Shelter	297 people
6. J. Wynne	San Diego, CA	June, 1984	Shelter	82 women
7. Soc. Serv. Div. Multnomah Co., OR	Portland, OR	1984	Streets, Missions, Soup lines, Parks, Camps, & SRO Hotels	131 people
8. V.Mulkern R. Spence	Boston, MA	1984	Streets & Shelters	250 people (132 shelters, 118 streets)

Table 4.1 (continued)

Prevalence Estimates	Type of Drugs Used
32% used alcohol daily or regularly 3% used drugs daily or regularly	
21.4% used alcohol regularly 6.2% used drugs regularly	1.9% used pills regularly 0.9% used cocaine regularly
38% used alcohol 1-2 days per week 26% used alcohol more than 3 days per week 18% used drugs 1-9 days per month 4% used drugs more than 20 days per month	
55% used drugs during last six months 31% were serious drug users	
35% used alcohol 13% used 1 or more drugs	8% used marijuana 2% used hallucinogens 4% used stimulants Less than 1% used sedatives narcotics 5% used other drugs
32% had "a drinking problem" 44% used drugs during previous 90 days	46% used marijuana 21% used minor tranquilizers 13% used cocaine
35% used alcohol daily 14% used alcohol more than 2 times per week 11% used drugs daily 4% used drugs more than 2 times per week	
30% of shelter guests used drugs 37% of street people used drugs 20% of shelter guests used drugs at least 1 time per week 25% of street people used drugs at least 1 time per week	

Table 4.2
Additional Studies with Data on Drug Abuse

Reference/Date of Study	Location	Study Site	Sample	Prevalence	Problem Definition	Method of Assessment
1. S. Hoffman/Jul. - Sep., 81 D. Wenger J. Nigro R. Rosenfeld/1982	New York, NY	Shelters	N = 107 100% male 85% minority Median age 36	26.0%	Drug abuse problem	Self-report interviewer assessment
2. F. Lipton A. Sabatini S. Katz/1983	New York, NY	Psychiatric Hospital	N = 90 75% male 53.9% minority 63% ages 20-39	41.0% 4.4%	Alcohol, drug, or alcohol and drug use Alcohol or drug dependence	Case record review
3. A. Arce/Winter 1981-82 M. Tadlock M. Vergare S. Shapiro/1983	Philadelphia , PA	Shelters	N = 193 78% male 53.9% minority 47% ages 18-39	3.0%	Drug abuse	Case record review
4. B. Jones D. Goldstein B. Gray/1984	New York, NY	Shelters Public Facilities Food Programs Streets	N = 158 59% male 70% minority 63% ages 18-39	38.0%	Drug use	Self-report anecdotal comments from interviewers
5. E. Bassuk/April 1983 L. Rubin A. Lauriat/1984	Boston, MA	Shelters	N = 78 83% male 23% minority Median age 33.8 (Range 4-68)	< 1.0%	Drug dependence	Diagnosis according to DSM-III criteria
6. J. Ball B. Havassy/1984	San Francisco, CA	Shelters Food Programs Drop-in Centers Streets	N = 112 81.2% male 21% minority Mean age 37.5 (Range 17-67)	8.7% .	Drug dependence problem	Self-report
7. E. Corrigan/Oct. 1974- March 1975 S. Anderson/1984	New York, NY	Shelter	N = 31 0% male 45% minority Mean age 46	58.0%	Drug use	Self-report
8. D. Roth/March--August 84 J. Bean N. Lust T. Saveanu/1985	Ohio	Shelters Food Programs Public Facilities Streets	N = 979 81% male 10.2% minority Median age 34 (Range 16-83)	32.2%	Drug use (includes medication)	Self-report

70

#	Authors / Dates	Location	Setting	Sample	Rate	Problem	Method
9.	M. Rosnow, T. Shaw, C. Concord, P. Tucker, J. Palmer/1985; Oct. 84–Feb. 85	Milwaukee, WI	Shelters, Streets	N = 237, 87% male, 40% minority, Median age 35	24.0%	Alcohol or drug abuse problem	Self-report
10.	G. Morse, N. Shields, C. Hanneke, R. Calsyn, G. Burger, B. Nelson/1985; 83-84	St. Louis, MO	Shelters	N = 248, 50.8% male, 64.9 % minority, Median age 28.7 (Range 17-62)	20.8% 6.0% 4.0%	Drug use/current Drug use/daily Drug abuse problem	Self-report
11.	P. Fisher, S. Shapiro, W. Breakey, J. Anthony, M. Kramer/1986; Winter 81-82	Baltimore, MD	Missions	N = 51, 94% male, 47.1% minority, Median age 38	19.6% 31.4% 70.6%	Alcohol or drug abuse & dependence/ current Alcohol or drug abuse & dependence/annual Alcohol or drug abuse & depend./life time	Self-report (DIS)
12.	S. Ladner, S. Crystal, R. Towber, B. Callender, B. Calhoun/1986; Nov. 82-Dec. 83	New York, NY	Shelters	N = 8061	16.5%	Drug abuse	Self-report client intake forms
13.	R. Farr, P. Koegel, A. Burnam/1986; Jl. 84-Mar. 85	Los Angeles, CA.	Shelters, Food Programs, Streets	N = 374, 96.4% male, 72.9% minority, Median age 35	10.1% 30.8%	Drug abuse and dependence/current Drug abuse and dependence/lifetime	Self-report (DIS)
14.	C. Mowbray, A. Solarz, V. Johnson/Winter 84; Apr.-May 84	Detroit, MI	Shelters		38.0%	Drug abuse problem	Key informants
			Psychiatric Hospital	N = 35, Mean age 32.7	44.0%	Drug use/current or former	Self-report
	E. Phillips-Smith, C. Combs (86)/ Jun.-Jul 84, Mar. 85		Shelters	N = 7, 71% male, 74.3% minority, Mean age 35.3	31.0%	Drug use/current	Self-report and health exam

a: Key informant study
b: Homeless patient interview
c: Health and mental health shelter screening

71

varied considerably, ranging from key informants' judgments to psychiatric eval-
uations. Most studies, though, relied on self-reported data that resulted in enormous variation in the prevalence estimates of "drug use," "drug abuse," and
"drug dependence." For example, the prevalence estimates for drug use varied
from 20.8 to 58 percent; for drug abuse from 3 to 38 percent; and for drug
dependence from 4.4 to 70.6 percent!

Estimates of drug use also varied widely depending on the inclusion or ex-
clusion of alcohol as a drug. For example, estimates of drug abuse were higher
when alcohol was included as a drug as in the work of Fischer et al. (1986),
where a combined alcohol and drug-use category yielded a 70.8 percent lifetime
prevalence estimate of drug abuse far higher than the 30.8 percent lifetime
prevalence estimate of drug abuse found by Farr et al. (1986) who excluded
alcohol. Estimates of drug use tended to be lower when case records or psychiatric
assessments were used, but this may have occurred because drug abuse rather
than occasional drug use was usually assessed with these techniques.

Despite this variability, some cautious generalizations about the prevalence
of current drug abuse among homeless people can be gleaned from these studies.
Prevalence estimates for current drug use among sheltered homeless people
ranged from 20.8 to 58 percent; for current drug abuse, estimates ranged from
3 to 48 percent; and for current drug dependence, the estimates were less than
1 to 10.1 percent. The data on current drug dependence are probably the most
precise, given the assessment techniques that were used. These included psychiatric assessments and the use of a valid diagnostic tool, the Diagnostic Interview Schedule (DIS), for getting DSM-III symptoms through self-reported
data (Robins et al., 1981).

Other attempts to document the prevalence of drug abuse among homeless
people fall within the ranges cited in Table 4.2. For example, Ladner et al.
(1986), reporting on data from city agencies and shelter providers, noted that in
Detroit, 38 percent of the shelter clients "showed evidence of drug abuse"; in
Los Angeles, 40 percent of the homeless men and 15 to 20 percent of the homeless
women had serious alcohol or drug problems; and, in Portland, 50 percent of
the shelter clients were alcohol or drug abusers. The Health Care for the Homeless
Project, funded by the Robert Wood Johnson Foundation and the Pew Memorial
Trust, reported a prevalence estimate of 10 percent for drug abuse among the
homeless people who used their clinics in 16 U.S. cities (Wright et al., 1987).
City officials, in a study done by the U.S. Conference of Mayors (1986), observed
drug abuse was prevalent in 88 percent of the homeless people in Portland, 50
percent in Minneapolis, and 45 percent each in Charleston, South Carolina;
Detroit, New Orleans, and San Francisco.

Level of drug use. The level of drug use among homeless people ranges from
occasional use to total dependence, but most studies do not distinguish between
levels. Morse et al. (1985) attempted to make distinctions. They found that
among homeless people with drug abuse problems, 11.1 percent reported a

"slight" problem, 3.2 percent a "moderate" problem, and 4.4 percent a "severe" problem.

Studies often do not mention the specific drugs that were used. However, the drugs that were used most commonly were marijuana, noted in nearly all the studies, cocaine, and heroin (Bassuk et al., 1984; Ladner et al., 1986; Morse et al., 1985; Mowbray et al., 1986; Rosnow et al., 1985). In addition, Corrigan and Anderson (1984) observed that tranquilizers and sleeping pills were used in some instances. Polydrug use also occurred among homeless populations that have been studied (Bassuk et al., 1984; Corrigan and Anderson, 1984).

Characteristics of drug users. Most of the studies do not report the characteristics of homeless drug users. Roth et al. (1985) is a notable exception. In this study, a homeless sample was divided into three categories: those in shelters, those in the streets and other public places, and those doubling up with friends and relatives. Thirty-five percent of the shelter users, 22.3 percent of the people living on the streets, and 28.1 percent of the people sharing domiciles reported current drug use (including the use of licit medication).

Despite combining drug and alcohol abusers together as substance abusers, Rosnow et al. (1985) provided some of the best data on the characteristics of users. Most of the substance abusers were male (98 percent); however 3 percent of the women and 28 percent of the men in the total sample used drugs. Men were almost 10 times more likely to use drugs than women were. Eighty-one percent of the substance abusers were living in shelters. Forty percent were minority, and 81 percent had been arrested at least once.

Ladner et al. (1986) also reported on the characteristics of drug abusers. They found a significant number of drug abusers were younger than 30. Like Rosnow et al. (1985), Ladner et al. (1986) found men were more likely than were women to be drug abusers (18.2 percent versus 10.7 percent, or nearly two to one). Minorities were almost four times as likely as nonminorities to be drug abusers (41.8 percent versus 12 percent). Most drug abusers had been arrested at least once (69 percent).

The inconsistencies in the findings on the racial characteristics of homeless drug abusers are partly attributable to how drug abuse is defined. For example, Rosnow et al. (1985) defined it as "substance abuse," including the use of alcohol. Alcoholics among the homeless have typically been older, white males and data on the current homeless population show this trend continues (Wright et al., 1987).

The simultaneous occurrence of drug and other psychiatric symptoms (comorbidity) has been reported in a number of studies. Farr et al. (1986), for example, found homeless drug abusers had symptoms of other mental disorders. In other studies, alcohol and drug abuse have often been found to be a secondary psychiatric diagnosis among homeless people who suffer from other mental disorders. Arce et al. (1983) found 18 percent of their sample had a secondary diagnosis of alcohol and drug abuse.

Methodological limitations. The methodological limitations of a number of these studies are very similar to those of the studies described by Mulkern and Spence (1984). Primary among these problems is the inadequate definition of drug abuse. Drug abuse was alternatively defined as drug use, drug abuse problems, drug abuse, and drug dependence. Consequently, a clear distinction between occasional use and dependence in homeless people cannot be made in these studies other than to note that occasional drug use is probably far more prevalent than is drug dependence.

Some studies have focused on substance abuse, putting alcohol and other drugs together (e.g., Arce et al., 1983); whereas others have looked at alcohol and other drugs separately (e.g., Jones et al., 1984; Lipton et al., 1983). When drug abuse and alcohol abuse were assessed separately, usually alcohol abuse was more prevalent among homeless people; however, this is true for the general population as well.

Very few studies differentiated among the total homeless population. The work of Roth et al. (1985), Arce et al. (1983), and Farr et al. (1986) were notable exceptions. However, only Roth et al. (1985) presented data on the relationship of categories of homelessness to drug abuse, and their measure of drug abuse is extremely limited. The use of over-the-counter and prescription drugs was included with the use of illicit drugs, so one cannot tell how significant a problem drug abuse was within this particular sample. Studies, for the most part, have focused on one subpopulation of the homeless defined in terms of the study site (such as adult shelter users), but without regard to other subgroups of homeless people defined, for example, on the basis of other components of homelessness, such as its temporal quality (e.g., episodic homelessness versus prolonged homelessness). Shelter sites were the primary setting where many of these studies were conducted; however, a few other sites such as psychiatric hospitals (e.g., Lipton et al., 1983) were also used.

The samples of homeless people in most of these studies were not representative of the total homeless population in their locales; the work by Roth et al. (1985) is a notable exception. The samples were predominantly male, with mean/ median ages under 39 years, and often were primarily minorities (Blacks and Hispanics).

Again, data on "who" used drugs were inadequate. Homeless drug users were not described adequately in terms of their demographic characteristics. Homeless drug users, though, seemed to be under 40, were usually male, and were often members of minority groups. Furthermore, because most samples were predominantly male, very little is known about drug abuse among homeless females.

Overall, as with the studies reviewed by Mulkern and Spence (1984), it is difficult to generalize about drug abuse among homeless people from these studies. It does occur and with some degree of frequency. The type of drug that is used the most frequently seems to be marijuana. The types of homeless people who use drugs are not clear, but demographic findings suggest that drug use occurs most frequently among minority men under the age of 40.

REMAINING RESEARCH QUESTIONS

A number of significant research questions remain concerning drug abuse among homeless people, given the methodological limitations of the studies reviewed. The first and most encompassing is: What comes first—drug abuse or homelessness? This is the "chicken or the egg" dilemma of causality that underlies almost all social science research on social problems. It is also the most difficult question to address in field research. One of the underlying assumptions that has guided this review was that drug abuse contributes to a lack of personal, environmental, economic, and social resources that in turn can lead to homelessness. But whether this process occurs and how it occurs is not known. This assumption suggests that drug abuse may lead to homelessness. However, the reverse—that homelessness may lead to drug abuse—could also be true.

Nonetheless, research has not been done to determine how drug abuse impacts upon the availability and use of personal, environmental, economic, and social resources. Specifically, how do service providers view homeless drug users and provide resources for them? How do homeless drug users view and utilize available resources? For example, focusing on environmental resources, how do service providers in the mental health or health care system target services for homeless drug users? How do homeless drug users gain access to the mental health or health care system? Focusing on social resources, what is the nature of the interaction of homeless drug users and their families and friends? How are homeless drug users perceived by and responded to by their families and friends? How do homeless drug users perceive and respond to their families and friends?

Also, research has not assessed the dominant level of drug use among homeless people. Is it occasional use, regular or frequent use, or dependence? Do different types or subgroups of homeless people have different levels of drug use? For example, in which group is drug use more prevalent—among displaced, episodic, or prolonged homeless people?[3]

Research has not examined how the "drug culture" operates among homeless drug users. Is it like the "drug culture" among other drug users? For example, how are drugs obtained by homeless drug users? How do the homeless drug users function and maintain themselves and their drug habits? Shelters discourage drug abuse, yet homeless people in shelters can still obtain and use drugs. How is this accomplished? These and other questions remain to be addressed in future research.

NOTES

1. Reviews on alcohol abuse among homeless people have been done recently. For example, see *Alcohol Health and Research World* 11, No. 3 (1987).

2. Some homeless people do have income from various sources, including Supplemental Security Income, part-time employment, and "hustling" activities, such as panhandling. This income, though, is insufficient to secure and maintain permanent housing.

3. The author is currently undertaking a study of drug abuse among adult shelter users to determine the level of drug use among subgroups of the homeless population. This research is funded by a grant (RO1DA04513) from the National Institute on Drug Abuse, National Institutes of Health, U.S. Department of Health and Human Services.

REFERENCES

Abelson, Herbert I., et al. 1977. *National Survey on Drug Abuse: 1977—A Nationwide Study—Youth, Adults and Older People* (DHEW Publication No. ADM 78–618). Washington, D.C.: U.S. Government Printing Office.

Arce, Anthony A., et al. 1983. A Psychiatric Profile of Street People Admitted to an Emergency Shelter. *Hospital and Community Psychiatry* 34 (9): 812–816.

Bachrach, Leona L. 1984. Interpreting Research on the Homeless Mentally Ill: Some Caveats. *Hospital and Community Psychiatry* 35 (9): 914–917.

Bahr, Howard M. 1969a. Family Size and Stability as Antecedents of Homelessness and Excessive Drinking. *Journal of Marriage and the Family* 31 (3): 477–483.

———. 1969b. Lifetime Affiliation Patterns of Early and Late Onset Heavy Drinkers on Skid Row. *Quarterly Journal of Studies on Alcohol* 30 (3): 645–656.

Bassuk, Ellen L., et al. 1984. Is Homelessness a Mental Health Problem? *American Journal of Psychiatry* 141: 1546–1550.

Baxter, Ellen and Kim Hopper. 1982. The New Mendicancy: Homelessness in New York City. *American Journal of Orthopsychiatry* 52: 393–408.

Blumberg, Leonard, et al. 1970. The Skid Row Man and the Skid Row Status Community. *Quarterly Journal of Studies on Alcohol* 32: 909–941.

Caplow, T. 1940. Transiency as a Cultural Pattern. *American Sociological Review* 5: 731–739.

Corrigan, Eileen, and Sandra C. Anderson. 1984. Homeless Alcoholic Women on Skid Row. *American Journal of Drug and Alcohol Abuse* 10 (4): 535–549.

Cross, W. T., and D. E. Cross. 1937. *Newcomers and Nomads in California*. Stanford: Stanford University Press.

Culver, B. F. 1933. Transient Unemployed Men. *Sociology and Social Research* 17: 519–535.

Division of Substance Abuse Services. 1983. *Drug Use Among Tenants of Single Room Occupancy (SRO) Hotels in New York City*. Albany, N.Y.: Author.

Farr, Rodger, et al. 1986. *A Study of Homelessness and Mental Illness in the Skid Row Areas of Los Angeles*. Los Angeles: Los Angeles County Department of Mental Health.

Fischer, Pamela J., et al. 1986. Mental Health and Social Characteristics of the Homeless: A Survey of Mission Users. *American Journal of Public Health* 76 (5): 519–524.

Gray, F. 1931. *The Tramp—His Meaning and Being*. London: Dent.

Hoffman, Stanley, et al. 1982. *Who are the Homeless? A Study of Randomly Selected Men Who Use the New York City Shelters*. New York: New York State Office of Mental Health.

Hope, Marjorie, and Young, James. 1986. *The Faces of Homelessness*. Lexington, Mass.: Lexington Books.

Hopper, Kim. 1987. Rethinking Homelessness: A Seven-Year Perspective. Invited address presented at the 95th annual meeting of the American Psychological Association, New York, N.Y.

Jessor, Richard, and Shirley L. Jessor. 1977. *Problem Behavior and Psychosocial Development—A Longitudinal Study of Youth.* New York: Academic Press.

Johnston, Lloyd D., et al. 1979. *1979 Highlights Nation's High School Students, Five Year Trends* (DHEW Publication No. ADM81–930). Washington, D.C.: U.S. Government Printing Office.

Jones, Billy, et al. 1984. Psychodynamic Profiles of the Urban Homeless. Paper presented at the 137th annual meeting of the American Psychiatric Association, Los Angeles, Calif. (May).

Kerr, L. 1930. *Back Door Guest.* Indianapolis: Bobbs-Merrill.

Ladner, Susan, et al. 1986. Project Future: Focusing, Understanding, Targeting and Utilizing Resources for the Homeless Mentally Ill, Elderly, Youth, Substance Abusers and Employables (Report prepared for the National Institute of Mental Health). New York: City of New York Human Resources Administration.

Lamb, Richard H. 1982. Young Adult Chronic Patients: The New Drifters. *Hospital and Community Psychiatry* 33 (6): 465–468.

Lazare, A., et al. 1972. The Walk-in Patient as Customer. *American Journal of Orthopsychiatry* 42 (5): 872–883.

Levine, Irene S. 1984. Homelessness: Its Implications for Mental Health Policy and Practice. *Psychosocial Rehabilitation Journal* 13 (1): 6–16.

Levine, Irene S., and James W. Stockdill. 1986. Mentally Ill and Homeless: A National Problem. In B. Jones, ed., *Treating the Homeless: Urban Psychiatry's Challenge.* Washington, D.C.: American Psychiatric Association Press.

Levinson, B. M. 1957. The Socioeconomic Status, Intelligence and Psychometric Pattern of Native-born White Homeless Men. *Journal of Genetic Psychology* 91: 205–211.

———. 1963. The Homeless Man: A Psychological Enigma. *Mental Hygiene* 44 (4): 590–601.

Lipton, Frank, et al., 1983. Down and Out in the City: The Homeless Mentally Ill. *Hospital and Community Psychiatry* 34: 817–821.

Locke, H. J. 1935. Unemployed Men in Chicago Shelters. *Sociology and Social Research* 19: 420–428.

Martin, Marsha. 1986. *The Implications of NIMH-Supported Research for Homeless Mentally Ill Racial and Ethnic Minority Persons.* Rockville, Md.: National Institute of Mental Health.

Merton, Robert K. 1968. *Social Theory and Social Structure.* New York: Free Press.

Milburn, Norweeta G., and Roderick J. Watts. 1985. Methodological Issues in Research on the Homeless and Homeless Mentally Ill. *International Journal of Mental Health* 14 (4): 42–60.

Miller, Judith D., et al. 1983. *National Survey on Drug Abuse: Main Findings 1982* (DHHS Publication No. (ADM) 84–1263). Washington, D.C.: U.S. Government Printing Office.

Morrissey, Joseph P., and Deborah L. Dennis. 1986. *NIMH-Funded Research Concerning Homeless Mentally Ill Persons: Implications for Policy and Practice.* Rockville, Md.: National Institute of Mental Health.

Morse, Gary. 1986. *A Contemporary Assessment of Urban Homelessness: Implications for Social Change.* (Report #1986–2). St. Louis, Mo.: University of Missouri, Center for Metropolitan Studies.

Morse, Gary, and Robert J. Calsyn. 1985. Mentally Disturbed Homeless People in St. Louis: Needy, Willing, but Underserved. *International Journal of Mental Health* 14 (4): 74–94.

Morse, Gary, et al. 1985. *Homeless People in St. Louis: A Mental Health Program Evaluation, Field Study and Follow-up Investigation.* Jefferson City, Mo.: Missouri Department of Mental Health.

Mowbray, Carol, et al. 1986. *Mental Health and Homelessness in Detroit: A Research Study.* Lansing, Mich.: Michigan Department of Mental Health.

Mulkern, Virginia, and Rebecca Spence. 1984. *Illicit Drug Use Among Homeless Persons: A Review of the Literature* (Report prepared for the National Institute on Drug Abuse). Boston, Mass.: Human Services Research Institute.

Mulkern, Virginia, et al. 1985. *Homeless Needs Assessment Study: Findings and Recommendations for the Massachusetts Department of Mental Health.* (Report prepared for the Massachusetts Department of Mental Health). Boston, Mass.: Human Services Research Institute.

Outland, G. E. 1939. *Boy Transiency in America.* Santa Barbara, Calif.: Santa Barbara State College Press.

Priest, Robert G. 1976. The Homeless Person and Psychiatric Services: An Edinburgh Survey. *British Journal of Psychology* 128: 138–163.

Robins, Lee, et al. 1981. The National Institute of Mental Health Diagnostic Interview Schedule: Its History, Characteristics, and Validity. *Archives of General Psychiatry* 38: 381–389.

Robinson, P. 1894. Personal Communication. Boston, Mass.

Rooney, James. 1980. Organizational Success Through Program Failures: Skid Row Missions. *Social Forces* 58: 904–923.

Rosnow, Mark J., et al. 1985. *Listening to the Homeless: A Study of Homeless Mentally Ill Persons in Milwaukee.* Milwaukee, Wisc.: Human Resources Triangle, Inc.

Roth, Dee, et al. 1985. *Homelessness in Ohio: A Study of People in Need.* Columbus, Ohio: Ohio Department of Mental Health.

Segal, Steven P., et al. 1977. Falling through the Cracks. Mental Disorder and Social Margin in a Young Vagrant Population. *Social Problems* 24 (3): 387–401.

Siegal, Harvey A., and James A. Inciardi. 1982. The Demise of Skid Row. *Society* (January/February): 39–45.

Social Services Division. 1984. *The Homeless Poor.* Portland, Oreg.: Author.

Spradley, James P. 1970. *You Owe Yourself a Drunk: An Ethnography of Urban Nomads.* Boston, Mass.: Little, Brown and Company.

Stark, Louisa R. 1985. Strangers in a Strange Land: The Chronically Mentally Ill Homeless. *International Journal of Mental Health* 14 (4): 95–111.

U.S. Conference of Mayors. 1986. *The Growth of Hunger, Homelessness, and Poverty in America's Cities in 1985: A 25 City Survey.* Washington, D.C.: Author.

Watts, Roderick J., and Norweeta G. Milburn. 1987. *A Framework for Research and Action on Homelessness.* Unpublished manuscript.

Wiseman, Jacqueline P. 1970. *Stations of the Lost: The Treatment of Skid Row Alcoholics.* Chicago: University of Chicago Press.

Wood, Susanne M. 1979. The Social Conditions of Destitution: The Situation of Men With Schizophrenia or Personality Disorder. *Journal of Social Policy* 8: 207–226.
Wright, James D. et al. 1987. Ailments and Alcohol: Health Status Among the Drinking Homeless. *Alcohol Health and Research World* 11 (3): 22–27.

5

Homelessness as a Long-Term Housing Problem in America

Elizabeth D. Huttman

Homelessness is above all due to lack of affordable shelter (Hoch and Cibulskis, 1985). Those homeless, that is, without permanent shelter, are the most noticeable victims of a severe rental housing crisis in America. They essentially have the problem of being able to obtain only temporary housing in emergency shelters, under deplorable superficial coverage such as lean-to structures, under benches, bridges, or in doorways. For some the shelters are their cars, recreational vehicles, or tents. For the more fortunate it is doubling up with relatives or friends.

The homeless are those who have failed to locate long-term shelter either when they move to a new area or are released from a hospital, mental institution, or prison; it is those who voluntarily leave their past home due to conflict, abuse, or financial inability to pay (Hopper, 1984; Huttman and Huttman, 1988). Although they occasionally do not find alternative shelter due to their social problems or household characteristics, such as family size and age, the main cause is their inability to pay rent. This strain has forced them to temporary shelter.

For many *other* Americans this housing affordability crisis puts them *at risk* of homelessness. The prediction that many more will lack permanent shelter in the future comes from a number of writers (Hartman, 1987). The recent Conference of Mayors survey found a great increase in homelessness, especially the homeless families, in one year in the 26 cities studied. Cities that in 1983 saw the problem as a temporary one, and the homeless not likely to stay around, now admit it is likely to get worse due to the scarcity of affordable housing (Goode, 1986).

In this chapter we document the lack of supply of affordable housing in terms of decreased number of SROs (single room occupancy hotels) due to demolition and upgraded uses; lack of board and care facilities and other specialized types of shelters, even housing for the elderly; shortage in terms of apartments, both for large families and for singles, with reasonable rents (both existing and new starts), mentioning demolition, rehabilitation/gentrification, and condominium conversion as causes for the decreased supply. We also detail the decrease in subsidized housing. Lack of affordability is documented in terms of rent data for various cities, data on number of low-rent units, and vacancy rates for such units as well as location. Information on the income of the homeless and those *at risk* of becoming homeless is then given to show the crisis on rent/income ratio, with many poor paying half or more of their income for rent.

This material is supplied to point out the major role of housing affordability in causing homelessness, a fact obvious to most housing researchers (Marcuse, 1987; Van Vliet—, 1988), but certainly not to many service providers of the homeless, legislatures, or the general public. To many of them, the focus is on the social problem of the homeless, and their response has been in provision of services and temporary shelter that can cause as many problems as it solves. With an image of the homeless as alcoholic men or vagrants—often misrepresented as wanting a transient life (Hoch and Cibulskis, 1985) or drug abusers, many of these legislators and service providers fail to take serious the homeless population's need, and lack of, permanent accommodation. What differentiates even the "social problems" part of the group from the past is then they had some permanent shelter, whether a SRO, board and care home, or whatever; now they lack a roof over their head on other than a temporary basis. They now are, as community shelter workers in San Francisco said, poor on the low-rent merry-go-round that "keeps them from the streets to dormitory-like shelters operated by non-profit foundations for limited short stays, to the hotels and then back again" (Goode, 1986). Often they can not even stay in the shelters during the day. If living in cars, they must move them.

Such situations cause those who become homeless due to economic hardships to in fact develop social problems, whether psychological tensions, uncleanliness, inability to function in the job market due to lack of sleep, or to more major problems of alcoholism and drug abuse. In other words, for many of the new homeless the lack of permanent shelter causes the social problems rather than the reverse. Being homeless for a few weeks affects their habits and outlook severely enough to make them permanently homeless, and it deprives them of necessities for getting a job, such as a phone, a permanent address, clean clothing, and dignity.

The whole situation becomes a vicious cycle. The press portrays the extreme privations of the homeless—some is actually caused by their housing situation and not their personal traits. Yet this image locates the cause of the problem within the person (Hoch and Cibulskis, 1985) rather than seeing him as victimized by the rental housing situation today. Hoch and Cibulskis (1985: 11) stated:

Portrayed as a sick and vulnerable population, the homeless evoke public compassion and thereby stimulate the provision of care, but the very success of this approach means the same homeless people will be hard pressed to earn public respect . . . Instead of citizens with a shelter problem, the homeless become victims whose need defines their rights— a need subject to the interpretation of service providers. Thus, if the expansion of emergency and transitional shelter continues, justified solely on the basis of service need, the three-tiered plan [emergency shelter, transitional shelter, and permanent low-cost housing] will become little more than a rehabilitation program leading nowhere. The service agencies may receive additional funds to set up emergency and transitional shelters, but the homeless will have few options when "prepared" to leave the transitional shelter.

This criticism by Hoch and Cibulskis (1985) is even more valid in 1988, after Congress has put over a billion dollars into a mainly shelter and service bill for homeless (*New York Times,* 1987), and many states have also appropriated large sums for shelters. Hoch and Cibulskis's (1985: 6) prediction that "if the provision of permanent low cost housing . . . does not accompany the expansion of shelter, then the probability of emergency shelters becoming a form of reinstitutionalization increases enormously" seems to becoming true. As Hope and Young (1987: 1) say, the "homeless trend risks reviving the poor houses"; they describe the conditions in shelters as near those of former poor houses, "overcrowded, noisy, untidy and devoid of privacy . . . even if . . . allowed to stay during the day, there is little for them to do but sit . . . this is a dehumanizing way for anyone to live; it is devastating for children . . . they lose any sense of home. They are rarely alone with their mother or father." Hope and Young (1987) ask "Why do we continue our fixation with shelters?" They speak of a "shelter industry"; of the federal government considering a permanent office for the homeless; of the architects' association issuing a guide to shelters as an "emerging building type." Social workers too now have, as service providers, a stake in the service/counseling approach to the homeless.

SUPPLY OF AFFORDABLE HOUSING

Opposed to these approaches is the provision of permanent housing. The discussion first centers on lack of supply of such. In doing so, it first mentions that not all homeless have the same housing needs and thus want the same kind of housing. A significant number are singles who want small units; those include the aged, young workers, divorcees, and problem groups such as the alcoholics, mentally ill, and drug abusers. The three latter groups, many experts feel, are in fact better served by SROs, congregate housing arrangements with meals, or for the mentally ill, special service facilities. On the other hand, there is the increasing number of homeless families that need large apartments; some of these are immigrants, many are black and female-headed households (Hartman, 1988; Hopper, 1984).

SUPPLY OF SRO HOTELS

For the single person, whether elderly, a young man, an alcoholic or mentally ill, the single-room occupancy hotels have traditionally been a source of cheap shelter. However, in the 1970s their number decreased dramatically in major cities in the U.S. In San Francisco one study showed the loss of over 6,000 units from 1977 to 1985 (San Francisco Housing and Tenant Council Study, 1985). Many were lost to conversion to tourist hotels such as downtown Tenderloin area's Villa Florence hotel, renovated at $35,000 a room and now renting at around $100 per night (*San Francisco Chronicle*, 1987). Others were demolished for office space or converted to apartments. Some ironically were removed from the market, as the Mental Health Association (1987) reports, to be used by the City Department of Social Services for the homeless on a temporary basis; over 1,800 are used for this purpose. Thus these SRO units were converted from permanent to temporary shelter; in addition, the city, paying higher per-day rents for these units helped push up the rents at all SROs (Goode, 1986; Weeden and Linedan, 1987). Other SRO units have been rehabilitated for Section 8 use (Kasinitz, 1984). A different government action in New York City decreased the number of SROs; according to Kasinitz (1984) the city gave tax-abatement incentives to upgrade SROs; this caused the rent to go up and for them to be removed from the cheap rental pool. In general in New York City the number of SRO units dropped from 50,454 in 1975 to 18,853 in 1981 (Kasinitz, 1984), even greater than the 17 percent loss of 32,314 SRO units in San Francisco, 1975 to 1979, and continued loss due to loopholes in the city's moratorium on SRO conversion from 1979 on (Hartman, Keating, and LeGates, 1982).

Now in some parts of the country local governments are trying to bring in new SROs. For example, San Diego, through changes in its zoning laws and building codes, has encouraged developers to construct new 207- and 400-unit SRO hotels. With the city's financial help these units, with shared bathroom and kitchen facilities, rent for under $300 a month (Bay Area Housing Briefs, January 1988).

Board and care facilities used for the mentally ill as an alternative to mental institutions have also decreased in number. The Mental Health Association of San Francisco (1987) reports a loss of over 41 percent of the city's board and care beds since 1977, with major loss in the more desirable outer areas. This group feels this situation has caused increased utilization of acute care services, the most expensive type of treatment, and holdbacks on release from these facilities (costing $357 per day in local hospitals). This group, estimating that 30 to 60 percent of San Francisco's homeless are mentally disabled out of the 8,000–10,000 homeless (National Coalition for the Homeless survey, 1986), sees a need for both board and care (shortage of 330 treatment-related beds) and long-term housing (shortage of 1,500 to 2,000 units for the mentally disabled). With mental hospitals discharging a large number of their patients in the 1970s and lack of community facility replacements, a similar problem exists all over the country (Stoner, 1984; Hopper and Hamberg, 1984).

LACK OF LOW-RENT APARTMENTS

Demolition, rehabilitation, abandonment, and condominium conversion have lessened the number of low-rent housing units in most major cities. In San

Francisco over 17,000 units were lost from 1975 to 1985 due to demolition and conversion (San Francisco Housing and Tenant Council Study, 1985). Displacement nationally has been high, with the 1981 Annual Housing Survey showing 1.7 to 2.4 million persons displaced annually for a number of reasons. Lee and Hodge (1984) show it is the poor, elderly, black, and female-headed households that are the ones likely to be displaced. Palen (1988) states that displacement has been particularly severe in some inner-city areas, especially in Washington, D.C., and San Francisco. While studies show some find another home, many pay more because demolition, rehabilitation, and conversion have taken the cheap units out of the market. In many cities in the 1970s more than 5 percent of the rental stock was converted to condominiums (O'Connell, 1988). Former residents in almost a third of the cases paid at least 25 percent more rent than they did in their preconversion building (HUD, 1981). Rehabilitation for gentrification also means loss of cheap units; HUD in a study of six cities (particularly San Francisco) found renters and especially short-term residents (three years or less) to be the main sufferers from this situation (Palen, 1988). In San Francisco, with whole neighborhoods of Victorian houses gentrified, such displacement is a serious problem.

Abandonment also causes loss of low-rent units. In New York City, one-forth of the housing is on streets with at least one abandoned building (Marans and Colten, 1985). Rent control can cause such abandonment, although maintenance and operating costs are as likely, along with property taxes and city demands for code enforcement, to be among the factors causing small-time private landlords to abandon their property considered to be an extremely poor investment (Sternlieb, 1970).

STARTS OF NEW MULTIFAMILY HOUSING

If investors and landlords of existing rental units find they cannot make a profit, it is not surprising that developers are not eager to build new units for the middle- to low-income household. Construction costs in terms of materials and labor are both expensive, as is land. The construction industry, with its many small builders (Sumichrast, Ahluwalia, and Sheehan, 1979) and inability to use mass technology on many parts of the process (Stegman, 1969) has continually increased costs of direct labor and of subcontractor arrangements in this labor-intensive activity; the construction industry has a capital/labor ratio of 4.3:1 compared to 12:1 in electrical machinary manufacturing. In addition, materials are increasing in cost and land prices are increasing exorbitantly; land almost doubled in value from 1960 to 1980 (*Statistical Abstracts*, 195, in Van Vliet—, 1988). Scarcity of land in desirable inner-city locations has not only caused costs to go up for the in-filling possible or the land freed by demolition; it has caused developers to concentrate on less-expensive suburban sites, except in the case of luxury apartment developments. Even there development costs have gone up as opposition by homeowners, and especially limited-growth advocates, delays the buildings or increases open-space requirements or public amenities. This suburban opposition to multifamily rental-unit developments assumed to increase local municipal infrastructure and school costs, is reinforced through zoning ordinances and building codes outlawing multifamily units in many areas, or lowering densities. For example, in Livermore, California, they voted to reduce average density of a 2,900 acre area from 4.9 to 4.3 units per acre, mostly by reducing the densities allowed for apartments (*Bay Area Housing Briefs*, January 1988). These actions occur even though the New Jersey *Mt. Laural v. NAACP* Supreme Court case and the follow-up New York case (*Asian Americans for Equality v. Koch*) restrict the right of municipalities to exclude people by zoning/land-use regulations, as Massachusetts also does by legislative decree; or at a time when community general plans are to make provision for low-income housing.

The above problems around land scarcity and land cost for multifamily rental units is exceeded by another barrier to provision of low-cost units, that is, high interest rates, usually over 10 percent, both for up-front infrastructure costs and for the buildings themselves. In the early Kaiser Commission research (President's Commission on Urban Housing, 1968), the authors estimated that debt retirement (including interest) was a much greater part of the cost than construction and land costs. Based on construction-starts data, as interest rates go up, new construction decreases.

Developers, clearly unenthusiastic about the chance for profit from building multifamily rental units based on costs as well as the low income of potential tenants (see below), quickly reduce activity when rates go up. In addition, the new tax-reform bill's change in depreciation schedule has had a very negative impact on multiunit builders' future plans. Some studies show that 40 percent were very negative and about 75 percent at least somewhat negative about future plans (*Business Week*, 1987). This is now shown from national statistics on drops in starts in the first quarter of 1987, averaging only 464,000 annual rate compared to a high of 1.1 million family units in late 1985. In the San Francisco Bay area building permits for the first half of 1987 decreased 29 percent compared to 1987 for apartments and condominiums. For this whole large area of several million, only 8,539 apartment and condominium permits were issued for the first half of 1987. For San Francisco itself, while the total number of new units completed has been high in 1985–1987 compared to 1984 and many earlier years, when 589–790 units were completed, half of the new multifamily units are either luxury units or condominiums (*Bay Area Housing Briefs*, February 1988). In San Francisco at the same time they are proud that a third of all the 1986 starts were rental units for people with low and moderate income, and between 1980 and 1986, 2,300 rental and cooperative units were built for such. Yet they admit that this is not enough with as many as 2,600 new moderate- and low-income rental units needed in the city each year (*Bay Area Housing Briefs*, February 1988). As Harloe (1988) points out at the national level, what is being built is luxury apartments for the professional and managerial groups;

This is the same situation as in San Francisco (*Bay Area Housing Briefs*, January 1986).

SUBSIDIZED HOUSING STARTS

Production of new subsidized housing with federal funds has greatly dropped in the United States in the last seven years. At the same time subsidized units are being removed from this category due to government contractual arrangements with investors whereby after so many years the developer/investor can retire the units from the low/moderate income-use category. In the Bay Area this means the loss of 18,000 units of federally subsidized low-income housing (Section 236, Section 8 New Construction, and Section 202, *Bay Area Housing Briefs*, October 1987). Public housing, never sufficient in number with only 1,318,298 total units in 1983 (Huttman and Gurewitsch, 1988), is now limited to almost no new starts during FY 1987/88 and 7,000 in 1985 (*New York Times*, 1987). As for Section 8 existing housing certificate allocations, matters are equally bad, and Section 8 new construction and substantially rehabilitated is at a standstill. As the *New York Times* (1987) editorialized, federal funds for housing have dropped from 7 percent of the federal budget in 1978 to .7 percent today.

In addition, tax shelter benefits for investors in low- and moderate-income housing have been cut back by the Tax Reform Bill of 1986, though the bill's Low Income Housing Tax Credit may somewhat replace them (*New York Times*, 1988).

While the federal government's inactivity in subsidizing rental units has been somewhat offset by various state and local government measures such as housing bonds, some cities demand that developers provide a fraction of their units for low- and moderate-income groups; they also demand rehabilitation grants for low-income housing. As such, this has only supplied a minimal number of rental units compared to demand—nationally, 1–15 million new units annually (Hartman, 1988); or 640,000 units according to Downs (1983).

VACANCY RATES

The low number of starts of multifamily rental units, both private and subsidized, plus the loss of many low-rent units through demolition, conversion, and gentrification/rehabilitation, mean low vacancy rates in most central cities (except for Florida, Texas, and other southern areas where overbuilding occurred in the late 1970s and early 1980s). In 1987 San Francisco had a 1.6 percent vacancy rate (0.8 percent in 1985). Cities such as Washington, D.C., and New York also have low vacancy rates. These vacant units are often luxury units (*Bay Area Housing Briefs*, 1987; Harloe, 1988) or even awaiting sale, as the Federal Home Loan Bank Housing Vacancy Survey includes *all* vacant units, as does the Bureau of Census. The 7.7 percent national rental vacancy rate for

April 1987 includes luxury units, suburban units unavailable to the poor, especially minority and non-auto-owning poor. This means that vacancies in regions of overbuilding as well as units for sale are misleading measures of available housing to the poor (*Business Week,* 1987).

The overall data also do not indicate rental vacancies by size or rent of the unit. Few new rental units are built for large families; most are built for singles. In San Francisco only 11.1 percent of the rental units (1980) had three or more bedrooms. Not surprisingly, vacancies in such areas are very low. As research studies (Marcuse, 1987) show, landlords can easily discriminate against many large families, especially minorities. The lack of supply of rental units for families has contributed to homelessness among this group. The U.S. Conference of Mayors (1987) survey of homeless in 26 cities found that families had the greatest increase in 12 months in homelessness (which increased 20–40 percent in many cities in 12 months). They found one-third of the homeless in U.S. cities were children, and added that more than 70 percent of all cities surveyed said that families, more than any other group, were the most frequently excluded groups from emergency shelters—a complaint expressed by many experts (Sullivan and Damroch, 1987). In Los Angeles only 51 of the 215 shelters accept families, and of those only 16 accept families with fathers present (Fadiman, 1987). Many families live in cars, using parks as their night location, and public rest rooms as changing rooms and bathing facilities for washing their clothes (Fadiman, 1987). Or, as reported by Halstuk (1987) they overcrowd hotel/motel rooms paying $26.88 per day ($810 per month) in an outer Bay-Area location.

For these families lack of money is the main problem, though housing discrimination against families is another. Even if one member is working (but only at minimum wage, as is true for many female-headed households), on the average they bring home only $6,968 annually for a 40 hour per week job—while the very low poverty level for a family of four is $11,200 per year. Looking only at those on AFDC (Aid to Families with Dependent Children), California (1986) had 1.1 million children (*San Francisco Chronicle*, 1987). There are many more poor not on AFDC.

AFFORDABILITY OF HOUSING

The low-income people can hardly afford today's high rent, rents increased by the scarcity of housing. That applies to not only low-income families but also the single elderly, some of whom have become homeless (Weeden and Linedan, 1987), as well as many single younger people such as divorcees (Goldscheider and DaVanzo, 1985) and the mentally ill and the alcoholics or drug abusers. It certainly applies to the increasing influx of immigrants. In one San Francisco shelter 10 percent of the beds are for Central American refugees. With well over 1 million new immigrants entering the country legally and illegally each year, there is a sizable need for cheap rentals.

In most cities, cheap housing is impossible to find. In San Francisco in 1988 the median rent for two-bedroom apartments was $850 (*Bay Area Housing Briefs*, January 1988). While long-time renters pay less, especially if under rent control, newcomers may pay more. HUD's recent (1987) data for city and suburban county areas showed rent for two-bedroom units was $616 in Los Angeles; $670 in Nassau-Suffolk counties, N.Y.; $563 in Washington, D.C.; $503 in eight counties of New York (certainly not New York City alone); $419 in St. Louis; and $400 in Houston (McLeod, 1987).

Those qualifying, due to income for Section 8 housing find in many cases that they cannot find units for these rents. In San Francisco a study by the city housing authority showed that 60 percent of those with a certificate for Section 8 in 1986 could not use it as they could not find a place with an allowable rent, even though that was $710 per month for a two-bedroom apartment in San Francisco. Median rents rose almost twice as fast as median incomes from the mid–1970s to mid–1980s so that nearly 50 percent of low-income renters were paying more than 50 percent of income for rent, the 1983 annual housing survey showed, and last year the rental cost for a typical single parent aged 25 to 34 with children was 58 percent of income (*International Herald Tribune*, 1988).

Besides this group, minorities are worse off in having a high rent/income ratio (Hartman, 1988). By 1983, of all Hispanic renter households, 43 percent were paying 35 percent or more of their income in rent; and 26 percent were paying 50 percent or more. For all black households (not just low income) it was 44 percent and 28 percent respectively (from Annual Housing Surveys, compiled by Hartman, 1988). Singles were especially hurt by high rents in obtaining apartments or SRO hotel units. For San Francisco, the Mental Health Association (1987) bemoans that its clientele, often on SSI paying about $600 per month, must pay $300 for an SRO unit. If they were on General Assistance (county welfare) they only got $377 in 1987 in San Francisco and were indeed hard pressed to afford housing.

Income is indeed a major problem (Downs, 1983; Harloe, 1988); but it is more the extreme rental crisis coupled with scarcity of units and greatly increased rents of the available stock of housing (Huttman, 1985; Huttman, 1986) that are at the crux of the problem. The result is about one to two million homeless (statistics vary from the National Coalition of the Homeless, 1984, data to the U.S. House of Representatives Subcommittee on Housing and Community Development, 1984).

THE SOLUTIONS FOR DIFFERENT GROUPS OF HOMELESS

The need for these homeless is of course permanent housing. Affordable rental units are also a need of the many *at risk* of losing their present shelter. As Hoch and Cibulskis (1985) point out, eviction comes much faster today than during the Great Depression; so does foreclosure for those who cannot pay their mortgage on time (Hoffman and Heisler, 1988).

Temporary shelters for those already homeless are, as stated above, a very poor solution; and of course they cannot be the answer in terms of preventive measures to help those *at risk* to avoid loss of their shelter. That is not to say we can abandon them, for we need them until we can substantially improve the supply of low-rent permanent housing, a development unlikely to be forthcoming in the near future. The problem of seeking short-term solution traps many Americans and their children in a homeless state from which they are unlikely to recover.

The long-term solutions are to provide housing of many types. While housing policy analysts talk of subsidy strategies in terms of below-market interest rates, housing allowances, capital for construction, tax-shelter investments, state housing bonds (Hays, 1986; Huttman, 1986), one can also talk of housing assistance strategies for different homeless and at-risk groups. For the single alcoholic and drug abusers, SROs or congregate-housing arrangements are recommended. For the mentally ill the degree of illness can determine the most appropriate shelter, from treatment-service units to SROs to small apartments, as the Mental Health Association of San Francisco (1986) suggests. For some, the suggested three-tier system of emergency shelters, transitional shelters, and then movement to low-cost permanent housing may be needed, especially if they have been homeless for a long period. For families it would seem that immediate use of apartments is the correct channel of help. Children suffer from the trauma of shelter living and of short-stay accommodations and constant moving.

For the elderly homeless or those at risk, unless in a problem category, it would seem that, besides provision of apartments for the elderly, for some, congregate housing with meals and housekeeping services would be suitable (Huttman and Gurewitsch, 1988) as well as SROs for men (Weeden and Linedan, 1987). For female-headed households, shared housing of a commune type may provide a cheap solution, certainly better than the present ones (McChesney, 1986; Franck, 1988). This, as well as apartments, should be the solution for battered/abused women, although again special shelters are needed for immediate help.

REFERENCES

Bay Area Housing Briefs. 1986 (January). Trends and Information.
————. 1987 (April, special issue). Potential Loss of Subsidized Housing, pp. 1–3.
————. 1987 (October). Affordability, p. 7.
————. 1988. (January). Trends and Info: On the Home Front, pp. 1–3.
————. 1988 (February, special issue). Housing in San Francisco: Building for Affordability, pp. 1–4.
Business Week. 1987 (May 4). Reform Hurts Apartment Building, p. 28.
Downs, Anthony. 1983. *Rental Housing in the 1980s*. Washington, D.C.: Brookings Institution.
Economic Road Maps (Published by the Conference Board). 1986. Statistics on Productivity, p. 528.

Fadiman, Anne. 1987. A Week in the Life of a Homeless Family. *Life* (December): 31–36.

Franck, Karen. 1988. Women's Housing and Neighborhood Needs. In *Handbook on Housing and the Built Environment,* edited by Elizabeth Huttman and Willem van Vliet—. Westport, Conn.: Greenwood Press.

Goldscheider, Frances, and Julie DaVanzo. 1985. Living Arrangements and the Transition to Adulthood. *Demography* 22: 545–563.

Goode, Erica. 1986. Why S. F. Program for the Homeless Fails Work. *San Francisco Chronicle* (October 13): 6.

Halstuk, Martin. 1987. A Waitress Who Hides Her Troubles. *San Francisco Chronicle* (December 11): A4.

Harloe, Michael. 1988. Private Rental Housing. In *Handbook on Housing and the Built Environment,* edited by Elizabeth Huttman and Willem van Vliet—. Westport, Conn.: Greenwood Press.

Hartman, Chester. 1987. The Housing Part of the Homelessness Problem. In *The Mental Health Needs of Homeless Persons,* edited by Ellen Bassuk. San Francisco: Jossey-Bass (New Directions for Mental Health Services, no. 30).

———. 1988. Affordability of Housing. In *Handbook on Housing and the Built Environment,* edited by Elizabeth Huttman and Willem van Vliet—. Westport, Conn.: Greenwood Press.

Hartman, Chester, D. Keating, and R. LeGates. 1982. *Displacement: How to Fight It.* Berkeley: National Housing Law Project.

Hays, F. Allen. 1986. *The Federal Government and Urban Housing.* Albany, N.Y.: State University of New York Press.

Hoch, Charles, and A. Cibulskis. 1985. Planning for the Homeless. Paper presented at conference on Housing Policy in an Age of Fiscal Austerity. International Sociological Association Ad Hoc Committee on Housing and the Built Environment. Amsterdam.

Hoffman, Lily, and B. Heisler. 1988. Home Finance: Buying and Keeping in a Changing Financial Environment. In *Handbook on Housing and the Built Environment,* edited by Elizabeth Huttman and Willem van Vliet—. Westport, Conn.: Greenwood Press.

Hope, Marjorie, and J. Young. 1987. Homeless Trend Risks Reviving Poor Houses. *Cleveland Plain Dealer* (February 24): 1.

Hopper, Kim. 1984. Whose Lives Are These Anyway? *Urban and Social Change Review* 17 (Summer): 12–13.

Hopper, Kim, and J. Hamberg. 1984. *The Making of America's Homeless.* New York: Community Service Society.

Huttman, Elizabeth. 1985. Policy Approaches to Social Housing Problems in Northern and Western Europe. In *Housing Needs and Policy Approaches: Trends in Thirteen Countries,* edited by Willem van Vliet—, Elizabeth Huttman, and Sylvia Fava. Durham, N.C.: Duke University Press.

———. 1986. International Trends in Housing Policy in Western Europe and the U.S. Paper presented at the World Congress of Sociology. Delhi, India.

———. 1987. Homelessness as a Housing Problem in an Inner City in the U.S. Paper Presented at the International Symposium on Housing Affordability and Homelessness. International Sociological Association Ad Hoc Committee on Housing and the Built Environment. Hamburg, West Germany.

Huttman, Elizabeth, and E. Gurewitsch. 1988. The Elderly and Housing. In *Handbook on Housing and the Built Environment,* edited by Elizabeth Huttman and Willem van Vliet—. Westport, Conn.: Greenwood Press.

Huttman, Elizabeth, and J. Huttman. 1988. An Economic and Social Analysis of the International Private Rental Housing Crisis. *Housing and Society* 15 (2): 47–52.

International Herald Tribune. 1988 (April 8). For Fairness in Housing, p. 4.

Kasinitz, Philip. 1984. Gentrification and Homelessness: The Single Room Occupant and the Inner City Revival. *Urban and Social Change Review* 17 (1): 9–14.

Lee, Barrett, and D. Hodge. 1984. Social Differentials in Metropolitan Residential Displacement. In *Gentrification, Displacement and Neighborhood Revitalization,* edited by J. Palen and B. London. Albany, N.Y.: State University of New York Press.

Marans, Robert, and M. Colten. 1985. U.S. Rental Housing Policies affecting Families with Children. In *Housing Needs and Policy Approaches: Trends in Thirteen Countries,* edited by Willem van Vliet—, Elizabeth Huttman, and Sylvia Fava. Durham, N.C.: Duke University Press.

Marcuse, Peter. 1987. Isolating the Homeless. *The Nation* (April).

McChesney, Kay. 1986. Homeless Women and Their Children. Unpublished report submitted to the Ford Foundation.

McLeod, Ramon. 1987. Rent Subsidies for S.F. Poor Often Can't Be Used. *San Francisco Chronicle* (June 29): 8.

Mental Health Association of San Francisco. 1987. *A Place To Be.* San Francisco: Mental Health Association Housing Task Force.

National Coalition for the Homeless. 1984. *Survey of Homeless.* New York: National Coalition.

———. 1986. New Survey Shows Increase in Homelessness Since 1985. New York. Press release.

New York Times. 1987 (November 22). They're Still Cheating Housing, p. F26.

———. 1988. (January 8). Low Income Tax Housing Credit, p. A7.

O'Connell, Brian. 1988. Cooperative and Condominium Conversions. In *Handbook on Housing and the Built Environment,* edited by Elizabeth Huttman and Willem van Vliet—. Westport, Conn.: Greenwood Press.

Palen, John. 1988. Gentrification, Revitalization and Displacement. In *Handbook on Housing and the Built Environment,* edited by Elizabeth Huttman and Willem van Vliet—. Westport, Conn.: Greenwood Press.

President's Commission on Urban Housing (Kaiser Commission). 1968. *A Decent Home.* Washington, D.C.: Government Printing Office.

San Francisco Chronicle. 1987 (July 27). Behind the Boom in Rehab Hotels. Business Section, p. 5.

———. 1987 (December 13). Profile of Bay Area Poverty, p. 5.

———. 1987 (December 17). Conference of Mayors Survey Finds Rise in Homeless Families, p. B4.

San Francisco Housing and Tenants Council Study. 1985.

Stegman, Michael. 1969. Reducing the Cost of New Construction. *Journal of the American Institute of Planners* 35 (3).

Sternlieb, George. 1970. *Rent Control in New York City.* New Brunswick, N.J.: Center for Urban and Regional Studies.

Stoner, Madeline. 1984. An Analysis of Public and Private Sector Provisions for Homeless People. *Urban and Social Change Review* 17 (1): 3–8.

Sullivan, Patricia, and S. Damroch. 1987. Homeless Women and Children. In *The Homeless in Contemporary Society,* edited by Richard Bingham, R. Green, and S. White. Newbury Park, Calif.: Sage Publishers.

Sumichrast, M., G. Ahluwalia, and R. J. Sheehan. 1979. *Profile of the Builder.* Washington, D.C.: National Association of Home Builders.

U.S. Bureau of the Census. *Annual Housing Survey.* 1981.

U.S. Department of Housing and Urban Development. 1981. *Residential Displacement— An Update.* Washington, D.C.: Office of Policy Development and Research. Department of Housing and Urban Development.

———. 1984. *A Report to the Secretary of the Homeless and Emergency Shelters.* Washington, D.C.: Department of Housing and Urban Development.

U.S. House of Representatives. 1985. Subcommittee on Housing and Community Development. *Hearings.* May 24.

Van Vliet—, Willem. 1988. Housing in the United States. In *International Housing Policy,* edited by Willem van Vliet—. Westport, Conn.: Greenwood Press.

Weeden, Joel, and M. Linedan. 1987. *Elders and Housing Displacement.* University of California Institute for Health and Aging.

6

A Social-Psychiatric Perspective on Homelessness: Results from a Pittsburgh Study

Jeffrey C. Wilson and Anthony C. Kouzi

Psychiatric perspectives on homelessness have been the subject of considerable controversy in the social sciences. Critics have questioned the nature and prevalence of mental illness among the homeless. A "medicalization phenomena" or psychiatric bias has been described in reference to early reports of mental illness among the homeless. In a recent review Snow et al. (1986) challenge the assumption that a high proportion of homeless persons suffer from mental disability. In this important article, they cite numerous examples of medicalization, both in the popular press as well as in psychiatric literature. The assertion that most homeless persons are "interactionally incompetent, conversationally incoherent, occasionally menacing, and institutionally dependent, crazy" (Snow et al., 1986: 407–408), is in their opinion very misleading.

A well-known earlier trend in psychiatric homeless research was an over reporting of prevalence figures for mental illness in studies conducted primarily by psychiatric investigators. These studies can be viewed as initial efforts to characterize the problem when the state of knowledge in that discipline about homeless persons was relatively undeveloped. While sociological studies on homelessness date back many years (Anderson, 1923; Bogue, 1963; Bahr, 1968), the U.S. psychiatric community has only recently turned its attention to homelessness as an important area of investigation. In the early psychiatric studies, sampling methodologies were limited, and diagnostic procedures were conducted by clinicians with semistructured or unstructured instruments. Given the inherent biases of clinicians in reporting illness when more-structured assessment techniques are impractical or unavailable, such efforts were likely to suffer from a "medicalization effect."

Most of these studies were conducted in the early 1980s by well-intentioned community psychiatrists who were committed to serving the poor and disenfranchised mental patient. There are several examples of these earlier studies. In Philadelphia, out of 179 residents at an emergency shelter, 84 percent were diagnosed as having mental illness (Arce et al., 1983). In New York (Lipton et al., 1983), out of 90 homeless persons treated at Bellevue Hospital, 72 percent were diagnosed with serious psychoses and up to 12 percent were labeled with personality disorders. In Boston (Bassuk, 1984), over 90 percent of 78 residents at a shelter were given psychiatric diagnoses.

These three studies were widely cited in the literature and led to the following stereotypes: "The overriding fact about the homeless is that most are mentally disabled" (Bassuk, 1984: 44), or "The streets, the train and bus stations, and the shelters have become the state hospitals of yesterday" (Lipton et al., 1983: 821). These studies, while pioneering in their field, have led to considerable misconception. Critics have cited numerous other case studies that contradict these earlier medical reports. The homeless population is diverse, they contend (Marin, 1987: 40–41), including the following groups: alienated veterans, the mentall ill, the physically disabled or chronically ill, the poor elderly, the new poor, runaway children, substance abusers, immigrants, traditional tramps, hobos, and transients.

By labeling most homeless persons as mentally ill, critics contend, the root problems of homelessness are mystified and thereby ignored. Instead the problem should be framed in political and economic terms (Kerr, 1986), free from stigmatizing labels or "blaming the victim" approaches. Considerable animosity has developed among homeless consumers themselves, who feel the burden of stigmatizing labels. The homeless consumer movement has grown quite strong in opposition to such "medicalizations" of their problems. An example of such consumer indignation was a recent political demonstration and "heckling disruption" at a 1986 national conference on homelessness and mental illness at Harvard University.

The consumer movement has done much to advance the cause for fighting stigma and lobbying for necessary political reform for homeless persons. Their perspective is that structural features of the economy are to blame for their predicament, not widespread mental illness. Homeless consumers feel that the societal response to homelessness has been too often guided by misconception and ignorance, i.e. "widespread mental illness." This has in turn led to shortsighted and restrictive policies. Shelters are, at best, short-term solutions; they are highly regimented and run by bureaucratic agencies with operating rules that often reflect underlying prejudice and contempt for homeless persons.

While it is important not to exaggerate the prevalence or causal nature of mental illness among homeless persons, it is necessary to address recent reports of mental disorder and unique mental health service needs among the homeless. Research in the area of homelessness and mental illness has now entered a more mature phase as second- and third-generation studies with improved methodology are being reported (Levine and Lezak, 1985). Large epidemiological studies have demonstrated conclusively that a significant proportion of homeless persons suffer from mental disability.

In Ohio, a large-scale study of 979 homeless people in 19 counties (Roth and Bean, 1986) concluded that 31 percent of the sample had symptoms serious enough to require mental health services. In that study, 30 percent reported hospitalization at least once previously for mental health reasons. Two other studies with sophisticated probability sampling methods have been completed to date. The Los Angeles study (Farr et al., 1986), which utilized a probability sample of 379 individuals and structured diagnostic instruments, reported 28 percent who were categorized as chronically mentally ill. Another 34 percent were described as chronic substance abusers. In the Chicago study (Rossi et al., 1987), a probability sample of 722 homeless persons was studied with relatively high levels of mental illness reported. Almost one in four (23 percent) showed high levels of psychotic thinking with up to 47 percent displaying symptoms of depression. Nearly one in six (16 percent) had a history of previous suicide attempt, while 23 percent reported previous psychiatric hospitalizations. Among those with previous mental hospitalizations, 58 percent reported a history of multiple hospitalizations.

Other studies (Fischer et al., 1986; Human Services Research Institute, 1985; Morse et al., 1985, Rosnow et al., 1985) corroborate the above findings of significant mental health disability among homeless persons. In the light of these and other findings, considerable attention has been directed towards the service needs of this mentally ill homeless population.

Persons who are homeless and suffer mental disability pose considerable challenge for health planners. They often have extensive and multidimensional mental health needs (Bachrach, 1984; Ball and Havassy, 1984; Baxter and Hopper, 1982; Jones, 1983). More recently they have been described (Fischer and Breakey, 1986) as multiproblem clients, highly mobile, utilizing multiple services, with few social supports and frequently subject to victimization. In addition, they have been noted to have a critical lack of social margins to negotiate successful passage through informal and formal caregiving systems (Segal et al., 1977). The primary health care needs among this population are also noteworthy (Robertson and Cousineau, 1986; Schutt and Garrett, 1986).

While not solely responsible, deinstitutionalization and related policies have contributed to this issue. The extent of resources for long-term community care and support of the chronically mentally ill has been extensively criticized (Arnhoff, 1975; Bassuk and Gerson, 1978; Borus, 1981; Lamb, 1984). Social welfare and housing needs were not addressed as state hospitals declined in significance and their chronically mentally ill were released into the community. New community mental health centers often ignored or devalued care of the chronic patient in exchange for prevention programs (Goldman and Morrissey, 1985) and treatment of new, middle-class populations often described as "the worried but well." The American Psychiatric Association, in a recent review (Lamb and Talbot,

1986), has cited the implementation of deinstitutionalization as "disastrous" and causally related to both homelessness and criminalization among the mentally ill.

Currently, the issue of service provision for mentally disabled homeless has become an urgent priority as urban areas report alarming increases in the extent of the problem. The devolution of public health and welfare programs with a growing privatization has complicated the problem. Local groups are now carrying the burden of assisting the multiproblem homeless client, often in an uncoordinated and informal manner. The fragmentation of available services has necessitated collaborative efforts among all of the human services in order to provide the appropriate mix of services (Levine and Kennedy, 1985). Because of widespread public opinion, mental health agencies are now being forced to take proactive leadership roles in facilitating the development of innovative programs.

THE RESEARCH STUDY

The authors conducted an applied research study in the inner city of Pittsburgh during the winter and spring of 1985. The research project was designed to provide information for the planning and development of a new outreach consultation program servicing the operators and mentally ill clients of local shleters and soup kitchens. The study was intended to identify the demand for services among homeless persons with mental disability, to assess existing service resources and their relevance, and to provide a detailed community description of the social context of the problem. The initiative was sponsored by Community Human Services Corporation which operated in conjunction with area mental health agencies and private philanthropic groups. The geographic target area was defined according to the catchment policy of Allegheny County which divides the city into several different service areas. This service area, known as the 9C1 catchment area, contained a large poor population in the inner city.

The broad aim of the mental health outreach program was to deliver outreach case management and support services to displaced, poor persons with mental disability as well as their providers of emergency shelter and food. Both direct services to homeless mentally ill persons as well as ongoing consultation to preexisting caregiving systems were viewed as priorities. The latter process of ongoing consultation included training, education, and linkage functions designed to supplement the informal, temporary care provided by shelter and soup kitchen operators. These consultation services were planned to link informal, mostly private systems with formal, public systems through a process of network building, resource sharing, and interorganizational cooperation. The ultimate aim of the program was to influence the existing formal system of health and human services through raising awareness of the needs of the target groups.

In order to establish a planning data base, a study assessing provider and client needs, service network information, and social area context was designed. The specific goals of investigation were: (1) to assess provider needs for training, education, and networking/linkage; (2) to describe homeless clients' behavioral patterns and needs; (3) to outline agency interactions for planning purposes (i.e. strengthening interorganization communications, enhancing services, and promoting resource sharing); (4) to evaluate existing referral patterns with the goal of developing a more functional and comprehensive referral system; and (5) to appraise regional social, political, and economic trends relevant to the problem.

METHODS

Both qualitative and quantitative approaches were used to produce a triangulation of data. A multidimensional, less-structured approach was employed for several reasons, the first of which is the acknowledged difficulty in administering structured and lengthy diagnostic instruments to homeless persons. The most common reasons for these difficulties include the desire for privacy on the part of the homeless, difficulty establishing rapport, and the limited attention span of clients who were often incoherent or suspicious. Second, the small budget available for the local study precluded the use of well-standardized but time-consuming data-gathering procedures even if they were considered appropriate for this population.

The initial phase of research involved field analysis and participant observation in soup kitchens, shelters, and other locations where the homeless were known to congregate, such as street corners and bridges. Two masters's-level researchers were trained and served as participant observers. Field notes were collected from the identified sites for approximately four months. These procedures included observations, interviews, and personal impressions of providers and the clientele in the shelter/soup kitchen circuit. The initial phase was viewed as a necessary, exploratory introduction to sites and homeless persons looking for shared concerns, problems, and patterns of interaction. The field records were reviewed and analyzed qualitatively in a search for common themes and unmet needs.

On the basis of this field analysis, two semistructured research instruments were developed for the second part of the study. The first instrument was a 16-page semistructured questionnaire that was used to gather information from service providers. All operators (N = 10) of shelters and soup kitchens in the target area were interviewed. The semistructured interviews were conducted by mental health professionals experienced in mental health assessments. The providers selected at each site were those persons directly in charge and/or their assistants. These people had close involvement and interaction with homeless persons on a daily basis. Major areas covered in the provider questionnaire were the following: (1) facility characteristics: funding, facility service provision, staffing patterns, volunteer support, training needs, and information on facility providers such as education and training; (2) client characteristics: prevalence of mentally disabled persons, classification of types of mental illnesses, particular service needs; (3) referral system characteristics: referral patterns-agreements, types of resource sharing, and levels of cooperation between referring agencies.

The second semistructured instrument was used to interview a purposive sample of representative homeless individuals. The questionnaire was designed to include social, demographic, vocational, and mental health histories; patterns of service utilization, and immediate service needs. Eligibility criteria consisted of being both homeless or at high risk for homelessness and exhibiting symptomatology strongly suggestive of mental illness according to DSM-III criteria. Homelessness was defined as limited or no shelter for any length of time. Subjects were either referred by providers, self-referred, or approached by field workers. Subjects were offered $10 to participate in the interview.

Four categories of homeless persons formed the purposive sampling framework. These four categories were derived from field analysis, each category reflecting similar mental health histories, patterns of service utilization, and immediate service needs. The four categories were the revolving door, substance abusers, transients, and the untreated. These four groups were developed for heuristic purposes and as such were intended as descriptive guides to service planning.[1] Subjects who were felt to be representative of one of these four categories were asked to participate. A total of 14 interviews were conducted, 4 in each category except transients where only 2 could be located.

Information on referral chains for each shelter and soup kitchen were assessed with data collected from the provider interview. These referral sources were evaluated on a scale that ranged from helpful to least helpful and frequency of referral-source utilization. Referral maps were constructed that included major sources of interaction and cooperation. In addition to referral maps, a network profile was developed from resource-sharing patterns among shelters and soup kitchens.

Finally, secondary data sources and key informants were utilized to identify a set of environmental factors and trends that were viewed as having a potential impact on the local homeless problem in the present and future. This environmental dimension included economic forces in the community, social values of decisionmakers, political climate, and key governmental policies.

FINDINGS

Service Providers

Each site varied considerably in a number of areas regarding admission policies, house rules, staffing patterns, and levels of assistance/services to homeless mentally ill persons. All locations had formal admission policies, rules, and daily schedules that were strictly enforced. Staffing levels were generally very low, and significant overcrowding was mentioned in most sites. Social service advocacy was encouraged in some sites, available but not utilized in others, and was unavailable in still others.

Mental illness estimates by providers ranged from a low of 15 to 20 percent to a high of 50 percent with an average of 31 percent for all sites. Providers described mentally ill clients as demonstrating unpredictable and unusual behaviors, frequently acting out and disrupting house operations. The most commonly identified symptom groups reported were substance abuse, paranoia, delusions, and depression. All providers desired direct service (e.g., counseling, crisis intervention, assessment, and referral), while fewer requested training and consultation for their own staff in dealing with clients with mental health problems. A variety of additional support services ranging from assistance with entitlement, vocational rehabilitation, and leisure/education classes covering budgeting, child care, and family planning were requested. All sites discussed financial resources as significantly limiting the scope of services provided to mentally ill clients.

Homeless Persons

Substance abusers—persons abusing alcohol and/or street drugs who use shelters and/or soup kitchens. This group appears to be the most prevalent in the 9C1 catchment area. Providers' estimates of substance abuse ranged from 15 to 75 percent with an average of approximately 45 percent. All had long histories of abuse, including many unsuccessful attempts at detoxification in detoxification programs. All reported social inadequacies and depression as precipitant factors in abuse. Many had histories of psychiatric hospitalization and treatment. Their physical health is often poor, with high blood pressure, seizures, and gastrointestinal problems reported. Substance abuse was cited by the entire group as the cause of unemployment. Many had been involved in panhandling, hustling, and other such activities defined as criminal. Substance abusers were found to be the most likely to cause serious disturbances and to be involved in violence at the various sites.

Revolving door—individuals with repeated voluntary and/or involuntary admissions to psychiatric hospitals who are using shelters or soup kitchens. This group represented the long-time mental patients with backgrounds of psychotic illnesses and histories of institutionalization; all had at least seven-year histories of multiple admissions and outpatient treatment. Characteristics such as frequent bouts with homelessness, recurring need for hospitalization, and poor compliance with service intervention were found. These individuals reported frequent, often unsuccessful, contacts with various social service agencies for extensive periods. In constant crises, they were not able to maintain stable housing, finances, or other social supports. A paranoid and adversarial style predominated in their interactions, often indicating feelings of unfair victimization. Generally demanding and often belligerent, all were having problems in shelters because of hostility or uncooperativeness. They had unrealistic expectations of mental health services, often discontinuing services for delusional beliefs (e.g., feelings persecuted). Such persons are usually uncooperative with mental health appointments and often refuse prescribed medications, especially during bouts of homelessness.

Untreated—persons with identifiable psychological problems or psychiatric disabilities who have never been treated and are using shelters and/or soup kitchens. This category contains a very large and heterogenous group of individuals. It includes several different subgroups all united by psychiatric difficulties with no prior history of treatment. The first group is the traditional "street people" such as "bag ladies" and "bag men." These clients manifest withdrawn, antisocial, and avoidant behaviors while often giving the impression of being totally self sufficient, seemingly due to pride and difficulty with dependence. Rarely utilizing shelters, these "untreated" persons sleep on the streets and visit soup kitchens during the day.

The other subgroups of untreated encompass the situationally distressed who have been displaced by a variety of forces including domestic crisis, unemployment, poverty, and lack of affordable housing. These subgroups have increased in recent years; they are often referred to as the "new poor" or the "new homeless." While differing dramatically from "street people," they share their history of no prior treatment or contact with the mental health sector. Many of these individuals do not suffer from primary mental disorders but develop secondary mental disability resulting from the exigencies of street survival and the extreme stress associated with catastrophic displacement and homelessness. High levels of anxiety and depression were commonly observed among these people. The stress associated with homelessness often leads to a repetitive cycle of anxiety and indecisiveness followed by depression and feelings of loss of control, the cycle repeating itself once again.

Transients—persons using shelters or soup kitchens from out of state, in need of mental health services, who do not have or plan permanent residence in Pittsburgh. This group displays prominent and disabling psychiatric symptoms including paranoid ideation, delusions, and social withdrawal with histories of multiple, brief hospitalizations. Transients shared many features in common with the group of young adult chronics often cited in mental health literature both in terms of age as well as service utilization (Pepper et al., 1981). They demonstrate a marked pattern of venturous mobility and traveling. Generally they are not interested in mental health treatments. Their accounts of travel suggest moving in order to avoid the system at large, in particular the mental health system. They exhibit independent lifestyles, preferring to live on the streets as they move from city to city.

Existing Referral Systems

There was significant variation in referral patterns among individual sites. For the sites that provided little social service advocacy, referral chains were sparse to nonexistent while many referral sources were reported for other more active programs. All sites reported difficulty with mental health referrals. Local, community psychiatric mental health centers were generally resistent to accepting clients into outpatient or day programs. Emergency room services were available, but hospital staff frequently discouraged referrals, often requesting an involuntary commitment prior to evaluation.

There was a significant absence of adequate crisis mental health referral sources for all sites. In fact, the police were the most frequently cited source for dealing with disruptive mentally ill clients. Actively psychotic or paranoid clients were frequently subject to arrest and incarceration as the only means of dealing with their deviant and unmanageable behaviors. This is consistent with other reports in the literature that refer to the criminalization of the homeless mentally ill (Lamb and Grant, 1982). One common pattern reported was a 24-hour cycle that included police intervention, arrest of mentally ill clients, and release to the streets the following day with subsequent return to the original site.

Environmental Impact

The Pittsburgh region continues to suffer considerably as economic forces transform formerly robust manufacturing industries. From 1979 to 1983, almost 50,000 jobs were lost in primary metals (Mellon Bank Economics Department, 1984). Thousands of additional persons have disappeared from the work force for a variety of other reasons (Gruson, 1986), including a local recession. There has been constant and extensive transformation in the local workplace with higher proportions of jobs in white-collar and service industries. Blue-collar employment opportunities have steadily declined with wide-scale unemployment and dislocation appearing as a harsh reality for many local families in western Pennsylvania.

Structural changes in the society over the past 20 years have contributed to the increased severity of the homeless problem. Poverty and economic distress have become inescapable burdens for unprecedented numbers in the general population. The shift from a traditional manufacturing economy to high-tech automation and service industries has displaced large numbers of workers who are poorly equipped to compete in the changing work force. High unemployment is a more serious problem for those in the lowest socioeconomic strata. Polarization and disparity in income distributions have proceeded at an alarming rate.

Central city, urban areas have greater problems with increased concentrations of poor, aging, minorities, disabled, and single-parent families. Urban redevelopment programs and gentrification of city neighborhoods have compounded these problems by eliminating affordable housing opportunities in central city areas. Wide-scale disruption of the family unit has occurred secondary to these social and economic stresses.

Public housing programs have been cut back substantially during recent years. According to one analyst (Riordan, 1987: 26), the overall budget for HUD has been reduced from 35.7 billion in FY 1980 to 14.2 billion at present, with federal subsidies for low-income housing declining by 60 percent over this period. Few new housing projects are scheduled, and many more are predicted to vanish. It is estimated that in the next decade up to 900,000 of the existing 4.2 million federally subsidized housing units will be lost (Riordan, 1987: 26).

In addition to the above economic trends of poverty and sharp decreases in affordable housing, key trends are evident in the devolution of federal health and welfare programs for the poor and disabled. Major shifts in human service delivery have occurred since the conservative Reagan administration instituted block grant funding. The result has been a more pervasive degeneration of safety-net welfare programs, decreases in the availability of health care, and cutbacks in the human services. This transfer of responsibility to state and local governments has proven disastrous, especially for programs that serve the economically marginal. Between 1981 and 1984, social services were cut by 22 percent, employment training by 60 percent, and community development by 19 percent (United Way of Pittsburgh, 1985). While private philanthropy has increased, it has failed to compensate for the loss of public-sector funding.

Increasing privatization of community services has resulted in an absence of essential care in communities least able to afford them. Privatization here refers to the private-enterprise solution to community needs once provided by local, state, or federal government, i.e., the public sector. This trend has succeeded in saving taxes for well-to-do communities and residents who are able to provide community services on their own via private enterprise. Those living in adjacent, often inner-city neighborhoods are doing without as public sector is no longer providing a full range of services. These poorer areas cannot afford to contract for these services, i.e., private police, separate mental health, library acquisitions, fire and safety personnel, and the like.

In the area of mental health, critical developments are under way that also relate to the homeless problem. Shrinking program budgets and deinstitutionalization mandates have strained the delivery of comprehensive services to the poor and disabled. Financing of services for the seriously mentally ill living in the community is wholly inadequate. A large number of community mental health centers (CMHC) are eliminating services, (42%) while over one-third (36%) are reporting a decline in total services rendered because of funding reductions (Estes and Woods, 1984). Over two-thirds of state mental health budgets still support hospitals with less than one-third left for community care. The result is a growing discrepancy as service cutbacks occur simultaneously with increasing demands for services in the community. Thus the poor and disabled client is left by default in a vulnerable position, having to compete for services with those who have monetary resources.

SUMMARY AND DISCUSSION

There are several noteworthy trends that are evident from the results of the assessment of facility/provider, clientele, and existing referral system and environmental scan. First, there is a high proportion of homeless persons, up to one-third of whom exhibit symptoms of mental disability, who utilize the shelters and soup kitchens in the target area. This percentage was based on provider estimates and confirmed by field analysis. A recent survey (Bromet et al., 1986) in Allegheny County reports comparable estimates of mental illness in shelters ranging from 31–60 percent for diagnosis of either schizophrenia or depression at different sites. If substance abuse and other diagnoses are included, the prevalence estimates are much higher.

Among the group of mentally ill in the target area, there was considerable evidence of extensive unmet needs for mental health services. These groups are composed of individuals who pose challenges for the planning and delivery of services. Generally, homeless mentally ill clients were found to be isolated and withdrawn, leading extremely noncommunicative lives, often suspicious of and resistant to ordinary social interaction. Uprooted traumatically, they appear totally unconnected to any visible supports. They exhibit a marked mobility with no fixed addresses and few predictable patterns of shelter/soup kitchen utilization. Movement between shelters and other sites occurred frequently and was therefore difficult to trace. They wander frequently, filled with distrust and paranoia, using corners of the social landscape to hide and avoid contact.

There is currently a loosely organized group of service providers all united by a strong commitment to serve the destitute and homeless. These providers all express feelings of being overwhelmed by the unmet needs of their mentally ill clients. Restrictive measures and bureaucratic rules are required at these sites because of short staffing and overcrowding. They admit to virtually no training in dealing with serious mental illness. They report feeling abandoned by the local mental health system. The providers describe this as a sense of isolation from mental health support resources, often commenting that the services offered are inadequate or inappropriate. The most common examples were the excessive reliance on inpatient hospitalization and involuntary commitments instead of outpatient programs such as supportive housing and vocational training.

Crisis behaviors (violence and acting out) were frequently reported among their mentally ill clients. These behaviors are disruptive, often leading to dangerous situations and police intervention. The providers must function without previous experience and training. Lacking adequate support, they often view police intervention as their only recourse. In addition to these more extreme behaviors, they report relatively high levels of depression, anxiety, substance abuse, and psychosis among their homeless clients. Consultation, education, and training in dealing with mental illness are urgent needs for this group of service providers. In addition there is a strong desire for coalition development and networking with other agencies and health systems.

The existing mental health referral system for homeless persons is poorly organized and functionally inadequate. The catchment policy and its resultant territoriality phenomenon severely constrain most attempts to provide continuous and comprehensive treatment. Residential and housing referrals were the most significant elements missing or in short supply. Community residences that provide structured services and rehabilitation for the mentally ill were in short supply relative to the demand. Instead, board and care homes often in poor repair with restrictive rules, and custodial environments appeared as the only alternatives.

The mental health systems emphasis on inpatient hospitalization, mostly involuntary, is costly, often inappropriate, and culturally irrelevant. Current policy favors reimbursement of hospital-based, acute services. These approaches compartmentalize treatment within hospitals and neglect the overwhelming environmental impacts of desperate poverty, social isolation, and helplessness. Clients are given medications and then discharged often with inadequate provisions to remedy their vulnerability to subsequent homelessness. These short-term, ''medical model'' treatments in general-hospital settings focus on symptom remission. This however, is a relatively weak predictor of successful community adjustment after discharge.

A more important element of community adaptation is a continuum of support services such as residential and day programs, drop-in centers, and outreach case management teams. These outpatient programs however, essential for the long-term rehabilitation of homeless mentally ill clients, are poorly funded and hence largely not available. When available, they are usually inaccessible to this population or insufficient in quantity and resources to meet the demand. In addition, many mental health agencies have biases against homeless mentally ill, preferring to treat ''more desirable'' clients such as those with fewer, less complicated problems and better prognoses who are also more likely to have medical insurance.

Traditional mental health systems with their conventional office-bound or hospital-based approaches to treatment are poorly equipped to deal with the complexities of service delivery to this population. A flexible, street-bound, mobile case-managment approach appears necessary to reach out, locate people in the community, and begin the arduous and slow rehabilitation process. Such an approach will have to be ''street wise'' and innovative, and its success will depend on creative alliance with a network of community ties.

Initiating treatment is a painstakingly slow process, often delayed by the barriers of mistrust, isolation, and frequent movement of clients. Case finding is difficult because of the lack of place stability among members of this highly mobile and often transient society. Furthermore, the profound anxiety and depression associated with social alienation and economic dislocation necessitates another time-consuming procedure. This is the preliminary or pretreatment process—the establishment of rapport or a trusting alliance. The creation of a relationship with homeless individuals involves continuous availability and an emphatic, supportive, and interpersonal approach. This process of finding new cases and then engaging them in treatment is highly unique and distinct in the demands it places on the mental health system.

The immediate task in homeless mentally ill service provision is the coordination of services within a network of agencies and the allocation or reallocation of adequate funding. Cutbacks in social services and safety-net welfare programs further threaten services to this vulnerable group. Increased interagency cooperation in combination with necessary funding is essential if the complex needs of this population are to be addressed. Much ignorance (and political resistance) hampers constructive allocation or reallocation of resources to meet the vast unmet needs of homeless mentally ill persons. Accurate reeducation and information dissemination to policymakers, professionals, and program administrators is needed to counteract systemwide resistance.

The existing system relies on a somewhat vague policy with altruism and informal agreements as a basis for interagency collaboration and resource sharing. These however are not sufficient to ensure cooperation for this difficult population in an era of fiscal austerity and scarce resources. Instead, a formal resource-sharing network is needed where there are negotiated rules regarding minimum resource commitment.

CONCLUSIONS

The social response to deinstitutionalized and homeless mentally ill persons in the Pittsburgh region is both unique and yet, in many respects, common. The problems associated with a rust-belt local economic recession are somewhat unique. The local provision of mental health and support services is, however, fairly representative of most urban, American communities. The response is marked by the following: (1) overcrowded shelters and soup kitchens operating as short-term solutions, often with restrictive policies and highly bureaucratic rules; (2) low staffing levels in most sites with limited social service advocacy capability; (3) a remarkable resistance on the part of local psychiatric facilities to share resources or reallocate program budgets to address the problem; (4) police crisis intervention and a criminalization phenomenon among mentally disabled clients; (5) economic constraints and governmental cutbacks further compromising service delivery.

Scarce resources resulting from small community mental health budgets and large hospital budgets are a common and harsh reality for the deinstitutionalized mentally ill. Psychiatric hospitals with their advanced institutional technologies and research programs have divested from local community problems such as the homeless mentally ill. Nowhere is this more apparent than in Pittsburgh, where one of the country's leading psychiatric treatment and research centers stands practically unmoved by its local homeless mentally ill problem.

The dogma associated with modern neurobiological psychiatry has redefined the problem of homeless mentally ill and has given large university (and publicaly funded) psychiatric centers an escape clause, abdicating themselves from any responsibility for this "messy affair." In the biomedical paradigm, the role of hospital complexes, which possess over two-thirds of mental health budgets, is to treat "hard disease" and correct neuroregulatory and biochemical defects. The multiple, social consequences (often victimizations) associated with the mental disease are ignored and passed on to a myriad of loosely knit, underfunded community agencies. These social consequences such as poverty, homelessness, and criminalization, however, represent the real human experience of mental disease and as such constitute the total illness. This illness experience demands a more-adequate psychiatric response (i.e., holistic psychosocial care), above and beyond short-term hospital treatments and pharmacologic prescriptions.

Such an adequate response, however, is unlikely as political and economic forces drive psychiatry further down the road of community divestment in pursuit of more advanced and expensive technologies and hospital treatments. The elder statesman of the biopsychosocial model in medicine, Engel (1984: 54) has described these forces well: "The power of vested interests, social, political, and economic, are formidable deterrents to any effective assault on biomedical dogmatism. The delivery of health care is a major industry, considering that more than 8 percent of our national economic product is devoted to health. The enormous existing and planned investment in diagnostic and therapeutic technology alone strongly favors approaches to clinical study and care of patients that emphasize the impersonal and the mechanical."

NOTE

1. Similar to the principles of DSM–3 nosology (i.e., current classification system in American psychiatry), taxonomy here works to provide a recipe or prescription for type of treatment; types of homeless refer to unique needs, problems, issues in treatment. The groups are not mutually exclusive, nor are they understood as encompassing all homeless mentally ill subtypes.

REFERENCES

Anderson, N. 1923. *The Hobo*. Chicago: University of Chicago Press.
Arce, A. A., et al. 1983. Psychiatric Profile of Street People Admitted to an Emergency Shelter. *Hospital and Community Psychiatry* 34: 812–817.
Arnhoff, F. N. 1975. Social Consequences of Policy Towards Mental Illness. *Science* 188: 1277–1281.
Bachrach, L. L. 1984. *The Homeless Mentally Ill and Mental Health Services: An Analytical Review of the Literature*. Washington, D.C.: DHHS.
Bahr, H. M. 1968. *Homelessness and Disaffiliation*. New York: Columbia University Press.
Ball. F. L., and B. E. Havassy. 1984. A Survey of the Problems and Needs of Homeless Consumers of Acute Psychiatric Services. *Hospital and Community Psychiatry* 35: 917–921.
Bassuk, E. L. 1984. The Homeless Problem. *Scientific American* 251: 40–45.
Bassuk, E., and Gerson, J. 1978. Deinstitutionalization and Mental Health Services. *Scientific American* 238: 46–53.
Baxter, E., and K. Hopper. 1982. The New Mendicancy: Homeless in New York City. *American Journal of Orthopsychiatry* 52: 393–408.

Bogue, D. 1963. *Skid Row in American Cities*. Chicago: Community and Family Studies Center, University of Chicago.

Borus, J. P. 1981. Deinstitutionalization of the Chronically Mentally Ill. *New England Journal of Medicine* 306: 339–342.

Bromet, E., et al. 1986. Mental Illness among the Homeless in Allegheny County. Paper presented at the Annual Meeting of the American Pschiatric Association. Washington, D.C.

Engel, G. L. 1984. The Need for a New Medical Model: A Challenge for Biomedicine. In *Culture and Psychopathology*, edited by J. E. Mezzich and C. E. Berganza. New York: Columbia University Press.

Estes, C. L., and J. B. Woods. 1984. A Preliminary Assessment of the Impact of Block Grants on Community Mental Health Centers. *Hospital and Community Psychiatry* 35: 1125–1129.

Farr, R. K., et al. 1986. *A Study of Homelessness and Mental Illness in the Skid Row Area of Los Angeles*. Los Angeles: Los Angeles County Department of Mental Health.

Fischer, P. J. and W. R. Breakey. 1986. Homelessness and Mental Health: An Overview. *International Journal of Mental Health* 14: 6–41.

Fischer, P. J., et al. 1986. Mental Health and Social Characteristics of the Homeless: A Survey of Mission Users. *American Journal of Public Health* 76: 519–523.

Goldman, H. H., and J. P. Morrissey. 1985. The Alchemy of Mental Health Policy: Homelessness and the Fourth Cycle of Reform. *American Journal of Public Health* 75: 727–731.

Gruson, L. 1986. Steel Towns Discharge Police and Reduce Services Sharply. *New York Times* (October 16): 1, 14.

Human Services Research Institute. 1985. *Homelessness Needs Assessment: Study Findings and Recommendations for the Massachusetts Department of Mental Health*. Boston: Massachusetts Department of Mental Health.

Jones, R. 1983. Street People and Psychiatry: An Introduction. *Hospital and Community Psychiatry* 34: 807–811.

Kerr, P. 1986. The New Homelessness Has Its Roots in Economics. *New York Times* (March 16): E–5.

Lamb, H. R. 1984. Deinstitutionalization and the Homeless Mentally Ill. *Hospital and Community Psychiatry* 35: 899–907.

Lamb, H. R., and R. W. Grant. 1982. The Mentally Ill in an Urban County Jail. *Archives of General Psychiatry* 39: 17–22.

Lamb, H. R., and J. A. Talbott. The Homeless Mentally Ill: The Perspective of the American Psychiatric Association. *Journal of the American Medical Association* 256: 496–501.

Levine, I. S., and C. Kennedy. 1985. The Homeless Mentally Ill: A Consultation Challenge. *Consultation: An International Journal* 4: 52–63.

Levine, I. S., and A. D. Lezak. 1985. *Research on the Homeless Mentally Ill: Current Status and Future Directions*. Rockville, Md: National Institute of Mental Health.

Lipton, F. R., et al. 1983. Down and Out in the City: The Homeless Mentally Ill. *Hospital and Community Psychiatry* 34: 817–821.

Marin, P. 1987. Helping and Hating the Homeless: The Struggle at the Margins of America. *Harpers Magazine* (January): 39–47.

Mellon Bank Economics Department. 1984. *Mellon Economic Update*. Pittsburgh: Mellon Bank.

Morse, G., et al. 1985. *Homeless People in St. Louis: A Mental Health Program Evaluation*. Jefferson City: Missouri Department of Mental Health.

Pepper, B., et al. 1981. The Young Adult Chronic Population: Overview of a Population. *Hospital and Community Psychiatry* 32: 463–469.

Riordan, T. 1987. Housekeeping at HUD: Why the Homeless Problem Could Get Much, Much Worse. *Common Cause Magazine* (March/April): 26–31.

Robertson, M. J., and M. R. Cousineau. 1986. Health Status and Access to Health Services among the Urban Homeless. *American Journal of Public Health* 76: 561–563.

Rosnow, M., et al. 1985. *Listening to the Homeless: A Study of Homeless Mentally Ill Persons in Milwaukee*. Milwaukee: Wisconsin Office of Mental Health.

Rossi, P. H., et al. 1987. The Urban Homeless: Estimating Composition and Size. *Science* 235: 1336–1341.

Roth, D., and G. J. Bean. 1986. New Perspectives on Homelessness: Findings From a Statewide Epidemiologic Study. *Hospital and Community Psychiatry* 37: 712–719.

Schutt, R., and Garrett, G. 1986. *Homeless in Boston: The View from Long Island*. Boston: City Department of Health and Hospitals.

Segal, S. P., et al. 1977. Falling Through the Cracks: Mental Disorder and Social Margin in a Young Vagrant Population. *Social Problems* 24: 387–400.

Snow, D. A., et al. 1986. The Myth of Pervasive Mental Illness Among the Homeless. *Social Problems* 33: 407–423.

United Way of Pittsburgh. 1985. *Toward Tomorrow: An Environmental Scan for the United Way of Allegheny County*. Pittsburgh: United Way.

7

Sweat and Blood: Sources of Income on a Southern Skid Row

R. Bruce Wiegand

The homeless live in abject poverty. Yet the social programs that have proliferated in the last decade do not give them money. Instead, these programs distribute food, shelter, and clothing. In the short run, they provide basic provisions in ample supply to those who care to use them. Shelter vacancies are common, even in cities where there are large concentrations of homeless (U.S. Department of Housing and Urban Development, 1984), and soup kitchens feed the multitudes every night.

But the homeless need more than a hot meal and a roof overhead. Their self-respect, privacy, safety, health, and personal grooming depend on money. The common impression that the homeless are idle and have no need or desire for money is a far cry from what I found in my study. These individuals do have budgets. I found that these men spend on average $30–50 per week.

Frequently complaining about the theft that occurs in public shelters and having no safe place to store personal belongings, homeless men often rent lockers in bus stations. Bus lockers cost about $7 per week. They also spend their money on hotel rooms. Renting a private room in a hotel is a luxury to someone who is accustomed to sleeping outdoors or in a shelter with maybe 600 other men. The rented room, which costs approximately $50 per week or $8–10 per day, allows one to relax his guard in a way that does not occur in large shelters where violence is common.

The homeless also seek money for toiletries, telephone calls, and transportation. Like other Americans, they even like to treat themselves to food and drink. A 35-year-old man told me that when he can afford it he likes to eat at

McDonalds. Another, a 22-year-old American Indian said that he spends between $10–30 per week, depending on whether or not he is drinking.

Besides using money to buy things, money symbolizes social position in the homeless community. Street life is socially stratified, and fine distinctions are made with respect to the amount of money one has and how it is acquired. It is irionic to see one homeless man berating another for "bumming" cigarettes or picking cigarette butts up off the ground to smoke. The socially correct thing to do is to buy one's own cigarettes, which can add as much as $5–10 to a weekly budget.

There is little known about how one goes about earning cash at this bottom rung of our economic ladder. What we know in general about the "homeless economy" comes from several different surveys and enumerations (Rossi et al., 1986; Institute for Research on Poverty, 1987–88; Roth et al., 1985). Although these studies focus on different cities, they reach similar conclusions. A quick review shows that: (1) the homeless are not part of the official labor force and on average have not worked a steady job in several years; (2) only 5–10 percent have worked full time in the past month, but as many as half have worked part time in that period; (3) males are more active than females in the homeless economy; and (4) single, white men are the least likely of the homeless to receive monthly government assistance (i.e., income from pensions, welfare, disability programs, and child support).

It is the economic pursuits of single, homeless men that form the focus of this study. I am specifically interested in describing their main source of income. Since the government generally is not one of these sources, the men must face the option of remaining penniless or finding a job in the urban economy. These jobs border on the brutal.

ETHNOGRAPHY AND THE PARTICULAR FEATURES OF SKID-ROW JOBS

Ethnography is a research technique used for studying the culture of a social group (For an elaboration of this idea refer to Spradley, 1970: 7–10; Howell, 1973: 368–83; Gold, 1958: 217–23). It calls upon the researcher to abandon his indigenous culture and subjectivity in favor of the perspective native to the group he wishes to study. This shedding of one's culture comes about as the researcher gains admittance into the group and assimilates its unique perspective. This acquiring of a new perspective gives the ethnographer a way of experiencing the world as it is experienced by members of the social group.

Lower Broadway, the skid-row area of Nashville, was the location of this ethnographic study. It is eight blocks long, eight blocks wide, and has a relatively stable homeless population in terms of size and demographic composition (Wiegand, 1988; Peterson and Wiegand, 1985). There are around 1,000 homeless people living there, most of them single men.

This study was begun in 1983 with funding provided by Housing and Urban Development (HUD). The entire project took 20 months, as the field work progressed through distinct stages. The first three months of the project were used to become familiar with the physical characteristics of Lower Broadway, such as its river bank and railroad yards, and to map out where skid-row men gathered at different times of the day and night. I began visiting these points as a way of gaining entry into their community. The group generally knew that I was a researcher studying them but they seemed not to alter their conduct as a consequence. One way that I ensured their conduct was unaffected by my presence was to interact with them repeatedly over long stretchs of time. A conservative estimate would be that I spent 20–30 hours per week in the field during this stage of the project. I started a field journal then and made entries in it several times a week.

The second stage of the project involved the collection of 60 oral histories. The interviews were recorded over the course of nine months and dealt with the work lives of the men. A loose outline around the themes of work experience and skills, income and expenditures, and lifestyle was used to allow for in-depth probing. The interviews were conversational in tone, and each lasted 30–60 minutes. The men who were interviewed were not selected with any criteria other than to explore the possible economic adaptations to skid-row poverty. They were men whom I met in the field or who had been referred to me as interesting cases (i.e., snowball sampling).

The third stage of the project began when I took up residence on Lower Broadway. I moved into a small hotel and lived there for eight months. During this time I continued the personal relationships that I had formed in the earlier stages of research and, in some sense, I assumed the rhythm and routines of skid-row men.

The taped oral histories were reanalyzed for this chapter, and the ethnographic perspective that I gained from the field experience serves as its foundation. Let us turn to a discussion of the skid-row economy.

Rossi et al.'s (1986) study of Chicago's homeless identifies two different sources of income. Regular sources of income, such as checks issued by the Social Security Administration, are received on a monthly basis. Occasional income, on the other hand, is received at no set or fixed interval. It is principally income that the homeless earn doing temporary jobs. These jobs may be as short as an hour or as long as several days. The livelihood of some 42 percent of the city's total homeless population comes from occasional sources of income (Rossi et al., 1986).

Among the skid-row homeless men on Lower Broadway, occasional income plays an even more important role. About 90 percent of the men depended on it primarily, whereas only 10 percent received regular monthly checks. Their occasional income came from jobs that exhibit three particular features that make them suitable to the population. Generally speaking, to function as viable sources

of income, the temporary jobs must correspond to the physical and social characteristics of homeless men. Moreover, social programs designed to substitute
for the jobs must exhibit the same particular features as well.

The first feature of skid-row jobs is that they pay in cash every day. Given
their urgent poverty, skid-row men cannot wait the customary two weeks before
getting paid. It is difficult for them to cash paychecks without a personal address,
and for this reason the men find it futile to seek "better jobs." This complication
also discourages homeless men from finding work through unemployment offices.

The second feature of skid-row jobs is that they accomodate a vagabond
lifestyle. The men, especially the younger ones, travel incessantly back and forth
from one city's skid row to another. They speak proudly of their "tramping"
and liken it to freedom. The jobs they seek are short lived and ones for which
they can be hired on the spot. Being hired for them does not imply a promise
of staying in the area for any length of time. Skid-row men would consider
painting the trim on a house, which might take two weeks, a big job. Something
more suitable would be unloading a truck, which might take six hours. Jobs
such as this do not require the men to produce personal identification, character
references, or a detailed job history.

The third feature of skid-row jobs is that they demand only marginal levels
of strength. The physical condition of the men on Lower Broadway is for the
most part deteriorated. Although the younger inhabitants are more fit than the
older and capable of doing heavy lifting and strenuous work, this is not to say
they are able-bodied or in good shape. Almost without exception, these men
smoke at least a pack of cigarettes per day which, combined with their tendency
to sleep outdoors, gives them chronic chest congestion. This cuts their wind and
endurance. Moreover, poor diets and lack of medical care make it physically
difficult for the young men to maintain a schedule of heavy labor for extended
periods. When skid-row men reach their mid forties, the thought of doing strenuous physical work for any more than several days a month becomes exceedingly
impractical. Their failing strength and concentration simply will not allow it.
Therefore, the older men develop survival strategies that are less demanding but
in turn yield less cash income. There is, in other words, a premature crowding
out of workers from skid-row labor markets. For those who exit the economy
altogether, there is nowhere further to fall. Without a source of income, the men
have lost themselves. About 1 percent of the population on Lower Broadway
have reached this depth. The others still have enough endurance and strength to
do hard physical labor at least on a temporary basis.

There are five categories of skid-row jobs: "junking," panhandling, street
hustling, spot labor, and selling plasma. The first two are truly marginal means
of subsistence and guarantee low status within the group. Junking is slightly
more respected than panhandling as it does not involve public begging. But it
hardly provides more income. One may spend an entire morning looking for
scrap metal and find only 24 empty beer cans. The cans weight about two pounds
and will sell for less than $1. Junk car batteries, which sell for a dollar each,

are more difficult to find. The men occasionally come across old appliances, automotive parts, and newspapers which can also be sold as junk. One man in our sample estimated that he made around $10 per week this way.

Street hustling is a more lucrative source of income. The men show real imagination in the different hustles they conduct. A young black man who was waiting for his first paycheck from a minimum-wage job as a tree surgeon made his hotel rent and food money by selling "nickle" ($5) bags of marijuana. In another instance, a 74-year-old homeless man was given yardsticks and several dollars each time he cleaned up the litter in a city parking lot. He set up a sidewalk stand and sold the yardsticks for whatever money people gave him. The problem with these hustles is that they are either illegal or too irregular and dependent on chance circumstances to be counted on.

The preferred and most prevalent jobs on Lower Broadway are working as spot labor and selling plasma. These jobs, by and large, pay the most and are usually available throughout the year. We will examine these two sources of income with respect to the job characteristics discussed above.

SPOT LABOR AND SELLING PLASMA

Skid-row men inevitably beat a path to the temporary hiring hall and the plasma center. These institutions are the economic mainstays of Lower Broadway. They are also both part of industries that are enjoying a boom across the country. In fact, the temporary employment service was the fastest growing industry in the United States between 1982 and 1984 (Carey and Kazelbaker, 1986). By 1985, there were nearly 8,000 such halls nationally, most of them being situated in urban industrial areas and southern states. The blood plasma industry is growing in response to the tenfold increase in plasma transfusions over the last decade. There are 400 centers in 225 cities (personal correspondence with the president of the American Blood Resources Association, 1988). Nearly a third of the centers are in California, Texas, and Florida—states having, perhaps not coincidentally, large homeless population (Momeni, 1988). The American Blood Resources Association estimates that there are 11 million donations per year, and most of the plasma donors are unemployed, students, or homeless (personal correspondence, 1988).

Lower Broadway has one temporary hiring hall and one plasma center. The hiring hall is where men go to find jobs. Some 30–50 men are hired on the spot every day. Sixty percent of the Lower Broadway inhabitants routinely obtain work at the hall. The plasma center typically handles 40 paid donors per day. Forty-six percent of the men told me they sell their blood plasma for a living. Thirty-four percent say they work as spot labor and sell plasma on a weekly basis. These two jobs are so basic to the skid-row economy that they deserve further inspection.

Both jobs meet the first job requirement of providing the men with daily cash income. The spot labor company pays minimum wage or around $25 for eight hours of work. However, there is no guarantee that the job will last a full day. Social Security tax is then deducted from the day's wages, reducing the men's take-home pay to around $18. Still, this is considered a fairly large sum of money on Lower Broadway.

The men begin arriving at the hiring hall around 6:30 A.M. They linger outside smoking and talking or go in the small cafe next door for coffee. From time to time, when there is especially strenuous work to be done, the manager of the hiring hall will arrange to have the cafe feed the languid laborers a breakfast of biscuits and gravy. It is for sustenance. If one were to buy the meal, it would cost $0.80. No lunch is provided. At the end of the day, the men are returned to the labor hall and given their checks. By this time the banks have closed, and most commercial establishments are unwilling to cash checks for homeless men. One of the bars has a policy of cashing these paychecks provided the men spend $5 there. The bar's menu is dollar beer and chili. After drinks and a meal, the men have spent nearly all of their pay and leave the bar broke though still in their work clothes.

The blood plasma center compensates the men in cash after each donation. The price for a pint of plasma varies from center to center. On Lower Broadway, it sells for $10. However, giving plasma four times over a nine-day period ups the price to $15. I interviewed men in their twenties, thirties, and forties who sold plasma eight times per month. They earned $120 per month in this way.

Donating blood plasma involves extracting the whole blood, separating the light yellow fluid or plasma from the red blood cells which carry oxygen, and then putting these red blood cells into a saline solution and back into the body. Each donation takes 45–60 minutes.

Spot labor and selling plasma are economic activities well suited for the nomadic lifestyle of skid row, although the former tends to favor local residents over men who have just arrived in town and are strangers in the community. A number of the homeless men I spoke with felt that the hiring hall manager discriminated against them because he did not know them personally. While this factor does affect who will be hired, especially in instances in which the temporary job is expected to last more than one day, it appears to be of only passing importance. The men on average are employed more than 50 percent of the times they go to the hiring hall. Owning a car to haul men to the job site is another factor that determines one's chances of being hired.

The spot labor company is required by federal law to verify the worker's identity by checking two forms of identification. One of them must show a picture of the man and the other his social security number. There are federal fines for employing a person without proper identification. The men we spoke with said that the hiring hall on Lower Broadway was not very strict in this regard. A social security card was all they were asked to show. There were cases in which men lost their wallets but were still hired. One fellow even used

Table 7.1
Age Distribution of Skid-Row Men, by Source of Income (%)

Age	Selling Plasma	Doing Spot Labor	Doing Both Jobs
20-30	38	33	25
31-40	37	33	58
41-50	19	10	11
50+	6	24	5
Total	100	100	100
Aver. Age	34	38	32

* N = 60

a personal letter from his sister that gave his Lower Broadway address as legal identification.

If spot labor is conducive to the nomadic lifestyle of the skid-row tramp, so too is selling plasma. Not only can plasma centers be found in practically every skid row in the country, but a donor is virtually assured of earning income with each visit. The Lower Broadway center is open every day of the week but Sunday, and donors are not required to set appointments. One of the attractions of selling blood plasma is that it does not tie up a person's entire day, thereby leaving him free to seek income from other sources and to participate in noon feeding programs. Moreover, only one piece of current identification is required.

Selling plasma, as an economic adaptation to skid-row conditions, is more physically demanding than doing spot labor. By the age of 50, the men have all but given up on the idea of selling their plasma, even though nearly a quarter of them still go to the hiring hall. To do both jobs on a routine basis requires a level of health that most of the older homeless men do not possess. In fact, our data show that by the age of 40 the men are less inclined to do either or both of these skid-row jobs on a regular basis. (See Table 7.1)

Of the Lower Broadway sample, the average age of blood plasma donors is 34, and the average age of spot laborers is 38. The average age of the men who worked both jobs is 32. Three-quarters of the plasma donors are under 40, whereas two-thirds of those who did spot labor are under 40. Eighty-three percent of those who did both jobs are also under 40. These distributions seem to indicate the relatively early age at which homeless men become physically unsuited for the two main sources of skid-row income.

Every time the men donate plasma they must pass a physical examination. Minimum health standards, established by the Food and Drug Administration (FDA) in 1973, require that the donor's blood pressure, temperature, and urine be tested for hepatitis, syphillis, and AIDS, and that his protein and enzyme values be examined (Personal correspondence with the president of the American Blood Resources Association, 1988). But these federal standards are sometimes ignored by the plasma centers. The FDA has successfully prosecuted several centers recently for overbleeding the donors and infusing them with someone else's saline solution (Thompson, 1985: 38). The FDA has also won convictions against plasma centers for keeping false records that show the donors to be healthier than they were, for failing to examine a donor, for falsely showing that equipment had been sterilized, and for accepting pregnant, feverish, and intoxicated donors (Thompson, 1985). While there is no evidence that the plasma center on Lower Broadway violated the law in any way, these convictions do suggests a need to monitor this growing industry.

The FDA standards, one might argue, do not go far enough in protecting the donor's health. While they do prevent many of the older skid-row men with high blood pressure from donating, neither the examination nor the FDA standards ensure anything resembling good health among plasma donors.

I interviewed several men in their twenties, for example, who drank beer and strong wine every day and who ate out of garbage cans. They were chronically malnourished, underweight, and, in some instances, underdeveloped physically. Yet their decrepit lifestyle and poor health did not prevent them from selling plasma once or twice per week. Furthermore, there are no federal guidelines to protect the mental condition of the donors. Selling plasma is demeaning and not an activity a person with economic options will gladly choose. But the psychological affect of selling blood plasma is not even considered in the screening of potential donors. There are instances in which the donor may not possess the psychological stability to do something as demeaning as selling plasma. For example, a man in his mid–40s told me how he and his wife had been recently attacked while they were sleeping in a boxcar. He was hit over the head and needed 20 stitches to close the wound; his wife was raped. The assailant was never identified. During their recuperation, the husband began to sell plasma for extra income. In another case, a Vietnam War veteran with a history of delayed stress syndrome and suicidal tendencies told us that selling plasma was how he sustained himself while awaiting the outcome of his application for admittance into the Veteran's Administration hospital. One would be hard pressed to argue that either of these donors was psychologically prepared to sell blood plasma.

Not all the spot labor jobs on Lower Broadway are physically demanding. The homeless men of the area would not be able to do them if they were. The work tasks are manual and unskilled. They typically include such light labor as cleaning up construction sites, doing yard work, or operating machinery; or, they involve somewhat heavier labor such as unloading trucks and moving vans, farm work, or construction work. Though the work generally is not physically difficult, it often is dirty and dangerous.

Several young skid-row men we interviewed were hired to work at a glass plant. The regular workers had gone on strike and had formed a picket line in front of the plant. The homeless crossed the line. Once inside, the men went about the job of cutting glass. Safety glasses were issued to everyone, but some of the men who wore short-sleeved shirts later complained of minute glass splinters getting into their skin. In another case, a 34-year-old man told us of a temporary job he once had cleaning hot grease off a machine. The machine had exposed gears that grabbed his finger and tore it off. The compensation that he received from the spot labor company for the injury was minimal. In the man's words, "My finger was worth $178."

There is another kind of injury that spot laborers are subject to as well. This injury is the relative deprivation that they experience by doing the identical work of a permanent employee but being paid much less than the regular wage.

Companies find it profitable to employ spot labor for different reasons, not the least of which is to reduce their labor costs. Spot labor contractors supply low-wage workers to these companies at an hourly rate that is less than the cost of employing someone permanently. Consequently, the temporary workers receive lower pay rates than the regular employees doing the same kinds of jobs (Carey and Kazelbaker, 1986). The labor contractor is responsible for hiring the men, withholding their social security taxes, and is liable for their health and safety (Carey and Kazelbaker, 1986). By assuming these responsibilities, the contractor saves the company recruitment and administrative costs, which run quite high for these low-paying, high-turnover positions. Moreover, temporary industrial workers such as the skid-row men are rarely offered full-time, permanent positions with the company.

The men we spoke with disliked having the spot labor contractor make money at their expense. As one young man in his twenties said, "I made $25 a day while guys who were doing the same thing as me earned $8 an hour." As he figured it, the labor contractor was making more per hour than he was. This feeling of being underpaid relative to the permanent employees is a work disincentive for skid-row men. It certainly discourages the hope of integrating these men into productive economic roles.

In summary, I have described in this section the two main sources of income on Lower Broadway. They are the selling of plasma and doing spot labor. I have examined these two income sources in terms of three characteristics of skid-row jobs. I have also tried to convey my feeling that reform of the skid-row economy is necessary. The concluding section offers some thoughts as to how that economy might be made humane.

A NAIVE POLICY AND A PRACTICAL COMMENT

The homeless have needs that are not being met by the existing social welfare system. The homeless are destitute but the system does not give them money. They are thus forced to seek it elsewhere. For homeless men who are able to work, this means participating in the skid-row economy, which offers various employment options, and the men are in some sense free to devise their own particular source of livelihood. But the only real option being offered to the men is whether to live penniless or suffer a work system that many Americans may have thought disappeared with the muckraking reforms of the early twentieth century. The challenge, as I see it, is to institute a policy that will give homeless men money without brutalizing them in the skid-row economy.

A naive policy might be one that proposes to give the men money directly. Such a policy, to be sure, is naive in two ways. First, it totally misgauges the potency of the reformist movement which has advanced the cause of homelessness in contemporary American society. Quite obviously, the national attention that has been critically trained on this issue for the better part of a decade indicates the movement's success at galvanizing the diverse interest groups involved. But none of these reformers has even proposed a "give-money" policy. And even if they were to do so, it would fail because the reformers do not have the political currency that it would take to commit the federal government to such a costly program.

Second, the "give-money" policy is hamstrung by the still widely held sentiment that the homeless, especially young homeless men, are "bums." The tradition in reformist circles, as Ringenbach (1973) points out, has been to distinguish the "deserving poor" from the "undeserving poor." While reformers zealously advocate welfare programs for those who cannot help themselves, they are reticent about assisting persons who are able but do not choose to work. These are the poor who are seen as getting only what they deserve. Skid-row bums are the classic illustration of being undeserving. Therefore, to suggest simply handing them money as a way to solve their immediate problems would call forth a moral outcry from all points on the political spectrum. Besides, as the seasoned skeptic would surely claim, such a program is tantamount to buying booze for bums and cigarettes for winos. I recognize the naivete of the policy and seek a more practical course of action.

My general recommendation is to increase the federal government's supervision and regulation of skid-row industries. As a principle of reform, the increased supervision would spawn numerous and specific legal changes, improving working conditions for the men at relatively bargain-basement rates for the government. Some of the specific recommendations are listed below.

We recommend developing a voucher system in which coupons could be picked up by the men and redeemed for a wide range of inexpensive products such as soap, shampoo, and prepared food. The merchants who redeem the coupons are reimbursed by the government. To ensure the system's success, the vouchers should be made available to the men daily, in small allocations, and require nothing more than personal identification. Special consideration may be given to the older homeless men who are unable to supplement the vouchers by earning income in the skid-row economy.

The men would be prevented from buying certain items such as cheap wine with their vouchers. Indeed, it may even prove wise in the long run to reconsider the kinds of liquor that stores are permitted to sell to the public. At the very least, liquor laws should reflect the government's concern over the easy access skid-row bums have to cheap booze. One possibility might be to institute a vice tax, if you will, against these skid-row wines; another possibility is to regulate where these products can be legally sold.

I recommend that spot labor companies be required by law to pay a wage that is pegged to the wage rate of the full-time employee, or to the hourly rate charged by the company. This would raise the amount of money skid-row men earn doing spot labor. It may even ignite some lost spark of work incentive. The federal government should guarantee that temporary workers be given a realistic compensation in the event of injury on the job.

Finally, the emergency shelters should have private lockers with keys for the men and the plasma centers should be more closely monitored. Unannounced inspections by FDA field workers at the plasma centers should be stepped up, and penalties for violating the existing codes should be increased. Moreover, the number of times a person is legally permitted to give blood plasma should be reduced, and the amount of payment per donation should be increased. In this way, skid-row men will be receiving more money though giving plasma much less often.

These recommendations are admittedly just the first step. It is a step that anyone who has ever had personal experience with skid rows will realize is long overdue.

REFERENCES

Carey, Max L., and Kim L. Kazelbaker. 1986. Temporary Growth in the Temporary Help Industry. *Monthly Labor Review* 109 (April): 37–44.

Gold, Raymond L. 1958. Roles in Sociological Observation. *Social Forces.* 36 (December): 217–223.

Howell, Joseph T. 1973. *Hard Living on Clay Street: Portraits of Blue Collar Families.* Garden City, N.Y.: Anchor Books.

Institute for Research on Poverty. 1987–1988. Tracking the Homeless. *Focus* 10 (4): 20–25.

Momeni, Jamshid A. 1989. *Homelessness in the United States: Volume I, State Surveys.* Westport, Conn.: Greenwood Press.

Most Blood Plasma Used Not Needed. 1984. *Science News* 126 (October 13): 237.

Peterson, Richard A., and Bruce Wiegand. 1985. Ordering Disorderly Work Careers on Skid Row. *Research in the Sociology of Work.* Volume 3, Greenwich, Conn.: JAI Press.

Ringenbach, Paul T. 1973. *Tramps and Reformers: The Discovery of Unemployment in New York, 1873–1916.* Westport, Conn.: Greenwood Press.

Rossi, Peter H., Gene A. Fisher, and Georgianna Willis. 1986. *The Condition of the Homeless in Chicago.* Amherst, Mass.: Social and Demographic Research Institute.

Roth, Dee, Jerry Bean, Nancy Lust, and Traian Saveanu. 1985. *Homelessness in Ohio: A Study of People in Need.* Columbus, Ohio: Ohio Department of Mental Health.

Spradley, James P. 1970. *You Owe Yourself a Drunk: An Ethnography of Urban Nomads*. Boston, Mass.: Little, Brown and Company.

Thompson, Richard C. 1985. Plasma Scam. *Food and Drug Administration Consumer* 19 (October): 37–38.

U.S. Department of Housing and Urban Development. 1984. *A Report to the Secretary on the Homeless and Emergency Shelters*. Washington, D.C., HUD, Office of Policy Development and Research.

Wiegand, R. Bruce. 1988. *The Number of Homeless in Tennessee*. Washington, D.C.: Unpublished Manuscript, Department of Justice, Law, and Society, American University.

8

Homeless Children and Their Caretakers

Sonjia Parker Redmond and Joan Brackmann

Over the past decade, the social problem of homelessness has received much attention by the public and human service professionals. The economic downturn of the late seventies and early eighties and inadequate federal housing policies have coalesced to create a situation in the eighties where not only transients and "societal drop outs" are homeless, but also thousands of long-term workers and their families are without permanent domiciles as well. The estimate regarding the number of people who are homeless varies. Estimates from the National Coalition for the Homeless suggest that between 3 and 4 million people in the United States are homeless, while government figures seldom approach 1 million (Kozol, 1988).

Among these homeless persons is a group that is especially vulnerable because of their lack of political power, the children. It has been estimated that homeless children number over 500,000 and that small children represent the fastest growing segment of the homeless (National Coalition for the Homeless, 1987). Homeless families are estimated to be as high as 25 percent of the overall homeless population, with 94 percent of the families consisting of single mothers with two to three children (Bassuk, Rubin, and Lauriat, 1986). While much attention has been devoted to the survival of homeless adults, much less attention has been paid to the plight of homeless children. This study contributes to the available knowledge in this area by examining the socioenvironmental factors related to homelessness among children as well as the socioemotional impact of such homelessness upon their lives. It examines mother-child relationships as well as attitudes, impressions, and concerns of their professional caretakers in shelter situations.

LITERATURE REVIEW

The literature revealed several recent studies that examined the condition and effect of homelessness on children. The small number of studies ranged from highly structured psychological studies to participant observation studies of homeless children. Literature discussing homeless mothers and children can often be categorized in two ways: (1) those studies of families rendered homeless by economic hardship; and (2) those studies of mothers and children seeking refuge from battering situations.

An evaluative study by Phillips, et al. (1988) at a large emergency shelter for homeless families in New York found a troubled group experiencing multiproblem situations. The descriptive profile of the families indicated that one-third of the mothers reported having mental illnesses or trouble with their nerves, 19 percent had been hospitalized for mental illness, 25 percent of the children experienced difficulties in school, 12 percent of the children had physical disabilities, and 20 percent fought very often with siblings.

A major report of homeless families in shelters in New York in 1984 showed a pattern of disrupted young lives due to long periods in temporary shelter in unfamiliar and sometimes dangerous situations. The report claims negligence by public and voluntary service agencies that seem to have overlooked the social, emotional, and recreational needs of the children (Citizens Committee for Children of New York, 1984).

Using psychological screening instruments, another group of researchers found developmental delays, severe depression and anxiety, and learning difficulties among homeless children at an alarming rate. When compared to emotionally disturbed children, the homeless children scored equal to or higher than the mean on the following factor scales: sleep problems, shyness, withdrawal, and aggression. The study suggested an intergenerational cycle of family disruption and emotional problems (Bassuk, Rubin, and Lauriat, 1986).

The literature suggests that children rendered homeless by domestic violence are even more vulnerable to negative socioemotional effects. Barad and Hughes (1983) reported a below-average self-esteem score for preschoolers, more aggressive behavior in school-age shelter boys than girls, and a tendency for mothers to rate their children less positively than the professionals. In a more recent study, Hughes (1986) listed several characteristics of children in shelters for battered women. They included restlessness and nervousness, poor academic performance, reticence in discussing violence, and fantasies about a different homelife. Gender-specific traits were reported showing boys exhibiting violent behavior by age three, with girls being withdrawn and passive. Preschoolers were found to have the most difficulties including school phobia, bed wetting, somatic complaints, nightmares, and insomnia.

In a recent book, Kozol (1988) writes compellingly about children in New York's shelter system. He writes of the horrid conditions under which many exist and fails to see positive futures for those who experience long-term homelessness. He has found that homeless children often fall asleep in class because of rest deprivation, are usually two to three grades behind, and display withdrawn, hyperactive, or disturbed behavior. He sees homeless children as having lost their innocence, becoming filled with anger and having an extremely increased probability of turning to juvenile and eventually adult crime.

From these studies, it becomes clear that children without homes, regardless of the reason, suffer profusely. The present study complements existing knowledge in the area of homeless children in several ways not found in the literature. The study not only examines negative attitudes or behavior but makes an effort to identify strengths or positive attitudes and behaviors that exist among homeless mothers and their children. Secondly, not only does the study report data from direct observations and interviews with the children and mothers, but it also gives a look at homeless families through the eyes of shelter staff. Therefore this research seeks to examine the homeless experience for children by not only observing them, but also by gathering information from those who are their caretakers, the mothers and the professional shelter staff who have responsibility for their care.

METHODS

The research design involved three segments utilizing formal interviews as well as participant observation. First, over a period of six months, interviews were completed with 20 mothers and 35 children in a Northern California Bay Area homeless shelter that accepted mothers and their children rendered homeless either because of economics or battering situations. The mothers and children were interviewed both separately and together. Data were obtained regarding prior sociodemographic, economic, and emotional status as well as attitudes regarding present homelessness. The mothers ranged in age from 20 to 41, while the children's ages were 4 to 16.

The second segment of data collection involved participant observation in which one member of the research team participated as an unpaid staff member of the shelter for a period of one year. During this time the researcher was able to gain insight into the general operation of the shelter as well as informal interactions between mothers and children and between shelter staff and clients.

The third research segment of this study involved formal interviews with 10 staff persons from six shelters in the Bay Area of Northern California who had primary responsibility for direct work with the mothers and their children. The majority of the staff interviewed were in the fields of psychology or social work and represented numerous years of experience working with homeless mothers and their children. Each intensive interview with a shelter staff lasted approximately one hour. Among some of the topics covered were information regarding their work with homeless children, what they saw as major strengths and problems with both mothers and children, and their suggestions for addressing these problems. Proper research precautions were taken to protect the identity of all subjects and institutions involved.

FINDINGS

Interviews with Mothers

Several of the women initially seemed nervous at being questioned about their children since many homeless women fear the possibility of having their children taken away. The women were reassured that the data collected was being sought with the intention of learning more about the needs of homeless children, that their confidentiality would be respected, and that they had the right to discontinue the interviews at any time.

Some of the women expressed feeling ashamed of their homeless status, while others expressed a sense of pride and competence in being able to find alternatives to their predicaments. All of the women in the study came from low socioeconomic backgrounds, were receiving Aid to Families With Dependent Children, or were in the process of applying. Over 50 percent of the mothers reported problems related to the scarcity of affordable housing. Women with more than two children especially had difficulty finding affordable housing that would accept children.

Although the shelter in which the study took place was not a battered shelter specifically, approximately one-third of the women were homeless for that reason. Over half of the mothers reported that their children had witnessed violence towards their mothers. Over half of the women revealed having been physically or emotionally abused when they were children, while slightly less than half reported that their children had been physically abused. A relatively high number of the women, one-third, reported that they had been sexually abused as children. Approximately one-third also reported that their children had been sexually abused. Virtually all of the mothers believed in physical punishment with varying levels of harshness as a means of disciplining their children. It was evident through the mothers' responses that their homeless children had experienced a substantial amount of violent behavior in their lives either directed at themselves or others whom they loved.

Interviews with Children

Interview/conversations with the children centered mostly around their feelings about being in the shelter, their perception of what homelessness meant for themselves and their mothers, and how they were handling the situation. When questioned specifically about why they were at the shelter, most of the children said they did not know. It was unclear whether these ''don't knows'' were attempts to protect the mothers or whether very little information had been shared with the children about the specifics of their homeless states. Some children did, however, make general statements about having no other place to go.

When asked about how things were going for them at the shelter, most children expressed positive feelings about being there. Most of the children talked about feeling safe at the shelter, having other children to play with, having toys to play with, enjoying child care with the volunteers, and liking the staff. These answers suggest a depth of appreciation of these children for a safe, stable, and caring environment.

The research sought information about how the children handled sadness or anger. A majority of the children indicated that when they felt sad or angry, they would deal with it alone. They expressed not liking to talk about things that were bothering them. Most had little experience communicating their concerns or their hurt constructively or they had little experience of being listened to.

Participant Observation

Participant observation yielded the following findings. Behaviors exhibited by children in the shelter were varied, but some patterns were recognizable. Most children seemed either to be severely withdrawn or to exhibit intensely aggressive and violent acting-out behavior. Most of the children in the study displayed great needs for attention and affection which the staff honored as often as possible.

Other behaviors observed were extreme shyness and an inability or unwillingness to communicate. This quiet and shy behavior occurred most often with younger children. The school-age children had developed a greater sense of independence and were more willing to communicate. The older the children, the more they tended to display angry and acting-out behaviors.

It was not always possible to separate the effects of homelessness from the effects of prior socioenvironmental influences on the children. It did become clearer, however, that the less traumatized the child upon entering the shelter, the more normalized the interactions and adjustments at the shelter. Another observation was that the parenting and coping skills of the mother, for example, quality of attention and ability to take charge of a situation, were directly related to the level of social adjustment of the child. All of the children seemed acutely aware of their mothers' whereabouts and moods, reflecting the strength of their bonding and the need to remain close to the one consistent aspect of their lives. Both mothers and children displayed high levels of commitment to each other.

Child Care Staff Interviews

Data obtained from the 10 child-care staff in six different shelters reflect the knowledge and experience gained from numerous years of working with homeless and battered women and their children. When asked to describe the most noticeable characteristic or behavior of homeless children, 9 out of 10 staff (in separate interviews) identified anger and acting-out behavior. The second most frequent characteristic described was the preponderance of attention and affection-seeking behavior among the children.

In order to balance the profile, staff were also asked to identify strength

Table 8.1
Responses from Children's Services Professionals

Issue	Response*
A. Most noticeable characteristics or behaviors displayed by the children	Anger-acting out behavior and need for attention
B. Most noticeable strengths or positive behaviors observed in the children	Independence and flexibility
C. Most pressing emotional problems faced by the children	Anger-acting out behavior and feelings of insecurity
D. Most prominent fears observed in the children	Fear of abandonment and fear of violence
E. Estimates on level of violence and abuse experienced or witnessed	At least half of the children had witnessed or experienced violence
F. Professionals' greatest fear and concerns regarding homeless children	That most will be trapped in the cycle of poverty and violence
G. Most positive characteristics observed in mother-child relationships	High levels of commitment between mother and children

*Responses—The high level of agreement of responses among professional staff (in separate open ended interviews) was striking. Agreement ranged from 80 percent to 90 percent among the professionals for the responses shown.

characteristics displayed by the children. Strengths or positive behaviors most often cited as being displayed by homeless children were independence and flexibility. They felt that these children have learned to a great degree to "roll with the punches," at least outwardly, and share responsibility for themselves and their siblings with their mothers.

The most pressing emotional problems being faced by the children according to staff respondents were the inability to control their anger and acting-out behavior and feelings of insecurity stemming from repeated losses of home, father, and friends due to their displacement.

The staff were asked to discuss the fears of homeless children. The fear of abandonment was seen by all but one of those interviewed as the most prominent fear observed in the children. Fear of rejection was the next most frequently fear mentioned by staff.

Although none of the staff persons interviewed had statistical data on levels of abuse, all of them gave estimated percentages based on their experiences. All of the staff respondents indicated that more than half of the children had witnessed violence in their homes, either through abuse of the mother or physical or emotional abuse of themselves.

In terms of their ability to share and cooperate with other children, the most frequent response given was that most of the children needed to be taught to share, and that once they were given rules about sharing and why they were expected to share, most of the time they were able to do so. Uncooperative behavior often changed as the children adjusted to being in the shelter and began to understand the rules. About half of the staff felt that most of the children had never experienced living with consistent rules and boundaries, but that they learned quickly in the shelter.

In considering the child's ability to cope as related to the mother's ability to cope, all but one of the staff indicated that they saw a strong relationship. The types of relationships seem to vary, however. A mother who coped well usually had children who coped well. A mother who did not cope well sometimes had children who also did not cope well, or she might have had a child who became "parentified" that is, who assumed the role and mannerisms of a parent. There was general agreement however, that the child's behavior most often reflected the quality of the relationship with the mother and her coping style.

As may be noted from the summary data presented in Table 8.1, when asked to discuss their greatest concerns regarding the children who come through their shelters, the overwhelming response expressed by staff persons was the fear that most of the children will have no chance to escape from the cycle of poverty, violence, and drug abuse. They were also concerned that the children would not have a chance of receiving a good education, that they would never have stability in their lives, and that many of them would be abused after they leave the shelter either by persons in their environment or by societally induced homelessness.

Children's Services Provided by Shelters

All of the agencies interviewed provided food, shelter, and clothing to the women and children. The shelters also required that school-age children attend school. All of the shelters have arrangements with local schools that enable children to be admitted even if certain paperwork or records have not been completed. About half of the shelters offer counseling to children if they show a "great" need, and all of the shelters offer extensive referral services. Just over half of the shelters offer some kind of weekly group activities for children aside from child care.

The aspects of the various programs considered by shelter staff to be most effective are providing shelter, providing a safe and stable environment, getting the children into school, providing referrals to health and housing services, and providing some positive attention for the children.

Recommendations for additional or improved services for homeless children were always prefaced by the need for more money and more staff. The various recommendations included additional child care, day care for preschool-age children, more individual counseling, more interactions of staff with mothers and children, communication and parenting skills sessions for mothers and chil-

HOMELESSNESS IN THE UNITED STATES

dren, tutoring programs, more men involved as volunteers, and special friends programs.

A sense of frustration and anger was conveyed by most of the professional staff at a system that seems to have turned its back on the children. The professionals surveyed are dissatisfied with what is considered band-aid approaches to the problem. They often work in dismal surroundings with limited resources with persons who often themselves have measured capacities for dealing with life situations. The professionals are dedicated and seem to have special talents for working with homeless mothers and children. They are realistic in knowing that many of the problems faced by the families before entering the shelter will continue. Affordable housing will remain elusive. Many will return to battering situations. Nevertheless they are also hopeful that the temporary respite for mothers and their children will help to lead them toward a better life with suitable and affordable shelter, less violence, and more confidence and ability to manage available resources.

DISCUSSION AND CONCLUSION

A major source of bias that has implications for the reliability and generalizability of this study lies in its small sample size. As an exploratory field study, the research provides much-needed insight into a heretofore often neglected segment of the homeless population. What the study loses in reliability, it gains in validity. Examining the plight of homeless children on three levels—participant observation, interviews with mothers and children, and interviews with the professional children's services personnel, provides a view of homeless children that is multidimensional. It enabled the researcher to test and compare findings. For the most part, the validity of responses was supported and verified by the checks-and-balances type of design utilized in this study.

This research supports many of the earlier findings related to socioenvironmental and socioemotional effects of homelessness on children. While it is true that some children who must enter shelters come from stable backgrounds, the children in this study were much more likely to have suffered traumatic experiences prior to the experience of homelessness. There was a high probability that they had experienced emotional, physical, or sexual abuse and that their mothers had had similar experiences (Bassuk, 1986). Many had witnessed violence to their mothers or were victims themselves.

While the children would rather be in their own homes, they expressed liking the shelters because of their safety, having other children to play with, and the attention given them by the staff. The interviews as well as observations revealed extremely high levels of attachment of the children to their mothers, regardless of the quality of parenting involved. Observations and interviews also revealed high levels of commitment of mothers to their children; again regardless of the quality of parenting (Kozol, 1985). In this study, both mothers and children showed signs of having stormy existences (Phillips et al., 1988; Citizens Committee for Children, 1984; Bassuk, 1986).

Interviews with the professional staff confirmed reports from initial mother-child interviews and impressions from participant observations. Professional staff saw the children as suffering emotionally from the traumatic experience of homelessness, displaying withdrawn or acting-out behavior, and having fear of abandonment as their major worry.

This research has highlighted the hurt, pain, and anger being experienced by homeless children in shelters as confirmed by the caretakers, mothers, and professional staff in the shelters. Future research could explore in more detail these findings along with intervention strategies at all levels of the social systems.

Although the children's services professionals were dedicated and provided as many services as resources would allow, they were realistic about their ability to make significant changes in the lives of most homeless children. They expressed concerns that even if the micro-level problems such as improvements in parenting skills, reduction in the influence of drugs, and improvements in life-management skills were addressed, the macro-level problems of insufficient affordable housing, poor educational preparation, low paying jobs, sexism, and discrimination would still remain.

The problems of homeless children will continue until the major micro and macro issues are addressed. Homeless children know what the major issues are for themselves. When asked if they had three wishes, what they would wish for, most gave the following responses:

"That we can all be safe and happy."

"To have a better life."

"That we can all have some place to stay."

As a society, we must begin to think that affordable housing is as much a right as education and the freedoms of speech and press. For children to be "safe and happy," all of our basic social systems must operate effectively. A severe breakdown in one inhibits accomplishments in another. Homeless children have difficulty in school. Uneducated children often do not know their rights and have difficulty communicating them. It becomes a vicious cycle requiring intervention.

There are many social problems that we do not know how to address. We do, however, have technology to construct affordable housing. Housing must be made a social and economic priority. Kozol (1988) writes that with homeless children and shelter children in particular, we are raising a generation of children who will not forget how they were treated by a society of plenty. The children's services professionals in this study continuously emphasized anger as the major characteristic they noticed in the children. Uneducated, hungry, and homeless children are angry, and without intervention, have a high probability of becoming angry adults. The answer is clear. This nation must give these children a chance at survival by ensuring them the security of permanent housing.

REFERENCES

Alameda County Task Force on Homelessness. 1987. *Homelessness in Alameda County.* Alameda Task Force on Homelessness.

Armstrong, D. 1986. Shelter-Based Parenting Services: A Skill Building Process. *Children Today* (March/April): 16–20.

Barad, S., and H. Hughes. 1983. Psychological Functioning of Children in a Battered Women's Shelter: A Preliminary Investigation. *American Journal of Orthopsychiatry* 53 (3): 525–531.

Bassuk, E., and L. Rubin. 1986. Homeless Children: A Neglected Population. *American Journal of Orthopsychiatry* 57 (2): 279–286.

Bassuk, E., L. Rubin, and A. Lauriat. 1986. Characteristics of Sheltered Homeless Families. *American Journal of Public Health* 76 (9): 1097–1101.

Brill, N. *Working With People: The Helping Process.* 1985. White Plains, New York: Longman, Inc.

Citizen's Committee for Children of New York, Inc. 1984. *The Third Report on Homeless Families with Children, Seven Thousand Children: The Crisis Continues.* New York: Citizen's Committee for Children of New York.

Davis, J. *Help Me I'm Hurt: The Child Abuse Handbook.* Dubuque, Iowa: Kendall/Hunt Publishing Co.

DeLange, C. 1986. The Family Place Children's Therapeutic Program. *Children Today* (March/April): 13–15.

Hughes, H. 1986. Research With Children in Shelters: Implications for Clinical Services. *Children Today* (March/April): 21–25.

Kozol, J. 1988. *Rachel and Her Children.* New York: Crown Publishers.

Layzer, J., B. Goodson, and C. DeLange. 1986. Children in Shelters. *Children Today* (March/April): 6–11.

National Coalition for the Homeless. 1987. *National Neglect/National Shame: America's Homeless: Outlook* (Winter).

Phillips, M., N. DeChillo, D. Kronenfeld, and V. Middleton-Jeer. 1988. Homeless Families: Services Make a Difference. *Social Casework: The Journal of Contemporary Social Work* 69: 48–53.

Zelkowitz, P. 1987. Social Support and Aggressive Behavior in Young Children. *Family Relations* 36: 129–134.

9

Programs Dealing with Homelessness in the United States, Canada, and Britain

Gerald Daly

You cannot disregard them if you accept the civilization that produced them.

—GEORGE ORWELL
The Road to Wigan Pier

Much of what has been written on the subject of homelessness is strangely repetitive and limited in scope. The popular press has portrayed the homeless in terms of the dreary, sad, and often frightening experience of those compelled to use emergency night shelters in places like New York City. In a few scholarly and literary journals considerable effort has been expended on analyses of the causes of homelessness and on debates over the numbers of homeless individuals and households in various cities and countries.

This discussion has served to heighten public awareness and has persuaded some government officials that the problems of homelessness cannot be swept under the rug. The objective of this study is different, however. It will examine an area that has been effectively ignored—that is, the identification of public and private programs that have evolved to address the myriad of needs associated with the homeless population. It represents a direct response to the challenge issued by Robert Hayes of the Coalition for the Homeless. He argues that "the numbers are transparently political . . . More time should be spent on trying to figure out what to do to resolve the homeless crisis, and less on arguing about the numbers."

Over the past few years I have had the opportunity to examine programs for homeless individuals and families in the United States, Canada, and Britain.

This chapter summarizes those observations; its primary objective is to describe and compare the strategies and the types of programs that have been developed in the three countries. It suggests that the variety of projects and breadth of services offered in Britain are deserving of further analysis for possible adaptation to Canadian and U.S. cities.

It is argued, moreover, that the definition of homelessness used in Britain is equally applicable to North America and that our description—statutorily and in practice—should be broadened to include not only those on the streets and in shelters, but also those, like battered women, who are potentially homeless. It should encompass those who are characterized as "at risk" as well as those who lack security of tenure beyond the next 30 days.

The causes of homelessness are similar in all three countries. This issue could be debated endlessly. When one cuts through the rhetoric, though, it is striking how much of the so-called "new" homelessness is attributable to government policy and to underlying economic conditions.

Among the principal causes and underlying trends are: (1) an acute lack of affordable housing; (2) severe cuts in public spending on housing and public assistance programs; (3) decline in the private rental sector and in housing condition; (4) loss of single-room occupancy units (SROs); (5) increasing unemployment; (6) a widening rift between "haves" and "have-nots"; (7) declining average wage levels relative to housing costs; (8) demographic changes, leading to an increase in the number of households and greater demands on the existing housing stock; (9) the feminization of poverty; and (10) a continuing movement toward deinstitutionalization without a corresponding increase in community care facilities to attend to both physical and mental health needs.

It is noteworthy that the United States, Britain, and Canada have all been governed by conservatives during most of the 1980s. One should take notice, as we briefly examine trends and programs relating to the problems of homelessness in the three countries, what strategies have been developed by these governments and how the voluntary or not-for-profit sector has reacted to public-sector cutbacks.

THE UNITED STATES

Because the extent of homelessness in major urban centers is so appalling, there has been an understandable concentration in U.S. cities on emergency shelters and crisis intervention. Consider the situation in New York City. It now has 28,000 people—including 12,500 children—in shelters. This does not include an unknown number "sleeping rough," living on the street, or incarcerated in jails and various institutions. The common thread running through the cases of homelessness in New York City is poverty as well as a severe shortage of affordable accommodation and a tendency for minorities to bear the brunt of the problem—about 90 percent of the homeless families in New York City are black or Hispanic (Kozol, 1988: 71).

Each year the number of homeless individuals in the city increases. The thrust of public and private efforts has been to warehouse families in shelters, while single individuals are compelled to shift for themselves and often end up spending nights in the city's 1,200-bed armory or similar emergency centers. The municipal government now spends $275 million annually—up from $18 million in 1980—on shelters, on grotesquely expensive "welfare hotels," and on short-term lodgings for the homeless (Kozol, 1988: 73).

Meanwhile, the supply of affordable housing in New York City has dwindled, and rents are skyrocketing. In the decade between 1971 and 1981, 30,000 dwellings were abandoned, and countless others were gentrified. During the same period, with government acquiescence, the city lost 87 percent of its 110,000 single-room occupancy hotels (SROs) (Hartman, 1987: 17).

New York City's situation is particularly dramatic, but the problems of homelessness plague most cities, large and small, across the United States. As a planner, I am naturally curious about the reaction to-date of planners who are presumably in a position to initiate remedial changes. The planning profession's response has been disappointing. A recent policy statement by the American Planning Association decried that:

At the present time, there exist an estimated 111,000 beds for the homeless on any given night throughout the nation. Even if the most conservative estimate of the number of homeless is used, this only addresses the needs of one third of the homeless population. (American Planning Association, 1987)

The issue is not one of beds, although a number of organizations (including Congress and the White House) have focused on the shortage of shelter beds. Debates over the number and size of these anachronistic institutions miss the salient point that shelters—which are essentially latter-day lodging houses—are not an appropriate solution; they address only part of a multidimensional problem. Moreover, if shelters help to perpetuate a cycle of "deinstitutionalization–sleeping rough–reinstitutionalization," they may well be counterproductive in the long run.

This limited focus begs the issue of long-term solutions and appears to emanate from a perception of the homeless as needing—solely or primarily—emergency shelter, associated detoxification, and minimal social services. In reality, for many the principal requirement is for a home, either immediately or after going through transitional phases.

What, then, has been the response of the federal government? Former theology student David Stockman set the tone for the Reagan administration:

"I don't think people are entitled to services," he testified to Congress. "I don't believe that there is any entitlement, any basic right to legal services or any other kind of services ... I don't accept that equality is a moral principle."

As soup kitchens proliferated, attracting considerable media attention, federal officials like Edwin Meese questioned the authenticity of the so-called "new homeless." Chiding them for cadging free meals at missions and shelters, he queried whether they were deserving of such hand outs.

Some in the administration followed the Orwellian strategy of minimizing problems by decreeing that reality conforms with its fantasies. The infamous HUD study of 1984 (U.S. Department of Housing and Urban Development, 1984), for example, found that there were only 250,000 to 350,000 homeless people in the entire country, while private groups and the U.S. Conference of Mayors (U.S. Conference of Mayors, 1987) estimated that the total exceeded 2 million. While the debate raged, HUD quietly lobbied behind the scenes to scuttle a proposed appropriation for emergency shelters.

Still other spokesmen for the Reagan administration attributed the problem of homelessness and severe overcrowding—which had become difficult to ignore or conceal—to ethnicity. Philip Abrams of HUD provided the following analysis: doubling up, he explained, "is characteristic of Hispanic communities, irrelevant to their social and economic conditions . . . It is a cultural preference, I am told."

This incident was followed by the sordid affair of the Department of Defense shelter program. Congress initially budgeted $8 million for a plan to make military facilities and services available to the homeless. The military's lack of enthusiasm was painfully apparent. In the end no substantive program was put in place, although a minimal emergency food and shelter program is being run by the Federal Emergency Management Agency.

The response of local governments in the United States has varied from utter neglect to real concern. A few cities, notably Washington and New York, are now required by local legislation or court orders to offer shelter to those who lack the means to provide for themselves. In general, there has evolved a growing awareness that homelessness is a nationwide problem—no large city or region is exempt. In fact, homeless individuals are now common in some rural areas as well. The United States Conference of Mayors' Task Force on Hunger and Homelessness has surveyed 29 cities for the past few years to discern trends and to focus attention on the subject. In December 1986 they reported:

By far, the most significant change in the cities' homeless population has been in the number of families with children . . . In 72 percent of the cities, families comprise the largest group for whom emergency shelter and other needed services are particularly lacking . . . Well over two-thirds of the homeless families are headed by a single parent. (U.S. Conference of Mayors, 1987).

Six months later, the task force survey found that "The number of families requesting emergency shelter during the last two years increased by an average of 31 percent" (U.S. Conference of Mayors, May 1987).

The relative positions of the different levels of government have also been more or less predictable. Jurisdictional wrangling is apparent among federal, state, and local bureaucrats and politicians. Federal officials contend that homelessness is a local problem. State and local governments have attempted without success to induce Washington to participate in joint efforts to solve issues of homelessness and housing supply.

The Reagan administration, however, argues that both of these issues are really matters of housing affordability that can be addressed by their "free market" experiment with housing vouchers. This strategy, however, presupposes an adequate supply of low-income housing stock. As the New York City case demonstrates, a central problem in major urban areas has been the drastic decline of affordable units as a result of cutbacks in subsidies, staggering increases in rents (at roughly twice the level of growth in wages), and loss of low-income housing due to fire, demolition, conversion, or gentrification. Meanwhile, cutbacks on public housing continue and the waiting list for public units is now a shocking 17 years in New York and 20 years in Miami, for example.

The General Accounting Office blandly characterized the government's passive posture in this fashion: "In summary, homelessness is likely to remain a problem for several years. What the federal role will be in providing services to homeless individuals is, however, unresolved" (U.S. General Accounting Office, 1985).

The federal position is forthrightly expressed by HUD in its recent Directory of Official U.S. International Year of Shelter for the Homeless (IYSH) projects. The agency's goal in selecting award-winning projects was "to identify exemplary local activities that explore new ways and means of improving the shelter and neighborhoods of low-income families through use of local initiatives that involve the private sector" (U.S. Department of Housing and Urban Development, 1987: v). Not surprisingly, the projects chosen emphasize emergency shelters and short-term services by private agencies and local government. Examples include: (1) The State Emergency Shelter Program in California "awards grants to charitable nonprofit organizations and local government agencies that provide emergency shelter . . . Of these, 97 percent are nongovernment, private sector programs" (HUD, 1987: 17). (2) The Urban Homesteading Program in Hartford, Connecticut provides "homeownership opportunities to moderate-income families" (HUD, 1987: 37). (3) The West Memphis (Arkansas) Private/Public Sector Home Improvement Program "makes it easier for low-income homeowners to obtain home improvement loans from private lending institutions" (HUD, 1987: 7). (4) Skid Row Development Corporation in Los Angeles "provides such temporary services as shelter, food, counselling, clothing and health care" (HUD, 1987: 12).

This is not to suggest that all programs undertaken in the United States have been so limited in scope. A number of innovative schemes have achieved some success. Among those that have been widely recognized are the Massachusetts program organized by the Office of Human Resources, as well as Governor Dukakis's Employment Training Program (Johnston, Kaufman, and Anthony, 1987: 54), the House of Ruth in Washington, D.C. which offers shelter and counseling but also finds jobs and housing for homeless women, and the Kentucky

Mountain Housing Development Corporation which attempts to prevent home-lessness by providing job training while constructing and rehabilitating housing for people with annual incomes as low as $4,000 (Kentucky Mountain Housing Development Corporation, 1986: 1). Others include: (1) The "cross-generational shared housing" and cooperative community programs of Innovative Housing in Marin County, California. (2) The second-stage or transitional housing model developed by the Women's Institute for Housing and Economic Development in Boston: "a multi-family residency program that includes a variety of support services for low income women who are heads-of-household and for their chil-dren" (Sprague, 1986). (3) The Minneapolis/St. Paul Family Housing Fund, a foundation-funded nonprofit corporation engaged in the development of SRO units and low-cost housing. (4) The Local Initiatives Support Corporation, also funded by private foundations, has accumulated assets of more than $100 million used to assist local nonprofit corporations to obtain financing in order to revitalize communities. (5) The Enterprise Organizations, funded by private foundations and businesses, attempt to develop housing and job training opportunities for low-income people. (6) Health Care for the Homeless, funded by the Robert Wood Johnson Foundation and the PEW Memorial Trust, provides medical and social services (often on an outreach basis) to the homeless in major cities (Navarro, 1985). (7) Covenant House, a nonprofit child care agency specializing in the care of runaways, urban nomads, and street kids, is located in several North American cities (Ritter, 1987).

The experience of the United States demonstrates that, to date at least, it has been necessary in most cases to rely on private funding to create innovative programs. In fact, many planners and housing reformers concerned with home-lessness have abandoned hope of involving the federal government in a substantial way. Nevertheless, it is essential that continuing efforts be made to actively involve federal, state, *and* local governments as well as the private and voluntary sectors in actively dealing with a problem of national importance. An awareness is gradually evolving of the need for permanent housing and related solutions in place of emergency shelters. But in most parts of the country this recognition has not yet been translated into actual programs.

Two recent federal initiatives do offer some hope, however. First, the National Institute of Mental Health and the Alcohol, Drug Abuse, and Mental Health Administration have funded CHAMP (a Clearinghouse on Homelessness Among Mentally Ill People). Second, a major piece of legislation, the Stewart B. McKinney Homeless Relief Act, was passed by Congress in 1987. It authorizes $442.7 million in FY 1987 and $616 million the following FY for housing, health, community service, and education, as well as nutrition programs for the homeless. Included are funds for drug and alcohol abuse treatment, community mental health demonstrations, and outreach services. The education component includes remedial and job-skills training, literacy classes, and counseling for homeless people, including children. Nutrition funds are being directed to the emergency distribution of surplus food (e.g. flour, cheese, and cornmeal) to the poor, including homeless persons.

PROGRAMS FOR THE HOMELESS IN CANADA

In comparison with Britain and the United States, the problems of the homeless in Canada are not particularly acute. Moreover, the safety net of health, welfare, and social services is significantly more refined and extensive than in the United States. Accordingly, the public sector has not felt a compelling need to develop innovative programs to assist the homeless. The national housing agency, Canada Mortgage and Housing Corporation, is attempting to devolve responsibility to the provincial and municipal level. Provincial and city governments, meanwhile, are just now awakening to the fact that there is a growing homelessness problem.

Perhaps the most striking characteristic of homelessness in Canada is the dramatic variation among cities. Certain regions are economically depressed and have witnessed increasing numbers of homeless as a result of recessions in the past decade. This phenomenon is particularly evident in Atlantic Canada and in a few western cities. Other parts of the country, notably southern Ontario, enjoy a buoyant economy that is responsible for the creation of most of Canada's new jobs. The converse of this situation is that the Toronto region has attracted thousands of unemployed individuals, hopeful of finding work in Canada's largest city. Extreme overcrowding has occurred as a result in the midst of a booming real estate market. Toronto's vacancy rate is nil; the city lost more than 10,000 units over the last decade to condominium conversion and gentrification; in the past year, real estate prices skyrocketed by over 30 percent so that the average selling price now is in excess of $200,000. In the meantime, Toronto's 2,500 hostel beds were occupied by 14,000 people in the past year. In addition to the large shelters run by the municipal government and organizations like the Salvation Army, a number of innovative programs have been developed (City of Toronto, 1987).

Homes First

Toronto's rooming houses are rapidly disappearing as land values escalate wildly. Homes First Society, a nonprofit developer with charitable status, created a "rooming house in the sky" in a new 11-story structure in the heart of downtown. The building has 17 self-contained apartments, each with four or five single bedrooms, as well as shared kitchen, dining, and living rooms. Each apartment is run as a separate household with its own ground rules.

Funding is provided by the national housing agency, which has written down the mortgage interest rate to 2 percent. Operating subsidies are offered by the provincial government (Ontario Ministry of Housing) so that residents pay only 25 percent of their incomes for rent. Average rental rates in the Homes First building are $320 per month, in marked contrast to rooming houses in the neighborhood, which charge about $450–$500 for a bare-bones single room. The Homes First building also houses a counseling program financed jointly by the provincial and municipal governments.

Christian Resource Centre

A shared-housing model program has been developed over the past 12 years by the Christian Resource Centre, funded jointly by the Province of Ontario, religious groups, and the federal government's national housing agency. The center now operates 13 homes, scattered throughout Toronto. Each has five occupants who manage their own dwelling. Residents, who include alcoholics, refugees, handicapped people, and drug addicts, have private bed/sitting rooms equipped with furniture and refrigerators. They share a kitchen and common rooms. Because the provincial government provides rent supplements, residents are required to pay only 25 percent of their income for rent. For those who are unemployed, the 25 percent rental payment is provided through public assistance. The center's homes are always full, with a waiting list of referrals from shelters and various social service agencies. Unfortunately, it is next to impossible to replicate this project in the urbanized areas surrounding Toronto because of restrictive by-laws and zoning codes.

Halifax/Dartmouth Metro Demonstration Project

Halifax, Nova Scotia, with a metropolitan population of only 600,000 has made significant progress in devising programs to deal with homelessness. This is due in part to the pressure applied by various grass-roots organizations led by MUMS (Mothers United for Metro Shelter) and the Housing for People Coalition. In 1984, when MUMS began to organize single mothers living in shelters, the city's vacancy rate was nil, the supply of low-cost private rentals was diminishing rapidly, and the ranks of the homeless were growing at an alarming pace.

In response to this initiative as well as calls for new housing from the region's municipalities, the federal, provincial, and local governments forged a unique agreement to provide the funding ($11.6 million) for 250 units of affordable housing. Five projects were initiated in 1987: these include a 50-bed emergency shelter, 50 units in rooming houses, 60 units in housing earmarked for single parents, 40 units for seniors, and 50 rental units designed to house families.

A significant feature of this project is that governments supply the up-front capital on a cost-sharing basis, but they will not be called upon to provide long-term subsidies. Front-end grants will have the effect of lowering rents to levels that can be managed by the low-income groups being served.

Association for Women's Residential Facilities (AWRF)

A few critics in Canada have questioned whether shelters are an appropriate response to the problems of homelessness. For the moment, though, the extent of transitional or second-stage housing is limited. An obvious gap exists between the present network of hostels or halfway houses and the private rental market. If one analyzes the typical case of a single mother working as a clerk-typist, the dilemma is evident. She may earn $1,000 per month, but after taxes, day care expenses for her child, and transportation to and from work, she is left with only $600 per month. In many Canadian cities she could not find adequate accommodation even if she were to pay up to two-thirds of her net income for shelter. Many women who fit this profile are housed in refuges or halfway homes; but the really thorny issue is what becomes of these single parents once they are compelled to find their own rental units in the private market.

One small program is being developed in Halifax to address this dilemma. AWRF has been designated to produce 15 units of transitional housing as part of the Metro Halifax Demonstration Project. Public funds from the federal, provincial, and municipal governments account for 50 percent of the total cost of $500,000; the remainder is being raised from foundations and private sources. The project will be a variation of shared housing, with 400-square-foot private rooms as well as common areas for meeting and socializing. Rents are set on a sliding scale according to income, although it is anticipated that most residents will be on social assistance. They may stay for 6 months to a year, during which time support services will be available on call 24 hours per day (Housing Networking Project, 1987: 2).

Hearth Homes Project

Northwest of Halifax is the scenic Annapolis Valley which attracts tourists from all over eastern Canada. This area, the wealthiest rural municipality east of Montreal, has an agricultural economic base. Farm workers are not covered by minimum-wage legislation, and most are extremely poor. They live in small settlements in the mountains on either side of the valley; social problems in the form of illiteracy, deprivation, overcrowding, and abuse are evident. In part, these problems are attributable to grossly inadequate housing. Typical structures are little more than shanties constructed of "found" materials, including truck and bus bodies.

The Housing Assistance Non-Profit Development Society (HANDS) was formed by local residents in an attempt to address the housing problems of the area's agricultural workers. Three important characteristics of their particular life-style were incorporated in the project: (1) wood is abundant locally and is the traditional source of heat; (2) families spend most of their time in the kitchen cooking, eating, and socializing; and (3) most do not want or need a "standard" National Housing Agency–approved home. Accordingly, each Hearth Home was built of wood, with a large eat-in kitchen, and was scaled down to two bedrooms, a living room, and four-piece bath (tub, toilet, shower and wash basin), at a total of 572 square feet, built in a 22' x 26' module. Units have a well and a self-contained underground septic system; they rent for $350 per month, with rents increasing at the rate of $10 per year. To date, 53 houses have been built in five counties. HANDS worked with residents, provided workshops on budgeting and maintenance, and arranged for financial assistance from the provincial government. The Nova Scotia Department of Housing contributes $50,000 per house over the life of the mortgage. Construction costs were $33,000 per unit, not including labor costs for fabrication, installation, and erection, which are covered by a grant from the federal government. Total development costs average $44,000 per house.

THE BRITISH EXPERIENCE WITH HOMELESSNESS

The British have publicly acknowledged and—albeit reluctantly—dealt with the issue of homelessness much longer than their North American cousins. Since 1948 local authorities have been obliged to provide temporary accommodation for ''persons who are in urgent need thereof'' (National Assistance Act of 1948). Nevertheless, the number of homeless households increased during the 1950s as a result of slum clearance and highway building projects, and continued throughout the property development boom of the 1960s.

In the ensuing decade the number of households in temporary shelters quadrupled to a total of about 50,000 people. The provision of accommodation and services for these families varied dramatically from place to place. Much depended upon the political will of the local authority and upon the relationship between members of the homeless household and their social worker.

Some councils resorted to travel vouchers to induce needy people to leave their jurisdictions. Others, starting with London boroughs in 1971, began to use bed-and-breakfast accommodations for temporary lodging of homeless families. By the end of 1976 there were 1,500 households in these establishments, at an annual cost of more than £1 million. Meanwhile, voluntary organizations were pressuring government for legislation that would clearly define the responsibilities of local authorities for accommodating both homeless singles and families.

The Housing (Homeless Persons) Act which passed in 1977 broadened the scope of local authorities' responsibilities. It defined homeless persons as ''those without accommodation they were entitled to occupy,'' and specifically included those (like battered wives) who were ''threatened'' with homelessness. As a result of amendments, however, the law excluded most of the single homeless as well as those whom local officials deemed to have made themselves intentionally homeless (by failing to pay rent, for example). Priority groups were defined: they include families with dependent children, pregnant women, those made homeless by fire or some other emergency, and those who are vulnerable through old age or mental or physical disability. The local authority is obliged to offer temporary refuge to high-priority households while the facts of the case are investigated. If judged to be a genuine case of homelessness, the family is entitled to council housing (CHAR, 1983).

From its inception, the Homeless Persons Act has been subject to widely different interpretations by councils. Some, for example, regard any cases involving family disputes or rent arrears—among the two principal reasons for homelessness—as outside the scope of the law because they represent evidence of "intentional" homelessness. Ironically, one's chances of being rehoused under the act depend more upon the community where one became homeless than upon the circumstances or reasons for one's plight.

The response of central government to the worsening problems of the homeless has been to claim that there is little that can be done. The Department of the Environment believes that "Homelessness is not a new phenomenon." The increase in homeless families is acknowledged, but the reasons are found in "profound changes in the nature of our society," including Europe's second-highest divorce rate, a dramatic increase in illegitimate births (from 6 percent in 1961 to 17 percent in 1981), and youth mobility: "Young people are leaving home earlier and with higher, if not always more realistic, expectations about what they might expect by way of housing" (Department of the Environment, 1987).

The Department of the Environment believes that there is only so much that government can do:

Because of these long term social problems and the fact that homelessness is to a very large extent a symptom rather than a cause, the scope for Government action is limited. (Department of the Environment, 1987)

Government's solution is to combine public and private finance to make funds go further, "to ensure that the fullest use is made of all existing dwellings," and to press for housing improvements and greater efficiency in housing management by local authorities and the private sector.

Despite the *laissez-faire* attitude, an impressive array of innovative and comprehensive programs have evolved in cities throughout Britain. How does one explain this phenomenon? Britain has a long history of philanthropic capitalism, charitable endeavors, and a public-private reform nexus. All parts of the ideological spectrum are involved in dealing with homelessness, which many see as a societal problem that must be dealt with by both public and private agencies. A number of local authorities, both Labour and Tory-controlled, have taken an activist role in creating programs to house the homeless. But the most interesting programs have been developed by private organizations in the not-for-profit sector with a combination of public and private funds.

In Britain there are many, many organizations involved with some aspect of homelessness, but this is a double-edged sword. A certain amount of stumbling about is apparent as agencies with a vested interest in "the homelessness problem" vie with one another to serve the same community. On the other hand,

and much more important in the long run, there are a variety of organizations and initiatives with specific briefs, equipped by dint of experience and motivation, to deal with a number of different aspects of problems associated with the homeless. This emanates from an understanding that the problems of homelessness are multifaceted; they are deep seated; further, the problems and the solutions are not the same for all segments of the homeless population. The homeless are actually a heterogeneous array of individuals and families with a diversity of housing, health, employment, and related concerns. An array of programs is thus required to address these needs.

An awareness has evolved that long-term solutions are required to deal with homelessness and related issues; short-term or band-aid fixes are considered passe. In recent years, government shelters have been closed. There is less emphasis on shelters or hostels than on community-based shared housing and a variety of ''staged'' accommodation to provide the homeless with a series of appropriate housing alternatives as they move from homelessness to resettlement within the community. Moreover, there is less emphasis on housing-only solutions (e.g. hostels) than on multidimensional housing, education, employment, and community reintegration schemes; these address a number of needs and provide a multiplicity of support mechanisms for those attempting to move from tenuous living arrangements to a more-secure place in society.

A central theme in many innovative British programs is the use of preventive measures and the concept of anticipatory planning. A number of projects, for example, deal with youths who are at risk of being homeless and of being in trouble with the law. These efforts are based upon the sound notion that preventive work will save many individuals from falling prey to the inexorable cycles of homelessness. Other efforts deal with prisoners, for instance, in a salutary example of anticipatory planning; arrangements for housing, employment, or education, and social service benefits are made before the individual leaves prison. Still others emphasize community care facilities; and many programs include elements of advocacy and lobbying. A thumbnail sketch of several programs will help to illustrate the variety and comprehensive nature of the schemes that have been developed.

Housing Aid Centers

An essential service for the homeless and the potentially homeless is provided by publicly and privately run housing aid centers, which are often dependent upon government funding. Predicated on the notion that homeless individuals and families require information and access in order to overcome their lack of power within the system, the centers are located in all major British cities. This concept assumes that the existing establishment, in the form of the health and welfare services, local governments, housing associations, and the like, is a continuing fact of life. If this presumption is taken as given, then homeless people must, in the interest of self-preservation, know whom to deal with and how to manipulate the system in order to secure their rights.

The housing aid center concept is particularly well developed in Britain. Principal among a plethora of small organizations is SHAC (The London Housing Aid Centre). It was established in 1970 by Shelter (National Campaign for the Homeless) and the Catholic Housing Aid Society. SHAC offers advice and assistance to the homeless and those with various other types of housing problems. The organization helps to focus national attention on housing and related issues by lobbying central and local government, by testifying to public bodies, by organizing and participating in conferences, and by conducting research and publishing its findings.

Among SHAC's research products are a number of reviews, like *Bed and Breakfast: Slum Housing of the Eighties* (1985), that shed light on housing and related issues, assist in educating the public, and help to focus the national debate. SHAC also engages in reform activities, attempting to effect fundamental changes in law and administrative practice. *A Fair Hearing* (1977), for instance, documents possession hearings and eviction proceedings against tenants and suggests radical reforms to the law.

SHAC receives 6,000 enquiries annually and gives advice to and/or attempts to find shelter for a diverse group: specifically, old-age pensioners and pregnant women as well as those "threatened with homelessness." Eventually, of the 1,650 cases taken on by SHAC annually, 30 percent are accepted by local councils for rehousing. The group often undertakes negotiations with local government officials (in 41 percent of its cases); in 8 percent it appealed directly to senior officers and elected councillors. Almost 40 percent of those households previously rejected were ultimately accepted by the boroughs following SHAC's intervention (Conway and Kemp, 1985).

It has been demonstrated repeatedly that, even with legislation on the statute books, the homeless population needs advisors and advocates. SHAC has been particularly successful in helping the elderly through the complex maze of regulations and negotiations with local authorities—46 percent of its elderly clients were assisted by the boroughs after SHAC's intervention. The organization was also helpful in those cases where people faced homelessness as a result of rent arrears or mortgage default. Detailed preventive work was undertaken in one-quarter of those cases; two-thirds of these attempts were successfully concluded.

Other groups, like MIND, the Housing Unit of the National Institute of Mental Health, perform similar advocacy functions on behalf of people with mental illness. MIND's principal method is to provide assistance and training programs to agencies managing or developing accommodation; this advice relates to finance, legislation, support services, resident selection, space layout, and residents' rights. In 1987 MIND launched a campaign, "A Better Life," for local mental health care. Its manifesto calls for action from government, from the voluntary sector, and from service users to recognize that mental illness should not be a barrier to the enjoyment of the full rights and responsibilities of citizenship. Staff members are particularly concerned with people who have been or are soon to be deinstitutionalized without proper housing and community supports. Too often hospital closures are not matched by the creation of adequate community care facilities. Instead people are shunted off to nursing and boarding homes. Through advocacy and education, MIND hopes to change this pattern (MIND, 1987).

Another interesting program is known as *The Bayswater Hotel Project*. Funded originally by the Greater London Council and now by the European Economic Community, staff members work with Bengalis and other refugees who are living in London bed and breakfast establishments—the British equivalent of "welfare hotels." Newcomers to London are assisted in learning the system, including how to secure one's entitlement from various government agencies. One of the project's principal tasks is to ensure that the local boroughs move these families into permanent council housing as soon as possible.

Housing Assistance for Prisoners

The prison population in Britain has grown dramatically in recent years, from 33,000 in 1966 to about 50,000 in 1987. Among the most troublesome problems for these people, as they prepare to leave prison, is locating housing and employment. The National Association for the Care and Resettlement of Offenders (NACRO) was established in 1966 to attend to these needs. With public and private funding NACRO employs 6,500 staff to run 260 projects across Britain, serving approximately 16,000 people. NACRO operates housing, employment, and education schemes. Its North London Education Project, for example, for the past seven years has provided education in a residential setting for ex-prisoners. In addition to offering remedial tutoring on-site, the center maintains several houses of shared accommodation, has a formal link with the North London Further Education College, and has a quota of permanent housing through local boroughs and housing associations. These dwellings are reserved for "graduates" of its educational program (North London Education Project, 1987).

Through its Prisons Link Unit, NACRO works with prisoners prior to their release in order to alleviate or preclude some of the problems typically encountered on reentering the community (one survey found, for instance, that 91 percent of serious repeat offenders encountered problems of homelessness). The unit has established relationships with prisons, with parole officers, and with community-based agencies to set up systems that provide advice and services to prisoners in housing, employment, education, and benefits while they are still in prison (National Association for the Care and Resettlement of Offenders, 1987).

Self-Help Housing Projects

The Empty Property Unit is a national, independently funded project, that brings empty properties back into use. By the end of 1987 approximately 16,000 dwellings had been reactivated by short-life housing associations, which provide a legal mechanism for the temporary use of dwellings that have been borrowed from their owners for one to five years. Owners are typically local authorities and housing associations as well as large organizations such as British Rail. Properties are licensed or leased to housing associations or cooperatives which are responsible for rent collection and management. This scheme has proven effective in housing the homeless; it is very popular with local authorities who save money on bed and breakfast bills and, at the same time, are able to delegate responsibility for maintenance and heating of their vacant council houses.

With sponsorship from the United Nations' International Year of Shelter for the Homeless (IYSH), the Empty Property Unit has established the National Fund for Self-Help Housing Projects, which provides resources to local groups to register as cooperatives. It offers loans for the purchase of tools and materials in order to repair dwellings to make them habitable. The Empty Property Unit has developed a set of model rules that it offers to prospective housing cooperatives and it assists members in establishing their cooperatives as legal entities. It also lobbies at national and local levels for legislation to facilitate the acquisition of empty properties (Fraser, 1986: 191).

Education Programs

Since 1981 the Housing Support Team, working in London, has been operating training programs for homeless individuals about to move from government resettlement units or hostels into conventional housing. It recently expanded these programs to include staff members within the referral and other service agencies to enable them to provide more effective advice for people preparing to be rehoused. During the past year over 300 people completed training, usually a three-day course, which covered Health and Social Services procedures and benefits; budgeting, banking, and saving; establishing links with a new community; and setting up housekeeping. The underlying principle for these efforts is to involve homeless individuals in shaping their own futures (Housing Support Team, 1987).

Programs for Women

Women are often referred to as the "hidden homeless." Battered wives with children are frequently compelled, out of economic necessity, to remain with a violent husband. Those who move out live in extremely cramped quarters with relatives or friends, rather than resorting to the sometimes dangerous life in shelters or on the streets. Hence, they are often excluded from statistics on the number of homeless people.

Housing choices for single women are particularly limited. They tend to be living on low incomes and cannot afford to buy a home or to rent one in the private sector. Female one-parent families represent a significant proportion of those homeless households placed in bed-and-breakfast accommodation or hotels. Because traditional hostels in Britain were typically limited to men, women's hostels are few in number; the ten largest in London are for men only.

Recently, a number of women's groups have been formed to assist those who are without homes or are potentially homeless. Some of the more progressive boroughs (e.g., Camden and Greenwich in London) have formed Women's Units to provide assistance. Other local authorities have produced lists of women's shelters and information handbooks describing how and where to obtain assistance in finding shelter and benefits. Several private initiatives, like Homeless Action and Accommodation (in London) and Welsh Women's Aid (in Cardiff) have been formed. Some provide advice and counseling. Others run refuges for battered women and their children (Witherspoon, 1985).

Handsworth Young Person's Accommodation Committee (HYPAC)

HYPAC was started in 1981 in the predominantly black area of Handsworth in Birmingham to provide interim accommodation for single homeless black offenders (ages 17–25) who were assigned to the law courts or were being discharged from penal institutions. HYPAC also helps young black people who are seen as being "at risk" of conflict with the law. These are judged to be particularly difficult cases; most are considered too "high risk" by already overburdened voluntary associations.

HYPAC is predicated on the assumption that black youths in the deprived inner-city areas of Birmingham—which have double or triple the national unemployment rates—encounter more than housing problems, though these may be the most visible. The organization provides accommodation for 86 tenants at one time; all black, about 80–85 percent male, about half younger than 20. Between 1981 and 1984 HYPAC fielded almost 400 referrals; about one-third were from prisons and probation officers, one-third from housing aid centers, one-quarter were self-referrals, and the remainder from other agencies. It is interesting to note that only 4 percent of these individuals were living with parents; the remainder were in some sort of tenuous living arrangement (prison, hostel, no fixed address, bedsits, etc.).

The typical HYPAC client stays in the offered accommodation for somewhere between six months and one year. The youths are given assistance in setting up their homes, in finding furniture, in receiving support, in representation with community agencies, and in acting as go betweens with the parole service.

Assistance for Low-Income Elderly Homeowners

One of the least-obvious groups of potentially homeless persons is elderly homeowners. Many exist on extremely limited incomes and live in marginal housing: 43 percent of people over age 75 who are living alone are in houses built before 1919; 55 percent of owner-occupied property with an outdoor toilet is owned by old people. Elderly widows, in particular, face enormous problems in trying to maintain such properties. When their homes become delapidated, they are put under closure orders and the occupants are forced to move into institutions. The result, for both people and the housing stock, is tragic and unnecessary.

Care and Repair Limited, supported by Shelter and the Housing Association Charitable Trust, operates 25 projects to assist elderly homeowners who are in danger of becoming homeless. The organization recently received a grant of £1 million from the Department of the Environment, provided that matching funds are obtained from individuals and private sources. The actual building repairs are paid through loans obtained from financial institutions and housing grants from local authorities. Hence, the monies provided from the public treasury are highly leveraged and have a substantial multiplier effect. Care and Repair Limited calculates that every pound contributed results in a total of £60–70 of repair and building work. The group intends to double its inventory of projects within the next two years. It is generally acknowledged to be successful in maintaining the nation's older housing stock and in enabling elderly homeowners to remain in their own dwellings (IYSH, 1987).

Outreach Programs

A key concern for homeless persons is to obtain access to health care. Some fail to secure proper service because they are rejected by health and welfare workers on the basis of their appearance or their behavior. Others cannot obtain benefits to which they are nominally entitled because they lack a fixed address.

In Britain there is some evidence of discrimination on the part of general medical practitioners against registering single homeless people. Often the process starts with receptionists, the first point of contact with the medical care establishment. This pattern may continue with indifferent treatment by the doctor. Such reactions are based upon stereotypes of the homeless individuals, their lifestyles, their appearance, or the address of a known hostel. In many cases doctors have simply asserted that their "lists are full," but have subsequently taken on new patients who did not give hostel addresses.

An exception to this pattern is the East London Homeless Health Project, which provides a primary health care team to meet the needs of the homeless, particularly those with no fixed abode. A salaried general practitioner works with a community psychiatric nurse, a district nurse, and an administrator. They also have access to a part-time alcohol counselor. The project has received a three-year funding grant from the Department of Health and Social Services. One of the project's aims is to encourage registration with GPs and to improve the involvement of medical professionals with local hostels and other residential establishments.

CONCLUSIONS

Many of the programs dealing with the homeless population of Britain are predicated upon the long-accepted concept of "housing as of right" as well as a network of related social services. Without this safety net and without a government policy of providing permanent housing for low-income households, it is difficult to come to grips with the long-term concerns of those who are homeless. It is important, too, to improve the delivery of existing services, to inform homeless individuals of their rights, and to provide them with information on how they can deal with the welfare bureaucracy. As demonstrated by British groups, advocacy is crucial to ensure that the homeless population becomes a powerful political constituency (Saunders, 1986).

An analysis of British programs reveals another important distinction. Battles won at the national level do not have to be refought (at least in statutory terms) at the local level. This is one of the most difficult aspects of dealing with such issues in the United States. Each state and municipality can in effect determine its own destiny, particularly when the federal government abdicates responsibility.

The experience of Canada, while similar to that of the United States, is different in at least one significant respect: it underscores the importance of the safety net of social services as well as the necessity of a national health service that is free to low income people.

In each of the three countries examined, problems vary from region to region, from city to city, and from neighborhood to neighborhood. Accordingly, locally devised programs are most appropriate. Yet, because homelessness is also a nationwide problem, the federal government must be involved and must provide sufficient funding on a continuing basis to assure permanent solutions. This is not to say that money should be thrown at the problem in hopes that it will disappear; rather, it must be recognized that the issues associated with homelessness are of such magnitude that long-term programs are essential to achieve any meaningful degree of success. The experience of New York, now spending over a quarter of a billion dollars annually on shelters and welfare hotels, dramatically illustrates the futility of programs limited to emergency shelter. As soon as beds are added, more homeless individuals join the queue.

The problems underlying homelessness represent institutional failures on a massive scale. Much of the homelessness dilemma is a reflection of urban economic development trends. Although not a new problem, it has dramatically increased in severity in all three countries since 1980. The traditional response to homelessness, then, requires critical rethinking. Governments and certain charitable organizations have been inclined to do things *for* the homeless, whereas many of the homeless individuals stress that they are a resource unto themselves. They want to be involved in building their own housing. The concept of cooperative or self-help housing should, then, be fully exploited as it represents a rare congruity among the homeless, liberal advocacy groups, and conservative governments.

A diverse mix of programs, provided or funded by an array of public and private organizations, are required to address the variety of problems grouped under the broad heading of homelessness. It is important to broaden the definition of homelessness, not just statutorily, but also with respect to the scope, type, and delivery mechanisms of services offered. We must recognize—in policy as well as in funded programs—that homelessness means more than simply the absence of shelter.

ACKNOWLEDGMENTS

The author gratefully acknowledges the contributions of Keith Cossey and Victor Helfand, both of York University, in researching Canadian projects.

REFERENCES

American Planning Association. 1987. *What Should APA's Position Be Regarding Planning and Zoning Considerations in Housing for the Homeless?* Washington, D.C.: American Planning Association.

CHAR (The Campaign for Single Homeless People). 1983. *In On the Act: The Homeless Persons Act—A Guide for Single Homeless*. London: CHAR.

Conway, Jean, and Peter Kemp. 1985. *Bed and Breakfast: Slum Housing of the Eighties*. London: SHAC.

Department of the Environment. 1987. *Homelessness Information Pack*. London: HMSO.

Fraser, Ross. 1986. *Filling the Empties: Short Life Housing and How To Do It*. London: Shelter.

Hartman, Chester. 1987. The Housing Part of the Homelessness Problem. In *Homelessness: Critical Issues for Policy and Practice*. Boston: The Boston Foundation.

Housing Networking Project. 1987. *People, Projects and Issues*. Toronto: Housing Networking Project (Spring/Fall).

Housing Support Team. 1987. *The Housing Support Team (1981–1985): The Development of a Small Training Organization*. Occasional Paper No. 3. London: Housing Support Team.

International Year of Shelter for the Homeless (IYSH). 1987. *Profiles*. London: IYSH.

Johnston, Philip W., Nancy K. Kaufman, and Amy A. Anthony. 1987. The Massachusetts Approach to Homelessness. In *Homelessness: Critical Issues for Policy and Practice*. Boston, Mass.: The Boston Foundation.

Kentucky Mountain Housing Development Corporation. 1986. *1985–86 Annual Report*. Manchester, Kentucky: Kentucky Mountain Housing Development Corporation.

Kozol, Jonathan. 1988. The Homeless and Their Children. *The New Yorker* (January 25).

MIND. 1987. Homelessness and the Plight of Mentally Ill People. London: The National Institute of Mental Health.

National Association for the Care and Resettlement of Offenders. 1987. *Annual Report 1985/86*. London: NACRO.

Navarro, V. 1985. The Public/Private Mix in the Funding and Delivery of Health Services: An International Survey. *American Journal of Public Health* 75 (11): 1318–1320.

North London Education Project. 1987. *Report, 1984–86*. London: NLEP.

Ritter, Bruce. 1987. *Convenant House: Lifeline to the Streets*. New York: Doubleday.

Saunders, Barbara. 1986. *Homeless Young People in Britain: The Contribution of the Voluntary Sector*. London: Bedford Square Press.

Sprague, Joan F. 1986. *Transitional Housing*. Boston: Women's Institute for Housing and Economic Development.

Toronto, City of. 1987. *Report of the Inquiry into the Effects of Homelessness on Health*. Toronto: Department of the City Clerk.

U.S. Conference of Mayors. 1987. *A Status Report on Homeless Families in American Cities*. Washington, D.C.: U.S. Conference of Mayors.

———. 1987. *The Continuing Growth of Hunger, Homelessness and Poverty in America's Cities: 1987*. Washington, D.C.: U.S. Conference of Mayors (December).

U.S. Department of Housing and Urban Development. 1984. *A Report to the Secretary on the Homeless and Emergency Shelters*. Washington, D.C.: Office of Policy Development and Research.

———. 1987. *Directory of Official U.S. IYSH Projects. Housing America: Freeing the Spirit of Enterprise*. Washington, D.C.: HUD.

U.S. General Accounting Office. 1985. *Homelessness: A Complex Problem and the Federal Response*. Washington, D.C.: US GAO.

Witherspoon, Sue. 1985. *A Woman's Place: Your Rights and Relationship Breakdown— A Guide for Married Women*. London: SHAC.

10

Public Policies for Reducing Homelessness in America

Terry F. Buss

As it has for the past several years, every fall season brings renewed concern that homeless people will suffer winter's hardships because there is not enough space for them in emergency shelters. Evidence for a shortfall in shelter capacity is provided by two independent reports issued recently:

1. A U.S. Conference of Mayors survey of 25 cities found, last winter, that in over one-half, some shelters routinely turned away people in need. Demand for shelter space had increased since the previous year in 9 out of 10 places, by an average 25 percent (U.S. Conference of Mayors, 1986).
2. The Partnership for the Homeless, a New York–based advocacy group, after surveying 23 localities, reached the even more alarming conclusion that as many as three of every four homeless people, including children, will be denied a shelter bed to them this winter.

The evidence regarding need is considerably more complex than implied by the figures cited above. A national commitment to a massive permanent system of emergency shelter would amount to accepting as a more or less permanent feature of American society the presence of large numbers of people with no place to call home. Before making such a commitment, a determination should be made whether or not effective policies can be developed for reducing homelessness—policies that the public would endorse and be willing to pay for.

NEED

Most homeless people do not stay in emergency shelters, and many would not do so on a regular basis even if beds were available. The U.S. Department of Housing and Urban Development (HUD) estimated in January, 1984, that there were about 111,000 shelter spaces nationally but probably between 250,000 and 350,000 homeless individuals (Housing and Urban Development, 1984). Yet, despite the obvious difference between the two figures and even though HUD's survey was conducted in the dead of winter, shelter operators reported, on average, that only 70 percent of their beds were occupied (74 percent in metropolitan areas of one million or more people). In the same survey, nearly one-half of the shelter operators reported turning people away—on average, just over two per night.

Turnaways may occur even when and where there are substantial shelter vacancies for varied reasons (Redburn and Buss, 1986). First, many shelters have restrictive admissions policies. Some do not take women and children. Others may not permit admission to unwed couples. Second, newly homeless people sometimes do not know about available shelter space. Those turned away from one shelter may, in many cases, find shelter elsewhere on the same night.

Shelter beds may go unfilled also because many homeless people avoid them or use them only reluctantly. The better shelters, offering specialized services such as psychiatric counseling or job referrals, are more likely than others to be fully occupied. Too many shelters, however, are dirty, uncomfortable, and even dangerous. There is a need to be concerned not only with the numbers accommodated in shelters but with what goes on there.

While the available evidence shows continued growth in demand for shelter in many places, shelter capacity has been expanding rapidly. Four out of 10 shelters surveyed by HUD in 1984 have been in operation for two years or less; and 2 in 10 had operated for less than one year. All signs point to a continued increase in the number of homeless in many areas.

The public sector has taken on increasing responsibility for establishing and operating shelters (Redburn and Buss, 1987). Prior to 1980, the task of sheltering the homeless fell almost exclusively on private charities and religious organizations. Now all but a few of the largest city governments assist those organizations by contributing funds to support shelters and other services for the homeless. In the last two years, cities spent over $100 million in federal Community Development Block Grant money to acquire and rehabilitate buildings for shelters or to provide services to the homeless. About $300 million in other federal funds have been distributed since 1983 for emergency food and shelter. A few states are, for the first time, spending specifically for the homeless.

The focus of these public efforts has been almost entirely on the immediate needs of the homeless, for food and shelter. Obviously though, the mere expansion of shelter capacity does not ensure that the nonshelter needs of the homeless are met. If the reintegration into the social mainstream of as many homeless as possible and, better still, the prevention of homelessness wherever possible was the objective of public policy, the present emergency shelter-based system of care would not be judged an adequate response.

To determine the proper course for public policy, the varying needs of the homeless population must be more clearly identified. Stereotyped images interfere with good public policy development and service delivery. The homeless of today are certainly a more diverse group than in the past, including larger proportions of families and youth. Significant proportions are mentally ill or addicted to drugs or alcohol. However, some observers have, intentionally or unintentionally, overstated the extent to which the homeless population is composed of such people.

Our research (Redburn and Buss, 1986) indicates that many of the homeless who exhibit bizarre behavior probably do not need prolonged drug therapy, counseling, or psychotherapy. Most of those with a history of institutionalization are not presently in need of treatment for psychiatric disturbance. Many of the seemingly ill homeless would benefit more from services aimed at achieving stable housing, employment, and income than from treatment focused on psychiatric problems. At the same time, our research and that of others indicate that a high proportion of those homeless who do suffer from chronic, severe psychopathology do not receive appropriate therapy. Provision of other services will not accomplish much for those with psychiatric disorders.

Our analysis of interviews with 1,000 homeless people conducted by the Ohio Department of Mental Health (ODMH) (see Roth et al., 1985) allows us to estimate the proportions of that state's homeless population who fall into each of four groups, each needing a different kind of help.[1]

There are three groups of homeless people whose needs for assistance clearly go beyond the need for temporary, emergency shelter. First, there are people who are unlikely to function outside a protected environment. They need permanent custodial care. In Ohio, by our estimate, 3 out of 10 homeless people cannot reasonably be expected to sustain independent residence over a long period. If they are not merely to survive but to be reasonably assured of meeting their needs for shelter, food, health care, and emotional support, then they must live in or be closely attached to an institution or agency dedicated to seeing that their needs are met. These include people whose age and employment history indicate that they have passed permanently out of the labor force, some who are physically disabled, and those with chronic, severe, psychiatric or behavioral disorders.

Second, there are homeless who have been unable to achieve economic self-sufficiency because of a major deficit (such as illiteracy) or a chronic problem (such as alcoholism) with which they cannot cope unaided. About one in four homeless people in Ohio do not need permanent custodial care but have identifiable deficits or remediable problems that must be dealt with before they can be judged likely to live successfully on their own. These include the homeless who have had serious problems with alcohol or drugs, those who have never worked, those with little formal education, and those who, while not severely ill, have been in and out of mental institutions on a regular basis.

Third, there are homeless individuals or families in crisis for a variety of reasons. In most cases, they will be capable of returning fairly soon to a more normal situation but need short-term crisis care, including counseling and other personal and sometimes financial support. One in five Ohio homeless does not have any apparent need for long-term custodial care nor any major deficit or problem such as those named above, but is demonstrably in crisis. These are people who have been homeless for relatively short periods and whose lack of permanent shelter is linked to family conflict or dissolution, an eviction or natural disaster, or being fired or laid off from their most recent jobs. This category includes the highest proportion of women, often accompanied by children.

Finally, there are homeless people with none of the above needs but who nevertheless need a temporary place to stay. This group consists of people who simply lack enough income to obtain permanent lodgings. It includes those on the move in search of work and those who prefer to keep moving. Some who properly belong in the other need categories, but whose need for other forms of assistance is not so obvious, may fall into this category. In Ohio, about 20 percent of the homeless appear to need emergency shelter only.

If it were possible to estimate what proportion of all homeless in the U.S. need each kind of assistance, the information would be very useful for policy-making. The data to determine this simply are not available. However, if the same proportions of the four need groups found in the Ohio homeless population were to hold nationally, then on the order of 100,000 homeless people sleeping in emergency shelters or "on the street" properly belong in permanent custodial settings ranging from in-community sheltered living arrangements to nursing homes, hospitals, or other institutions. This number is approximately equal to the total of emergency shelter beds that existed nationally in 1984. The comparison of these two numbers begins to suggest the limits of current public policies for the homeless.

CAUSES

Identification of need for shelter and other services is not a sufficient basis for making public policy. The other necessary component is an understanding of the causes of homelessness.

Among the often-advanced plausible reasons for the recent rise in U.S. homelessness are the following (General Accounting Office, 1985): (1) a severe recession in 1982 and persistent high unemployment in some regions; (2) reductions in national social program spending or new restrictions on program eligibility; (3) shortages of low-cost housing, perhaps exacerbated by changes in the governmental housing and urban redevelopment policies; and (4) the movement of state governments and the courts away from long-term hospitalization of the mentally ill, combined with the failure to create adequate community support systems for those who, in the previous era, would have been institutionalized. Evidence is not sufficient to say with certainty how much of the rise in homelessness is due to each of these or other factors.

Many have focused on the change in mental hospital admissions practices as the most likely cause of a short-term rise in homelessness (Lamb, 1984). Mental hospital populations did fall, from 505,000 in 1963 to 125,000 in 1981, but have since stabilized. Most research indicates that between 25 and 50 percent of the homeless are, in some way, mentally ill (Bachrach, 1984). Shelter operators surveyed by HUD estimated, on average, that 22 percent of their clients had such problems, and the rate of mental disorder among those not using shelters may be higher.

The rise in homelessness has been linked to changes in population characteristics and housing markets (Freeman and Hall, 1986). Increases in the number of female-headed families and substance abusers, along with deinstitutionalization, have gradually expanded the population at risk. Second, between 1979 and 1983, a rapid increase in the number of people with exceptionally low (below $3,000 per year) incomes has occurred. However, the continued rise in homelessness after 1983 resulted from an increase in very poor households accompanied by a decline in the low-rent units in central cities. Also a factor has been the recent elimination of many cheap boarding houses and single-room occupancy hotels that once sheltered the down-and-out (Kasinitz, 1984).

On a personal level, most people become homeless not as a result of a single catastrophic event but because of a series of misfortunes (Redburn and Buss, 1986). Most homeless people, it appears, had been poor and on the margin of the labor force before becoming homeless. Their present condition reflects not only their inability to earn income by working but also an unresponsive social welfare system.

Still unsettled is the extent to which the poverty and social marginality that characterize the homeless population are products of predisposing personal attributes—specifically mental illness and alcohol and drug addiction—and are not themselves primary causes of homelessness. A better understanding of causes and effects of homelessness will probably have to await the completion of longitudinal studies.

ALTERNATIVES

A more differentiated view of the homeless population—needs and causes— than that commonly taken necessitates the development of a new system of services and care with the goal of minimizing the numbers who, at any one time, are in emergency shelters or without shelter. This might be accomplished in a two-pronged approach: preventing some people from becoming homeless, and fostering the reintegration of some homeless with the society and providing permanent custodial care for others. The practicality of such an approach has yet to be tested.

To prevent homelessness, or at least to return people with a capacity for independent living to permanent housing as quickly as possible, requires a combination of services aimed not just at locating housing but at meeting other needs. Depending on the individual, this could include establishing a stable source of income, working through a crisis in personal relationships, or finding day care for children. Help in finding permanent housing could involve a combination of housing counseling, transportation, help in meeting landlords or housing authorities and completing applications, budget planning, and help in locating appropriate vacancies. A cost-effective effort of this sort would pay for itself in reduced shelter operating costs and capital cost-savings due to the reduced need for shelter space.

For those homeless needing prolonged rehabilitative or developmental services, the goal of reintegrating them with society will be harder to reach. In addition to help directed at remedying deficits such as illiteracy or alcohol and drug abuse, these efforts must involve counseling and close, temporary supervision designed to reverse behavior patterns that evolved as an adaptation to homelessness but would only produce rejection by employers or landlords.

In any case, a sizable fraction of the homeless population will continue to be homeless until they are given some kind of sheltered living arrangement. Institutional confinement may not be necessary. For most, it implies congregate or other sheltered services. For some, it may mean an independent, self-maintained residence with continuous close monitoring by others. One likely source of new insights on sheltered living arrangements for these homeless is a joint effort by HUD and the Robert Wood Johnson Foundation, begun in 1986, aimed at providing rental housing assistance, strengthening the system of community mental health services, better coordinating these with other city services, and purchasing and/or rehabilitating properties suitable for the chronically mentally ill who are homeless (Redburn and Buss, 1986).

If the prospect of meeting custodial care needs seems remote in an era of fiscal constraint, it is important to recognize the spending that is associated with the present situation, in which many of the aging and disabled homeless spend an increasing proportion of their existence in and out of hospital emergency rooms and out-patient facilities and claim a disproportionate share of attention from the staff of emergency shelters not designed to accommodate this range of needs. The true cost of homelessness is much greater than expenditures on shelter and soup lines would indicate.

UNACCEPTABLE ALTERNATIVES

Frustration with the inadequacy of present efforts to aid the homeless has led some to advance ideas that, if implemented, might do more harm than good. The idea that new laws are needed to protect some homeless from themselves threatens the civil liberties of many others. Another bad idea, the government sanctioning of cheap substandard housing would mean the abandonment of the long-held goal of bringing housing to one minimum standard.

In 1985, the politics of homelessness shifted toward questions of compulsion and rights. Issues being debated were whether cities, such as New York, could forcibly remove homeless people from the streets on cold nights on the presumption that they were incompetent to look after their own best interests; and whether homeless people with psychiatric disorders should be institutionalized against their will on the grounds that they were a danger to themselves. Both raise constitutional issues and run counter to the trend of judicial opinion in recent decades (Mitchell, 1986).

Forced Sheltering

New York City's policy of forced sheltering illustrates the first of these issues (see PBS, "MacNeil/Lehrer News Hour," December 23, 1985). When the wind-chill factor falls below 32° F, homeless people without a source of shelter and apparently disoriented are to be taken to public hospitals for psychiatric evaluation and forced into shelters. Those so detained are released the next morning.

The moral argument for such a policy has been captured by Charles Krauthammer:

There is a reason for forcibly removing the homeless mentally ill from streets: not society's fear of what the homeless are doing to us, but concern about what they are doing, cannot help doing, to themselves. In a society that aspires to be not only free but humane, removing the homeless mentally ill should be an act not of self-defense but of compassion. (1985: 104)

However, pressures on local officials from interests such as businesses and residents might lead them to expand the scope of a forced-removal policy to include other people under other circumstances.

A case against forced removal has been presented by the New York City chapter of the American Civil Liberties Union (ACLU). The ACLU argues both legal and practical considerations in protecting the homeless from forced sheltering by the state (see PBS, "McNeil/Lehrer News Hour," December 23, 1985). Although the ACLU accepts the legal right of the state to provide protective care for those who are mentally incompetent, it cannot accept the lack of due process of law. Under U.S. law, depriving a person of rights for protective purposes requires that the person be represented by counsel before a court. There are no exceptions. The ACLU argues that the homeless do not give up their rights but have all of the rights guaranteed to any citizen. To this argument Krauthammer responds:

Liberty counts for much, but not enough to turn away from those who are hopelessly overwhelmed by the demands of modern life. To permit those who flounder even in the slowest land to fend for themselves on very mean streets is an act not of social liberality but of neglect bordering on cruelty. In the name of a liberty that illness does not allow them to enjoy, we have condemned the homeless mentally ill to die with their rights on. (1985: 104)

To which another participant in this debate replies:

The law means well. All laws mean well. The authors of the Constitution, whatever else may be said of them, had a hearty distrust of guys... going about doing good. The freedom not to be carted off by cops without a specific warrant, or the presence of a crime, is an important freedom. It should not be fiddled with simply because in some rare case it might be a good thing. (Mitchell, 1986: 132)

Reinstitutionalization

At present, most states allow involuntary civil commitment only if an individual can be demonstrated to be "potentially dangerous" to himself or others. In practice this requires that objectively verifiable criteria be used before commitment is ordered. Usually, the criteria err on the side of noncommitment when difficult cases are encountered. Critics of deinstitutionalization would like to see the standards for commitment relaxed so that many of the homeless mentally ill could be moved "off the streets... and back in facilities designed for people in their condition" (Perkins, 1985).

The pendulum has recently begun to swing back in favor of looser commitment standards, a situation prevalent before the 1970s. The American Psychiatric Association's new model law (Holden, 1985), for example, proposes that states reject the "potentially dangerous" criterion and replace it with the concept of "significant deterioration" or "grave disability." This alternate concept focuses on whether the person is capable of tending to his or her physical needs rather than on potential dangerousness. It might also permit institutionalization of people who were not yet, but likely to become, gravely disabled. In addition to shifting the grounds for institutionalization, this broader standard would place decisions regarding commitment much more in the hands of the medical rather than the legal community.

Like the issue of forced shelter, the movement to broaden the grounds for institutionalization has implications not only for the homeless but for the rights of other citizens.

The "potential danger" criterion came into use because of concern generated by flagrant rights abuses occurring in the commitment of people to mental hospitals. Individuals often were not afforded due process under the law, including the right to counsel, to receive treatment, and to expect some limited duration of stay. Moreover, some viewed the typical mental hospital not as a place for rehabilitating people but as a warehouse for stockpiling them, often for an indefinite period. The criterion of "potential danger" forced the judicial system to commit only the most severe and unambiguous cases to the hospital system; and, once they were there, forced operators to provide some minimal treatment.

Those now favoring broader criteria have argued that the stricter standards are forcing people onto the streets who are dangerous—if not at the time of their commitment hearing, then later. Once there, they say, most of these people not only do not receive treatment but they are a source of danger and disturbance. In December 1985, for example, CBS reported that a woman was unable to have her daughter committed to an institution despite the fact that she had been diagnosed as schizophrenic and for several years was living on the streets of New York as a "bag lady." The daughter continues to live alone on the streets, tormented by internal voices that give her no peace. The conclusion that some draw from cases like this is that the standards for commitment are too loose and that too many people who should be institutionalized are harming themselves and others.

Civil libertarians counter that these are isolated cases (Holden, 1985) and that no one knows for certain or can readily determine the likelihood that an individual will be in danger if left free. Turning the arguments of those who favor a looser standard against them, civil libertarians have responded that if the current strict standards for commitment cannot sort out those who need or do not need treatment, then looser standards will suffer from same inexactitude. As with forced sheltering, the potential for broader harm seems to outweigh any possible benefits to the homeless mentally ill or others.

Shacks

Drawing a lesson from the squatters' camps of poorer nations, some (Burns, 1986) have proposed the legislation of such encampments or at least "turn a blind eye to building- and occupancy-code violations." This would provide a relatively cheap solution to housing problems that represent the failure of public housing programs.

This modest proposal is not unlike that pursued in many Third World countries. "In the developing nations, the key to unlocking the latent energies of the homeless was the discovery that prevailing views about squatters were substantially incorrect. Instead of the rascals and radicals that they were presumed to be, they were simply poor people, bewildered by the complexities of urban life. Given the opportunity, they had substantial potential for upward mobility (Burns, 1986)." Resistance to this idea is likely from "public servants whose job it is to make and enforce codes." Burns notes that one federal public housing official, asked why American Indians "had to be housed at prevailing, middle-class standards when relaxed standards would have produced housing for more families," responded: "We don't want to be accused of building second-class housing for second-class citizens." Burns's answer to this is: "Do it we must."

It would be easier to dismiss this idea as one having no application to the United States if there were no examples of government involvement in creating second-class housing for the homeless. However, in New York, where the average stay in the public shelter system has reached 11 months (Crystal and Goldstein, 1984) and where individuals and families may remain indefinitely in welfare hotels that are physically inadequate and dangerous, government is already deeply involved. Besides the direct harm done by holding people in such facilities, this fails to achieve the goal of providing everyone with housing that meets the same basic standards. Society has fallen short of this goal, but it should not be so easily abandoned.

The bad ideas have a common thread: they all view the homeless as being in a special category to which the usual protections and standards of treatment do not apply. This is a dangerous strain of thinking that could harm not just the homeless but many others.

RESPONSIBILITY

Fashioning an effective response to homelessness is a shared responsibility of local, state, and federal government and of the private nonprofit services sector. A response that is locally designed and administered stands a better chance of addressing problems in that locality. On the other hand, the very uneven geographic distribution of the homeless population and variations in local capacity and interest suggest a role for higher levels of government. In addition to providing financial support for impacted localities, the state and federal levels of government can support policy innovation. Given the fiscal constraints on action at the federal level, the states may be in a better position to sponsor innovative programs and their evaluation.

At the community level, an effective response will require new mechanisms to coordinate services for the homeless. Coordination responsibilities probably should not rest with a single shelter or service agency, since each deals with an unrepresentative fraction of the homeless population and may hold a specialized professional perspective. Given their highly successful performance in administering a portion of the Federal Emergency Management Administration emergency food and shelter program and its tradition of coordinating a diverse group of services at the community level, local United Ways may be the appropriate forum within which to organize a coordinated services response to homelessness. Two agencies that have played major parts in helping the homeless, the Salvation Army and the Red Cross, are generally under the United Way umbrella. Public welfare agencies and community mental health centers also must play a coordinating role if a coherent system of services is to be created.

Centralization of responsibility at the local level is a virtual prerequisite for the establishment of effective procedures. These procedures should include a comprehensive individual needs analysis and continuous tracking of service provision and its results. Since many of the homeless have multiple-service needs, the timing and delivery of help by various agencies should be centrally managed. Since this is a highly mobile population both within and between communities, shelters and other providers must be prepared to share information about their clients, given the clients' informed consent. Since the homeless frequently cross jurisdictional boundaries, state governments should authorize and encourage the exchange of information across localities.

States should lead in creating a coordinated system of services for the homeless at the community level. States also should sponsor and support demonstration efforts to meet the differentiated needs of the homeless, including prevention programs, crisis care and counseling, developmental services for those on public assistance, and an array of in-community custodial care arrangements. These demonstrations should be carefully evaluated and the best ones used as models for permanent state or federally funded programs.

CONCLUSION

If the American public accepts the creation of a permanent massive shelter system as the main response to homelessness, then it accepts also the permanence of a large population with no place to call home. A society that accepts this as a solution accepts its failure to develop effective approaches to prevention, its abandonment of reintegration as a goal for most of the homeless who need special help to live independently, and its failure to create new permanent custodial settings for those who have been debilitated by poverty and life on the streets.

NOTE

1. The Ohio study was funded by the National Institute of Mental Health, grant no. 1R18, MH 38877–01 to the Office of Program Evaluation and Research, Ohio Department of Mental Health. Dee Roth served as principal investigator on the project.

REFERENCES

Bachrach, Leona L. 1984. The Homeless Mentally Ill and Mental Health Services. In *The Homeless Mentally Ill*, edited by H. Lamb. Washington, D.C.: American Psychiatric Association.

Burns, Leland S. 1986. Third-World Models for Helping U.S. Homeless. *Wall Street Journal* (January 2): 32.

Crystal, S., and M. Goldstein. 1984. *Correlates of Shelter and Utilization*. New York: Human Resources Administration.

Freeman, Richard B., and Brian Hall. 1986. *Permanent Homeless in America*. Cambridge, Mass.: National Bureau of Economic Research.

General Accounting Office. 1985. *Homelessness*. Washington, D.C.: GAO.

Holden, Constance. 1985. Broader Commitment Laws Sought. *Science* 230: 1253–55.

Housing and Urban Development, U.S. Department of. 1984. *Homeless and Emergency Shelter*. Washington, D.C.: HUD.

Kasinitz, Philip. 1984. Gentrification and the Homeless. *Urban and Social Change Review* 17: 9–14.

Krauthammer, Charles. 1985. When Liberty Means Neglect. *Time*, December 2, 103–104.

Lamb, H. R. 1984. *The Homeless Mentally Ill*. Washington, D.C.: American Psychiatric Association.

Mitchell, Henry. 1986. Cold Facts About Our Civil Rights. *Washington Post*, January 3: B2.

Perkins, Joseph. 1985. New Institutions for the Homeless. *Wall Street Journal*, February 26: 33.

Redburn, F. Stevens, and Terry F. Buss. 1986. *Responding to America's Homeless*. New York: Praeger.

———. 1987. Beyond Shelter: The Homeless in the USA. *Cities*, February: 63–69.

Roth, Dee, et al. 1985. *Homelessness in Ohio*. Columbus, Ohio: Ohio Department of Mental Health.

U.S. Conference of Mayors. 1986. *The Growth of Hunger and Homelessness and Poverty in America's Cities*. Washington, D.C.: U.S. Conference of Mayors.

11

No Place to Go: A National Picture of Homelessness in America

Jamshid A. Momeni

The number of homeless in the United States in the 1950s was estimated at about 100,000 (Bogue, 1963). Since the early 1980s, however, homelessness has become a major and growing social and public health problem in the country. The estimate of the total number of homeless runs anywhere between 250,000 and 3.5 million. And, according to the U.S. Department of Housing and Urban Development (1989) the number of shelters grew by 190 percent between 1984 and 1988; the total number of shelter beds increased by 180 percent. As pointed out by Kozol (1989), the problem has grown so much that the American Institute of Architects is discussing "shelter architecture" for the homeless. As accurately indicated by Kozol (1989), we are now observing the evolution of new vocabularies and terminologies such as "shelter management," "homeless law," "shelter medicine," and "shelter residents." In Arizona, shelters are organized in terms of "Tier I" (short-term), "Tier II" (6–12 months), and "Tier III" (long-term) shelters for the purpose of housing a host of homeless persons ranging from transients to the long-term permanently homeless, respectively. The shelter residents are described as "guests" or "clients." "Transitional shelters" rather than housing are being built. A couple of regularly published periodicals dealing with the homeless issue (e.g., *Safety Network*) have also appeared. We even have the 1987 Stewart B. McKinney Act (or Law) providing financial aids to the shelters. Privately owned homeless hotels and motels have mushroomed in the major cities. Washington, D.C., and New York City have several such hotels and motels. While shelters are becoming the low-income housing of the 1980s, homeless hotels and motels are replacing the traditional hotels with Single-Room Occupancy units. Shelters represent an area with major growth in housing for poor people. Nationwide, the number of shelters grew from 1,900 in 1984 to 5,400 in 1988, and the total bed capacity for these shelters grew from 100,000 to 275,000, respectively (U.S. Department of Housing and Urban Development, 1989). Or, according to Kozol (1989), in New York City, for example, "every year since 1982, the city has undergone a loss of 14,000 units (houses or apartments) that poor people can afford. In the same years, the city has built a shelter empire holding 28,000 men, women and children . . . "

With its visible appearance on the streets, there has been a growing debate about the magnitude of homelessness. While conservatives have attempted to downplay its size, social activists, liberals, and democrats have tended to play up the problem and have viewed it as a national tragedy with dire consequences for society. While the debate has continued unabated, the most fundamental information, a reliable estimate of the total number of the homeless population, remains as yet unavailable. Largely as a result of differing views on the subject and its magnitude, the estimates of the size of the homeless population have varied greatly. The range is so wide that it would provide no useful information for policymakers, planners, or public agencies to deal with the problem. As a result, and in the absence of reliable data, the different perspectives on homelessness have hampered any genuine effort to help the neediest sector in society.

However, there has been a growing awareness of the issue which has led Congress to try to appropriate emergency funds to be disbursed through the states, local, and national board. But this is to be regarded only as a temporary measure. Any long-term planning requires more accurate information about the magnitude of the problem as well as its causes and consequences.

OBJECTIVES

The upper and lower limits of the size of the homeless population are given by two opposing groups, namely, the CCNV (Community for Creative Nonviolence, a homeless advocacy group) and HUD. Given the emotionally loaded and political nature of the problem, these groups, with competing views, have even exchanged verbal and legal assaults with one another. In view of the existing controversy the main objective of this chapter is to examine the following questions, if possible, both from empirical and theoretical points of view: (a) how is homelessness conceptualized? (b) how many homeless are there and who are they? (c) what are the major causes of homelessness? (d) how important is the role of mental illness and deinstitutionalization as a cause of the new wave in homelessness? (e) what proportion of the homeless are families? (f) how important are the economic factors and inability to obtain affordable housing in contributing to homelessness? and finally, (g) what has been done or is being done about it?

DATA AND METHODOLOGY

Because of financial resources and time constraints, this investigator had to resort to an innovative method of collecting the data. A one-page letter was sent to three groups: (1) Mayors of cities with a population of 40,000 or more. The January 1987 directory of *The Mayors of America's Principal Cities*, U.S. Conference of Mayors, was used to select the mayors; (2) the 50 state governors; and, (3) the U.S. senators—two from each state. About 1,200 letters were sent out, and the contents were uniform. The introductory paragraph contained a brief and simple statement of the problem and how important it was to collect the information. The letter went on to request statistical data, copies of publications, comments, or any and all information available regarding the extent, the nature, and the composition of the homeless population in the respondent's jurisdiction. Nearly 50 percent of the United States senators, all except five state governors, and about 30 percent of the mayors responded to the inquiry. As a result, this investigator received a large number of reports, publications, and comments contained in the respondents' letters.

METHOD

Given the volume and the diversity of the information collected, content analysis technique is used to summarize the data. At first an attempt was made to provide a state-by-state analysis of the massive amount of data collected. As the analysis progressed, however, it was realized that there were significant degrees of similarities in the reports from different states. Thus, it was decided that the analysis should concentrate on summarizing the major and *substantive* issues.

Conceptualization of the Problem

The current literature on homelessness, for being a "young" literature, bears the mark of lacking consensus on the most fundamental conceptual issue of defining homelessness. A cursory examination of the literature reveals that there is an array of definitions, ambiguities, and variations in conceptualizing the problem. This was also quite evident from the communications and the literature received from the respondents. The communications clearly show the lack of the basic guideline of who should or should not be defined as homeless.

Thus, a major problem in studying the homeless is the absence of a clear conceptualization of the issue. Rossi et al. (1986: 21) contend that "homelessness is not an all-or-none binary condition, but a continuum. Consequently, it is easy to achieve agreement on the extremes of the range from homed to homeless, but there is much disagreement on where the boundaries between the homed and the homeless should be placed. Homelessness is a condition that describes persons who do not have customary and regular access to a conventional dwelling, mainly those who do not rent or own a conventional dwelling.'' Even Rossi et al., in their study of homelessness in Chicago, used different definitions in different phases of their research. For example, in Phase I those under age 18 were counted among the homeless, while in Phase II no such age limitation was set if minors were unaccompanied by their parents (or guardians). Inconsistencies and ambiguities in definitions have led to varied interpretations. The problem in arriving at a reliable estimate of the number and characteristics of the homeless population has to do with different methods of conceptualizing homelessness. What is homelessness? How should it be defined? Should it include the homeless-vulnerable (or near homeless) population? Should it include minors not accompanied by parents or guardians? Should it include women and children who temporarily leave their homes as a result of family violence? Should it include runaway youth? Some of the runaway youth come from rich and well-to-do families; they are on the street not as a result of lack of affordable housing but as a result of poor, or lack of, communication with their parents. Obviously, a homeless person is one without a residence.

In a 1984 report, U.S. Department of Housing and Urban Development defined a homeless person as one who spends the night in public or private emergency shelters which take a variety of forms such as armories, schools, churches, government buildings, former firehouses, and where temporary vouchers are provided by public and private agencies, even hotels, apartments, or boarding homes. Included in the definition are those who spend nights on the streets, parks, subways, bus terminals, railroad stations, airports, under bridges or aqueducts, abandoned buildings, cars, trucks, or any other public or private space that is not designed for shelter (U.S. HUD, 1984: 291). Should the definition include persons who are staying with friends or families or who can afford to rent a hotel room on a temporary basis? In Arkansas the homeless are defined as ''those persons who are poor and without traditional or permanent housing, i.e. transients, abused elderly/children/spouses, persons with severe and/or persistent mental illness and run-away youth.'' In Connecticut, ''the definition of homeless constitutes those individuals who are in need of permanent dwelling. They can be either families or individuals. This family or individual should have resided within the city limits for a minimum of sixty (60) days before being determined homeless.''

In some states, the homeless are defined as the people on the street who, in seeking shelter, have no alternative but to obtain shelter from a private or public agency. Others simply define homelessness as the condition when the person/families do not have their own place to live in. Yet others view them as ''those people who hang around downtown and go through the rubbish cans.''

Some take a broader view and feel it should also include people who are evicted or have left their families because of difficulties. Still others define homelessness as being without shelter, but this definition reduces the seriousness of the issue and excludes a number of people deprived of ''homes.'' Unfortunately, while these examples may be accurate in defining a certain type or category of the homeless population, they do not delineate its parameters. That is, the current definitions or classifications of the homeless are of limited use, because at one extreme the homeless are defined as those who have lost their *housing*.

At the other extreme, some have defined it with some theoretical paradigm in mind. For example, Ropers and Robertson (1984) indicate that the most important dimensions of homelessness are duration and cause of homelessness, leading them to develop three major groups of the homeless: (1) short term; (2) long term; and (3) episodic. A much broader definition is provided by Caplow, Bahr, and Sternberg (1966) who defined it as a "condition of detachment from society characterized by the absence of attenuation of the affiliative bonds that link settled persons to a network of interconnected social structure." In this definition "home" is used as the focal point with its connotations: warmth, emotional attachment, social relationships, and a sense of belonging. This is perhaps what is missing in the most narrowly perceived definitions of homelessness.

Expressing great dissatisfaction with the fuzzy and blurring lines separating different groups of homeless people, Rosenthal (1987: 232) proposes that "we look at three dimensions of homelessness: paths (and social roots), demographics and lifestyles, and barriers to escape." He argues that "paths are important to understand in order to develop preventive strategies; demographics and lifestyles to understand what sorts of services, particularly shelters, are needed; and barriers in order to design escape strategies." Judging from the review of reports received, it appears that those in vulnerable economic situations, upon receiving an economic jolt, in the absence of "social margins" (savings, relatives, extended family, friends, etc.) become homeless. Also, these reports clearly show the great importance of economic factors in homelessness. Lack of economic resources appears to be the most common denominator in homelessness. "All of the . . . interviewees had an *economic path* [emphasis mine] to homelessness, through rent hikes beyond their incomes, unemployment, low wages, or some combination thereof. When asked what the solutions to homelessness were, three quarters of the . . . group responded with economic solutions involving improving the affordable housing stock and providing higher wages and/or more jobs" (Rosenthal, 1987: 600). Friedland and Marotto (1985) in their *Streetpeople and Straightpeople in Santa Cruz, California*, a study of the downtown area, emphasize the importance of economic factors in causing homelessness. "The findings show that most streetpeople rely on food stamps and private food services to subsist, and that their most salient unmet needs are economic resources and housing."

TYPOLOGY

A common understanding of who the homeless are or how homelessness should be conceptualized is vital to policy development and planning. Such conceptualization may be brought about through a typology that takes into account the salient variables.

All definitions considered, it appears that economic factors, duration of homelessness, and displacement and degree of detachment from the family constitute the major ingredients for conceptualizing homelessness. Based on these dimensions, the following typology has been constructed to explain various categories of the homeless and its degree of severity. As emphasized earlier, on the one hand some definitions look at homelessness from a broad perspective and have application for responding to the needs of the homeless. On the other hand, some researchers believe that "just because these people are out on the street doesn't mean they need more services." It is hoped that this conceptual scheme will aid in developing a framework of classification that could help to define clearly the homeless categories so that researchers would begin from a common ground. The following typology may be used to put recommendations regarding homelessness in context, for building a model of homelessness is a first step in looking at the problem in more depth.

Based on the typology presented in Figure 11.1, we have identified eight categories of homeless/homeless vulnerable. Under "poor" economic conditions (categories I to IV), depending on duration and the nature of displacement/ disaffiliation, we have those who may or may not recover, those in serious trouble, and those most seriously in trouble of becoming homeless. Under the "not poor" economic condition, depending on duration and detachment, there are another four homeless categories with the possibility of becoming homeless *permanently*. This typology, discussed later, shows the great importance of economic factor as the root cause of homelessness.

SIZE

Depending on how homelessness is conceptualized, one may arrive at different sizes for the homeless population. As discussed in the opening paragraph, the size of the homeless population runs between 250,000 (estimated by the U.S. Department of Housing and Urban Development in 1984) and 3.5 million (estimated by activist Mitch Snyder, director of CCNV [Community for Creative Nonviolence]). It is difficult to cut through the extensive controversy and political rhetoric regarding the true size of the homeless population. However, it is now quite obvious that neither HUD's estimate nor the activists' estimates are accurate reflections of the true size of the homeless population in the United States in 1989. According to Rep. Charles Schumer (D-N.Y.), chairman of the Ad Hoc Task Force on the Homeless and Housing: "On any given night there are 750,000 homeless people in the United States and by the end of this year [1988] between 1.3 and 2 million people in the country will have experienced homelessness. It is hardly just a very small number any more" (Committee on the Budget, House of Representatives, 1989). A 1988 study by the Urban Institute, a nonpartisan

Figure 11.1
Typology of Various Categories of the Homeless Population

Duration	Displacement/ Detachment	Economic Condition	
		Poor	**Not Poor**
Temporary	Minimum	I: May Recover	V: Not Serious
Temporary	Extensive	II: May Not Recover	VI: Least Serious
Permanent	Minimum	III: Serious	VII: May Pull Out
Permanent	Extensive	IV: Most Serious	VIII: May Become Serious

research organization in Washington, D.C., estimated that there were 600,000 homeless (Burt, 1988).

Based on the interview data determining the proportion of time the homeless remain on the street to the amount spent in shelters, some researchers have developed a multiplier to determine the total number of homeless. For instance, the total number of homeless persons was estimated from a count of homeless sleeping in shelters by applying a multiplier to this count. The multiplier was constructed by HUD (1984) in studies of Boston and Baltimore where both the homeless in the shelters and those on the streets were counted. The multiplier was computed as the ratio between the two counts. Freeman and Hall (1987) in a study of 500 randomly selected homeless persons in New York City concluded that there were 3.23 homeless persons for every homeless person using a shelter. Accordingly, if there were an accurate count of the shelter users, we could use the multiplier to determine the size of the homeless population. The problem is that we do not even have an accurate count of the shelter users on any given

night, nor do we know whether the multiplier 3.23 based on data from New
York City can hold true for the rest of the country. However, according to a
new report by the U.S. Department of Housing and Urban Development (1989),
the national shelter-bed inventory had grown to 275,000 in 1988. But HUD's
report contends that "on an average night in 1988, the Nation's homeless shelters
were, collectively, operating at 66 percent capacity." That is, on an average
night, only 181,500 of the beds were occupied. Applying the above multiplier
to the number of occupied shelter beds reported by HUD, there were an estimated
586,245 homeless in the nation in 1988. Homeless advocates have already taken
"issue with HUD's decision to calculate occupancy rates for shelters at a time
of year when fewest people seek shelter assistance. In August and early September, when the survey was conducted, homeless people in many areas eschew
shelters and sleep outdoors or in their cars. Occupancy rates in shelters are
generally higher in winter [especially in January], shelter providers report"
(National Coalition for the Homeless, 1989: 4).

   Some studies and reports clearly support the advocates' argument. "In the
last fiscal year [1988], 40,000 people—many of them forced out of their homes
by rising rents—were given emergency shelter in Maryland, and 30,000 requests
were turned down for lack of space, the state commission said" (Levy, 1989:
B7). The data released by the Maryland Department of Human Resources (Levy,
1989: B7) for four Maryland counties in the vicinity of Washington, D.C., for
FY 1988 shown below, clearly support the advocates' argument.

County	Number Sheltered	Unfilled Requests for Shelter
Montgomery	4,213	4,200
Prince George's	4,583	5,153
Anne Arundel	2,569	2,212
Howard	520	973

   The homeless problem in general and the question of unfilled requests for
shelter during wintertime is not in any way unique to Maryland. Reports from
several other states also indicate that during the cold season not only were the
existing shelters filled to capacity but many who requested shelter were either
turned down or the authorities had to direct them into public buildings to prevent
them from freezing to death. Accordingly, the argument against HUD's decision
to measure the occupancy rate in August and September is quite plausible; it is
during wintertime that shelters operate at a much more representative capacity.
The above figures for four Maryland counties clearly contradict HUD's finding
of 66 percent occupancy rate in the nation's shelters. If this is true, then by
applying the multiplier we arrive at an estimate of 888,250 homeless during the
peak wintertime in 1988.

   As of 1987, there were 37 metropolitan areas of 1 million or more population

(Level A); 94 metropolitan areas with a population of 250,000 to 999,999 (Level B); 125 metropolitan areas with a population of 100,000 to 249,999 (Level C); and 25 metropolitan areas with a population under 100,000 (Level D). Based on the content analysis of data collected in this study, the significant majority of the homeless are in the A and B level metropolitan areas, in some of which the proportion of homeless may be as high as 8 percent of the population. On the other hand, in smaller metropolitan areas (e.g., levels C and D), the proportion of homeless may be as low as 0.1 percent of the population. On the average, based on calculations not shown here, the content analysis of the data reveals that there are 3 to 5 homeless for every 1,000 people in the United States. Assuming a total population of 245 million in 1987, there were between 735,000 and 1,225,000 homeless in the United States. There are of course differentials by regions and city size. Our data also show states with mild climates tend to have a higher homeless population. Despite the fact that this estimate is somewhat less than the 1 percent-of-the-total population figure given by the advocates for the homeless, it is higher than the findings by Burt (1988) of the Urban Institute. In order to provide empirical justification for the above estimate we take a closer look at California, the harbinger of homelessness in the nation.

HOMELESSNESS IN CALIFORNIA

In order to demonstrate the validity of the above estimate, I have chosen to discuss homelessness in California in greater detail. California, the largest state in the union, with a 1984 population of 25 million, and its particular geographic, socioeconomic, and climatic conditions, may be considered as a state conducive to homelessness. Yet "the Department of Housing and Community Development (HCD) estimates [California's] homeless population to be between 50,000 and 75,000" (Camp, 1986: 1). This means 2 to 3 homeless persons for every 1,000 residents. Others have placed the total number of California's homeless population at 75,000 to 100,000. If we consider this extreme estimate as the true figure, given its population of nearly 25 million in 1989 it means 3 to 5 homeless for every 1,000 residents. The data for some of California's populated counties and cities are summarized in Table 11.1.

As the data in Table 11.1 show, there is a significant variation in the number of homeless persons per 1,000 residents. The rate of homelessness ranges between a low of 0.3 (Kings County) to a high of 33.2 (Mendocino County) per 1,000. But the average is about 5 per 1,000. In 1984 the California Homeless Coalition put the total number of homeless for the state as a whole at 50,000 to 90,000. Today, the estimates run to about 100,000. Given California's total population of about 25 million in 1989, it is clear that even in California there are less than 5 homeless persons per 1,000. California is one of the few states in the union known to have a large number of homeless people. When averaged for the nation as a whole the rate is certainly less than 5 homeless per 1,000.

Table 11.1
Number of Homeless Persons, Population Size, and Homeless Rate for Selected California Counties/Cities

Location	No. of Homeless	Population	No. of Homeless Per 1,000 Population
Berkeley	125	103,479	1.2
Contra Costa Co.	2,250	745,000	3.0
El Dorado Co.	1,000	113,800	8.8
Fresno Co.	9,176	597,400	15.4
Imperial Co.	2,521	109,500	23.0
Kings Co.	25	87,400	0.3
La Mesa	248	52,000	4.8
Los Angeles Co.	35,000	8,504,500	4.1
Marin Co.	3,000	227,700	13.2
Mendocino Co.	2,500	74,900	33.4
Monterey Co.	4,500	343,100	13.1
Oxnard	150	115,657	1.3
Pasadena	1,000	128,000	7.8
Redding	530	41,995	2.2
Sacramento	1,200	288,597	4.2
San Diego (City)	3,000	915,956	3.3
San Diego Co.	5,000	1,861,846	2.7
San Francisco	4,500	691,637	6.5
San Mateo Co.	6,000	587,329	10.2
Total	**81,725**	**15,589,796**	**5.2**

Source: Various reports received from respective jurisdictions. These reports are available upon request.

This study shows that the actual figure is anywhere between 3 to 5 persons per 1,000 (or, 0.3 to 0.5 percent).

Homeless Families

In California, as in the rest of the nation, homeless families represent the fastest-growing segment of the homeless population. The main reasons for this are twofold: (1) a cutback in the federally subsidized housing units; and (2) the increasing difficulty in qualifying for AFDC funds. According to some reports, in Los Angeles, there was a 50 percent increase in the demand for emergency shelters in 1986 and some 30 percent increase in the number of homeless families with children. These reports also point at significant increases in the number of homeless youth and recent Hispanic immigrants among the homeless in Los Angeles. In San Diego, it is estimated that women and children constitute about 15–25 percent of the homeless population.

DEMOGRAPHICS

An examination of the demographic characteristics of the homeless population clearly defy the typical notion of the homeless. The homeless of the 1980s, often referred to as the "new" homeless, do not fit the stereotype of middle-aged alcoholic and mentally ill men. Our analyses show that throughout the nation today's homeless are primarily unemployed/underemployed single men and women of *all* ages, minorities, immigrants, families, abused or deserted women often with young children, elderly pensioners, runaway or throwaway teenagers, and of course some chronically mentally ill persons. To illustrate the heterogeneous composition of the new homeless, a study of 3,169 homeless persons in Orange County, California, found 1,176 (37 percent) were children. About 39 percent were female; 47.5 percent of the males were reported as being single (Orange County Coalition for the Homeless, 1985: 3). Leonard (1984) examining the demographic characteristics of the people in need of emergency shelter in San Francisco, found that they were 78 percent male, 22 percent female; the mean age was 33.4 years (with median age of 31.4 years); 52 percent of the homeless were white, 28 percent were black, 11 percent were Hispanic, Asians and American Indians constituted 5 percent of the sample, and the ethnicity of the remaining 5 percent was unknown. Relative to marital status, Leonard (1984) reported 69 percent were single, 7 percent married, 22 percent widowed, divorced, or separated. According to the recent HUD report (1989), the racial/ethnic composition of the sheltered homeless was: 42 percent white (non-Hispanic), 44 percent black, 10 percent Hispanic, 2 percent American Indian, 1 percent Asian, and one percent "other."

Causes of Homelessness

There are striking similarities in the stated causes of homelessness throughout the 50 states. The causes of homelessness (those not homeless by choice) are multiple and broad in scope, some of which do not lend themselves to easy fixes. The most commonly cited causes are:

Housing shortage. Shortage of affordable housing for low-income families and persons is a major cause of homelessness. Hartman et al. (1982) estimate that 2.5 million people are involuntarily displaced from their homes annually. Most of them do find substitute housing. Yet a significant number cannot find affordable substitute units. Of the many factors that may be involved, financial strain is the overriding cause of securing housing. The recent increase in the number of homeless families is said to be primarily a function of this factor.

The decrease in the number of low-income housing units in the 1980s has been said to be the primary cause of homelessness. In San Francisco, the low-income housing stock declined significantly since 1980. Those on the list of assisted housing normally have to wait two and one-half years. The rental vacancy rate is less than 1 percent in San Francisco, and there has been a 20 percent increase in the number of homeless families with children. As a result of increasing demand for emergency shelters, San Francisco city authorities, with the support of Mayor Dianne Feinstein, has placed high priority on providing permanent housing for the homeless families with children who have been living in hotels and motels by placing them in the renovated units and paying for their moving expenses or by providing various services to children of homeless families. According to Levy (1989) in Montgomery County, Maryland, "five years ago, most of the homeless in this region were indigent men . . . Now, moderate-income families are being squeezed out of the rental market and onto the streets in dramatically increasing numbers, the state Housing Policy Commission said in its annual report to the Maryland General Assembly."

Deinstitutionalization of the mentally ill. This is a traditional reason, but no longer the main one. Deinstitutionalization, the movement to reduce sharply the number of state hospital beds across the nation, began about 30 years ago.

At the time, mental health professionals had convinced one another that *new psychoactive* medications and advance treatment techniques would permit local treatment when possible and would provide prevention as well as early intervention services, including brief hospitalization only when absolutely necessary. It was believed that that would almost eliminate the need for long-term confinement of mentally ill in state hospitals far from their own families and communities . . . The combined federal and state compaign to encourage deinstitutionalization was very successful. In the nation as a whole, state hospital beds dropped from 535,000 in 1960 to 137,000 in 1980. (Leavitt, 1984)

According to Leavitt (1984) in San Francisco "deinstitutionalization leaped ahead when President Reagan was governor (1966–1974), primarily because of the potential for state financial savings." Based on data presented by Leavitt, in 1960 when California's population numbered 16 million, there were 37,000 hospital beds for the mentally ill. By 1983 when California's population had increased to 24 million, instead of the expected 55,000 hospital beds there were only 5,000. Leavitt (1984) claims that about 10 percent of the mentally ill not occupying state hospital beds are on the streets. The analyses of the data collected through this study show that some researchers as well as service providers disagree with the problem being caused by deinstitutionalization, for its effect should have been felt 10 to 15 years ago. They maintain that its effect has diminished substantially over the years.

In addition to the increasing number of homeless families with children, Ropers and Robertson (1985) identified four groups of "new" homeless in Los Angeles: Vietnam veterans, the frail elderly, young "throwaways" [as opposed to willing "runaways"], and nonagricultural migrants.

The large-scale institutional discharge took place in the 1960s—nearly two decades ago. But homelessness, never as visible on the streets as today, has emerged as a public issue in the 1980s, extensively covered by the media, discussed in various political fora, and a subject picked up by advocates and activists. This mushrooming growth in homelessness cannot be attributed to deinstitutionalization.

A small proportion of the respondents and/or reports received indicated that some mentally ill patients benefited from deinstitutionalization by moving to community-based facilities, but the majority believed that it was poorly implemented. This has caused some mentally ill to join the rank of the homeless wandering the streets of America. However, the homeless mentally ill account for no more than 20–30 percent of the homeless in the United States today: the myth that mental illness is the principal cause of homelessness is simply not true. Today's homeless are not limited to mentally ill persons, as some believe.

Unemployment and underemployment. Lack of steady job (or income), inability to work (disability, presence of very young children, and fear of being deported in the case of illegal immigrants) are also partially responsible for the surge in the homeless population.

Lack of resources such as savings, skills, and training.

Substance addiction. Alcohol and drugs play a part in causing the mushrooming growth or the 1980s wave of homelessness. Drug abusers and alcoholics, once evicted, find it harder to get back into a normal life for they easily deteriorated under those conditions. However, some reports indicate that others, once on the streets, developed drug-abuse problems as a mechanism to cope with the problem. Drug problems may be thus both the cause and the consequence of homelessness.

Family violence. Family violence is a serious social problem occurring in almost every socioeconomic class. Every year millions of American women and children are involved in such violence. Although most battered women suffer in silence, an increasing number leave their homes to avoid the violence. Reports received from almost every city or state point at family violence and disintegration of the nuclear family as factors leading to homelessness. According to the U.S. Bureau of the Census (1986), the divorce rate in the United States increased from 0.22 percent of the population annually in 1960 to 0.52 percent of the population in 1980. Family violence, like any other factor with social roots, is due to the breakdown of traditional family norms and values. Commenting on the breakdown of social structures and social relationships, homeless advocates Hombs and Snyder (1983) state: "We no longer offer charity to the 'village idiot,' take our mother or uncle into our home with much frequency, or maintain relationships that are not working."

One great consequence of this breakdown in family relationships has been that the housed members of a family are hardly concerned about any member who is homeless—the homeless cannot rely on their family members to save them from becoming homeless by taking them into their homes. For some, the loss of an income-producing mate and increase in personal crisis resulting from family violence leads to homelessness.

Along with increases in family violence and break ups, there has been an increase in the number of runaway/throwaway children. According to Cuomo (1983), annually, an estimated 350,000 children who leave home have no place to go—they are homeless.

Cuts in public assistance programs. The increasing cuts in public assistance and the stringent new criteria to meet the eligibility requirements for public assistance has also contributed to the recent wave in homelessness.

Urban renewal. Urban renewal, often cited as a primary cause of homelessness, in some areas has resulted in a 60 percent reduction in the low-income residential hotel rooms in the past decade.

Rent escalation. Increases in rent have forced the very low income out of the rental market. Eviction for the lack of rent may lead to homelessness. A study by the United Community Services of Metropolitan Detroit concluded that after eviction by a landlord, the main reason for homelessness was the "inability to continue staying with friends or relatives" (*Safety Network*, 1984).

Curiosity about alternative lifestyles, or voluntary homelessness. Although the reliable data are not available, it is believed that this factor accounts only for a small proportion of the homeless population.

"Problems of homelessness are a phenomenon of the changes taking place in American society which have left many individuals without family or community support systems which have sustained them in the past. For this reason the problem must be viewed as defying immediate solution but is one which commands community-wide effort over a long period of time" (*A Report: The Phoenix Homeless*, 1985: 6). The debate over the "individual" versus "social" causes of homelessness lurks below the surface of many communications and reports received and literature reviewed. The U.S. General Accounting Office (1985) in a survey of literature ranked the factors contributing to homelessness by their frequency in the literature as: (1) increased unemployment; (2) deinstitutionalization of the mentally ill and the lack of available community-based services for the mentally ill; (3) increases in personal crises; (4) cuts in public assistance programs; (5) declines in the availability of low-income housing; and, (6) alcohol/drug abuse problems. Of these six most frequently cited causes of homelessness, only two (increases in personal crises and alcohol/drug abuse problems, which rank 3 and 6, respectively) may be considered as "individual" causes of homelessness. The remaining four factors point at social causes of homelessness. Those who emphasize the social causes of homelessness argue that in the 1980s the size of the homeless population at least tripled—from 100,000 in the 1950s (Bogue, 1963) to 200,000 in the late 1970s (Larew, 1980), to its current size, estimated to be between 750,000 and 1,250,000 according to this study. This tripling or quadrupling of the number of homeless after two decades of small growth and manageable numbers is seen to be due to major social changes or having social roots. Rosenthal (1987: 600) argues that there is an economic path to homelessness and that "these economic paths to homelessness reflect underlying social processes which affect far greater numbers of people than just the homeless. The homeless are merely the most visible victims of social trends, often the results of deliberate political decisions, which have rendered the lives of the poor that much more precarious in the 1980s." Rosenthal (1987: 601) further argues that "the conditions of being homeless are perpetuated by the social conditions homeless people *live under*, and the *effects* those conditions have on them."

SOME GENERAL OBSERVATIONS

As a result of examining the data, three general observations emerge: (1) about 80 percent of all respondents indicated that there is insufficient information about the size and the nature of homelessness in their communities or jurisdictions; (2) the homeless population has significantly increased in the 1980s and it continues to grow; (3) roughly, for every one homeless man seeking shelter there are two homeless women with children under 18; (4) the majority of the homeless population suffers from poor health; (5) the average age of today's homeless population is lower than the average age of the stereotypical homeless; (6) the homeless population is larger than most people expect in their community. There is a large segment that is not known to human service or government agencies; (7) the homeless population is quite diverse; (8) there is a segment of the homeless population considered chronically mentally ill: homelessness can also affect one's mental health; (9) the number of homeless children has increased significantly (this is in conjunction with an increase in the number of homeless females—especially single-parent females); and, (10) the number of homeless families has increased. Subgroups of the homeless population include: (a) transients—temporary residents who are job seeking, or street nomads; (b) mentally disabled—deinstitutionalized mentally ill persons unable to cope with society's demands; (c) substance abusers who are victims of crimes and committers of crimes (a major subpopulation); (d) the voluntary homeless—those who voluntarily choose homelessness as a life-style (this group may include juvenile runaways, social dropouts, and a criminal element that preys upon other homeless people; programs must concentrate on the teenagers who are easily victimized); and, (e) vagrants—aggressive persons who live on the streets primarily by illegal means.

DISCUSSION

Based on our discussion of conceptualization of the problem, economic factors are the major factors causing and perpetuating homelessness. It is a common denominator for all categories of homelessness. Thus, an improvement in the economic condition of the poor will help to reduce homelessness.

The effect of economic factors could be either direct or indirect. Even the *disaffiliation* (long-standing attentuation of social ties) theory advanced by Bahr (1969, 1970, 1973) and Bahr and Caplow (1973) is said to have economics as its precipitating factor.

The displacement theory set forth by some researchers and advocates (Ropers and Robertson, 1984; Cleghorn, 1984; and Hombs and Snyder, 1983) is also based on the argument that homelessness is a result of shifts in economic structure that have marginalized people beyond their control. Anderson (1961), Bogue (1963), Hombs and Snyder (1983), Cleghorn (1983), and Ropers and Robertson (1984) argue that homelessness is primarily caused by the economic factors that marginalize people and render them poor and homeless through social processes largely beyond their control.

A related concept is echoed by Goffman (1963), Wiseman (1970), and Segal et al. (1977), who speak of "social margin," referring to all resources and ties an individual can draw on in times of need. According to these researchers, homelessness results when the individual has exhausted his or her social margins—that is, he or she has no resources and ties to draw on to survive in society. The concept of "social margin" and "disaffiliation" are very similar in the sense that both emphasize the individual's pulling away from social ties. But clearly the latter concept implies a much lesser degree of internal psychological process than the former. Rosenthal (1987), in his study of homelessness in Santa Barbara, California, examined different explanatory theories of homelessness. He found that the predictive powers of disaffiliation, displacement, and social margin theories were 25 percent, 62.5 percent, and 33.3 percent, respectively. He concluded that

for many of the homeless, the typical path is a displacement through economic factors, followed by a period of homelessness or near homelessness in which one's social margin may be gradually used up, and ending with, for some proportion of the homeless, a reactive disaffiliation from a world which seems to have first abandoned them. (Rosenthal, 1987: 605)

However, Rosenthal (1987) is quite cognizant of the fact that disaffiliation, displacement, and social margin, the three stages in homelessness, "are not normally discrete, but *interactive*. A limited previous social margin leads to a greater impact of a [sic] economic event which potentially leads to displacement. Economic displacement leads to a lessening of the resources one has to trade in maintaining social margin. The shock of displacement leads to disaffiliation." Rosenthal (1987: 611) continues to argue that: "while the loss of social margin and the weight of economic dislocation are formidable barriers to overcome in order to escape homelessness, neither is even possible when disaffiliation sets in" (Rosenthal, 1987: 611). That is, once disaffiliation is established, income alone may not be the whole story. The conditions under which the homeless leave tend to perpetuate their conditions. The wealth of data I have collected and waded through also suggest that economic factors are most important in determining the extent and duration of homelessness.

Accordingly, "homelessness seems to generally be the result of economic displacement affecting people with few resources and little social margin . . . After some time being homeless, disaffiliation is likely to set in to varying degrees if there are not strong ties to the straight world, including jobs, children, partners, or a strong network of friends or relatives" (Rosenthal, 1987: 612).

Given the ambiguities regarding various definitions of homelessness, there is a definite need for developing a generally acceptable standard definition of the homeless. Such definitions are needed to identify those who do (or do not) qualify for public assistance. Such definitions are also needed for proper conceptualization of the problem as well as developing a standard measure of homelessness throughout the country.

It is not the size of the homeless population or the lack of funds to deal with the problem that has attracted so much public attention. Rather, it is the change in the composition of the homeless, from the stereotypical image of alcoholic, skid-row derelicts to single men and women, women with children, men with children, and intact families who have no place to go. These new homeless are primarily victims of poverty and unemployment rather than mental illness.

A more serious aspect of the problem is the fact that the 1980s wave of homelessness has not taken place at a time when the national economy is experiencing recession, but has occurred during a period when the economy has experienced upward growth. The implications of this observation are that current homelessness cannot be regarded as a temporary displacement of the poor at the bottom of the economic strata. The problem appears to be permanent and is expected to grow worse if there is an economic recession.

Furthermore, long-term policies must be developed to deal with the problem. The current temporary and curative (as opposed to preventive) methods of dealing with the problem may prove ineffective and very costly in the long run. The services provided by the voluntary organizations, advocates, activists, churches, and social service agencies, do provide short-term humanitarian solutions to the problem, but these services will not and cannot take the place of a long-term national policy to eradicate this national disgrace of a million homeless wandering throughout the country.

The nationwide approach to dealing with the homeless problem has been to concentrate efforts at the community level. Each community must identify its problems and the kind of services that it can provide. The private sector has played and should continue to play a major role. The federal and state governments must cooperate and facilitate the community efforts and provide some funds to deal with the problem.

The federal policy must be to approach the problem from a preventive rather than a curative point of view: attempts must be made to prevent people from running the risk of becoming homeless rather than merely trying to deal with the problem. This may be achieved by developing long-term policies of helping the indigent in areas where private-sector and community-based organizations cannot be of much help. For example, the federal government must require and encourage developers to allocate a certain proportion of units built for low-income groups.

ACKNOWLEDGMENTS

Many of the U.S. senators, state governors, and mayors of cities with a population of 40,000 or more, to whom I wrote requesting data on homelessness in their respective jurisdictions, responded enthusiastically. The contents of this chapter is primarily based on the data received. For this, I am truly indebted to everyone who responded to my inquiry. Due to a lack of space and the long list of contributors, however, I am unable to acknowledge their contributions individually.

REFERENCES

A Report: The Phoenix Homeless. 1985. Phoenix, Ariz.: City of Phoenix.

Anderson, Nels. 1961. *The Hobo: The Sociology of the Homeless Man.* Chicago: Phoenix Books.

Bahr, Howard. 1969. *Homeless and Disaffiliation.* New York: Bureau of Applied Research, Columbia University.

———. 1970. *Disaffiliated Man: Essays and Bibliography on Skid Row, Vagrancy and Outsiders.* Toronto, Canada: University of Toronto Press.

———. 1973. *Skid Road: An Introduction to Disaffiliation.* New York: Oxford University Press.

Bahr, Howard, and Theodore Caplow. 1973. *Old Men Drunk and Sober.* New York: New York University Press.

Bogue, Donald. 1963. *Skid Row in American Cities.* Chicago: University of Chicago Press.

Burt, Martha. 1988. *Projections of Our Estimate of Service Using Homeless People in U.S. Cities of 100,000 or More to All Homeless People in the United States.* Washington, D.C.: Urban Institute. Unpublished manuscript.

Camp, C. Catherine. 1986. *Report of the CSAC Homeless Task Force.* Monterey County, California.

Caplow, Theodore, Howard Bahr, and David Sternberg. 1966. Homelessness. *International Encyclopedia of the Social Sciences*, edited by David L. Sills. Vol. 6. New York: Crowell, Collier, and McMillan.

Chun, Paula, and David Takeuchi. 1983. *The Homeless in Hawaii: A Preliminary Study.* Honolulu, Hawaii: Health and Community Services Council of Hawaii.

Cleghorn, James S. 1983. *Residents Without Residence: A Study of Homelessness in Birmingham, Alabama.* Unpublished master's thesis. University of Alabama, Birmingham.

Committee on the Budget, House of Representatives. 1989. *Homelessness During Winter 1988–89: Prospects for Change.* Washington, D.C.: Government Printing Office.

Cuomo, Mario. 1983. *1933/1983—Never Again: A Report to the National Governor's Association Task Force on the Homeless.* Albany, N.Y.: State of New York.

Freeman, Richard B., and Brian Hall. 1987. *Permanent Homelessness in America Today?*

Cambridge, Mass.: National Bureau of Economic Research, Working Paper No. 21013.

Freidland, William H., and Robert A. Marotto. 1985. *Streetpeople and Straightpeople in Santa Cruz, California: A Report of the Downtown Study*. Unpublished Manuscript. University of California, Santa Cruz, Division of Social Sciences.

Goffman, Irving. 1963. *Stigma: Notes on the Management of Spoiled Identity*. Englewood Cliffs, N.J.: Prentice-Hall.

Hartman, Chester, et al. 1982. *Displacement: How to Fight it*. Berkeley, Calif.: National Housing Law Project.

Hombs, Mary Ellen, and Mitch Snyder. 1983. *Homelessness in America: A Forced March to Nowhere*. Washington, D.C.: Community for Creative Non-Violence.

Kozol, Jonathan. 1989. Here Comes Shelter Chic: We Need Homes for the Poor, Not an Empire of Poorhouses. *Washington Post* (April 2): C5.

Larew, Barbara I. 1980. Strange Strangers: Serving Transients. *Social Case Work* 61 (2): 107.

Leavitt, Alan. 1984. *The Impact of Deinstitutionalization in Ten San Francisco–Bay Area Counties*. San Francisco Community Mental Health Services.

Leonard, Donald. 1984. *Demographics* [of the Homeless in San Francisco]. San Francisco, Calif.: Office of the Mayor.

Levy, Claudia. 1989. Maryland's Homeless Increasingly Moderate-Income Families. *Washington Post* (April 18): B1, B7.

National Coalition for the Homeless. 1989. New HUD Report: Dramatic Increase in Homeless Families, Low Shelter Occupancy. *Safety Network* 8 (4): 1–4.

Orange County Coalition for the Homeless. 1985. *Survey of Shelter Needed and Shelter Provided*. Balboa, Calif.: Report of the Orange County Coalition for the Homeless, 1985.

Ropers, Richard, and Marjorie Robertson. 1984. *The Inner-City Homeless of Los Angeles*. Los Angeles: School of Public Health, UCLA.

Rosenthal, Robert. 1987. *Homeless in Paradise: A Map of the Terrain*. University of California, Santa Barbara, Unpublished Ph.D. dissertation.

Segal, Steven P., et al. 1977. Falling Through the Cracks: Mental Disorder and Social Margin in a Young Vagrant Population. *Social Problems* 24 (3): 387–400.

U.S. Bureau of the Census, U.S. Department of Commerce. 1983. *1980 Census of Housing (Santa Barbara-Santa Maria-Lompoc SMSA)*. Washington, D.C.: GPO.

———. 1986. *Statistical Abstract of the United States*. Washington, D.C.: Government Printing Office.

U.S. Department of Housing and Urban Development. 1984. *A Report to the Secretary on the Homeless and Emergency Shelters*. Washington, D.C.: HUD, Office of Policy Development and Research.

———. 1989. *A Report on the 1988 National Survey of Shelters for the Homeless*. Washington, D.C.: HUD, Office of Policy Development and Research, Division of Policy Studies.

U.S. General Accounting Office. 1985. *Homelessness: A Complex Problem and the Federal Response*. GAO-HDR 85–40. Washington, D.C.: General Accounting Office.

Wiseman, Jacqueline P. 1970. *Stations of the Lost: The Treatment of Skid Row Alcoholics*. Englewood Cliffs, N.J.: Prentice-Hall.

Select Bibliography

Adams, Carolyn Teich. 1986. Homelessness in the Postindustrial City: Views from London and Philadelphia. *Urban Affairs Quarterly* 21 (4): 527–549.

Alter, Jonathan. 1984. Homeless in America. *Newsweek* (January 20): 20–29.

Anderson, Nels. 1923. *The Hobo: The Sociology of the Homeless Man.* Chicago: University of Chicago Press.

Appleby, Lawrence, and Prakash Desai. 1985. Documenting the Relationship Between Homelessness and Psychiatric Hospitalization. *Hospital and Community Psychiatry* 36 (7): 732–737.

Arce, Anthony A., et al. 1983. A Psychiatric Profile of Street People Admitted to an Emergency Shelter. *Hospital and Community Psychiatry* 34 (9): 812–817.

Bachrach, Leona L. 1984. Interpreting Research on the Homeless Mentally Ill: Some Caveats. *Hospital and Community Psychiatry* 35 (9): 914–917.

Bahr, Howard M. 1968. *Homeless and Disaffiliation.* New York: Columbia University Press.

————. 1969. Family Size and Stability as Antecedents of Homelessness and Excessive Drinking. *Journal of Marriage and the Family* 31 (3): 477–483.

————. 1969. Lifetime Affiliation Patterns of Early and Late Onset Heavy Drinkers on Skid Row. *Quarterly Journal of Studies on Alcohol* 30 (3): 645–656.

Bahr, Howard M., and Kathleen C. Houts. 1971. Can You Trust a Homeless Man? A Comparison of Official Records and Interview Responses by Bowery Men. *Public Opinion Quarterly* 35: 374–382.

Ball, F. L., and B. E. Havassy. 1984. A Survey of the Problems and Needs of Homeless Consumers of Acute Psychiatric Services. *Hospital and Community Psychiatry* 35: 917–921.

Bassuk, Ellen L. 1984. The Homeless Problem. *Scientific American* 251: 40–45.

Bassuk, Ellen L., et al. 1984. Is Homelessness a Mental Health Problem? *American Journal of Psychiatry* 141 (December): 1546–1550.

Baumann, Donal J., et al. 1985. *The Austin Homeless: Final Report Provided to the Hogg Foundation for Mental Health.* Austin, Texas: Hogg Foundation for Mental Health.

Baxter, Ellen, and Kim Hopper. 1982. The New Mendicancy: Homelessness in New York City. *American Journal of Orthopsychiatry* 52: 393–408.

Bingham, Richard, Roy E. Green, and Sammis B. White, eds. 1987. *The Homeless Women and Children.* Newbury Park, Calif.: Sage.

Blumberg, Leonard, et al. 1970. The Skid Row Man and the Skid Row Status Community. *Quarterly Journal of Studies on Alcohol* 32: 909–941.

Bogue, Donald. 1963. *Skid Row in American Cities.* Chicago: Community and Family Study Center, University of Chicago.

Boston, City of. 1986. *Making Room: Comprehensive Policy for the Homeless.* Boston: Office of the Mayor.

Brown, Carl, et al. 1983. *The Homeless of Phoenix: Who Are They and What Should Be Done?* Phoenix: South Community Mental Health Center.

Caplow, Theodore. 1940. Transiency as a Cultural Pattern. *American Sociological Review* 5: 731–739.

Caplow, T., et al. 1968. Homelessness. *International Encyclopedia of the Social Sciences* 6: 494–499.

Cleghorn, James S. 1983. *Residents Without Residence: A Study of Homelessness in Birmingham, Alabama.* Unpublished master's thesis. University of Alabama, Birmingham.

Corrigan, Eileen, and Sandra C. Anderson. 1984. Homeless Alcoholic Women on Skid Row. *American Journal of Drug and Alcohol Abuse* 10 (4): 535–549.

Crystal, Stephen. 1984. Homeless Men and Homeless Women: The Gender Gap. *Urban and Social Change Review* 17: 2–6.

Cuoto, Richard A., et al. 1985. Healthcare and the Homeless of Nashville: Dealing With a Problem Without a Definition. *Urban Resources* 2 (2): 17–23.

Erickson, Jon, and Charles Wilhelm, eds. 1986. *Housing the Homeless.* New Brunswick, N.J.: Rutgers University, Center for Urban Policy Research.

Fadiman, Anne. 1987. A Week in the Life of a Homeless Family. *Life* (December): 31–36.

Fischer, Pamela J., et al. 1986. Mental Health and Social Characteristics of the Homeless: A Survey of Mission Users. *American Journal of Public Health* 76 (5): 519–524.

Freeman, Richard B., and Brian Hall. 1987. *Permanent Homelessness in America Today?* Cambridge, Mass.: National Bureau of Economic Research, Working Paper No. 2013.

Gist, Richard M., and Quintin B. Welch. 1986. *Estimates of Period Prevalence of Homelessness in Kansas City, Missouri, 1985. Report No. 27.* Kansas City, Mo.: Missouri Health Department, Office of Health Research and Analysis.

Governor's Task Force on the Homeless. 1983. *Report of the Governor's Task Force on the Homeless.* Trenton, N.J.: New Jersey Department of Human Services.

Green, Laura L. 1986. *Task Force on Homelessness: Final Report of Findings and Recommendations.* Nashville: Metropolitan Development and Housing Agency.

Hartman, Chester. 1987. The Housing Part of the Homelessness Problem. In *The Mental*

Health Needs of Homeless Persons, edited by Ellen Bassuk. San Francisco, Calif.: Jossey-Bass.

Hombs, Mary Ellen, and Mitch Snyder. 1982. *Homeless in America: A Forced March Nowhere*. Washington, D.C.: The Community for Creative Nonviolence.

Hope, Marjorie, and James Young. 1986. *The Faces of Homelessness*. Lexington, Mass.: Lexington Books.

Hopper, Kim. 1984. Whose Lives Are These Anyway? *Urban and Social Change Review* 17 (Summer): 12–13.

Hopper, Kim, and Jill Hamberg. 1984. *The Making of America's Homeless*. New York: Community Service Society.

――――. 1986. The Making of America's Homeless: From Skid Row to New Poor. In *Critical Perspectives on Housing*, edited by Rachel Bratt, et al. Philadelphia: Temple University Press.

Hopper, Kim, Ezra Susser, and Sara Conover. 1985. Economies of Market Shift: Deindustrialization and Homelessness in New York City. *Urban Anthropology* 14 (1–3): 183–236.

Hughes, H. 1986. Research With Children in Shelters: Implications for Clinical Services. *Children Today* (March/April): 1–25.

Kasinitz, Philip. 1984. Gentrification and Homelessness: The Single Room Occupant and the Inner City Revival. *Urban and Social Change Review* 17 (1): 9–14.

Kozol, Jonathan. 1988. *Rachel and Her Children*. New York: Crown Publishers.

Lamb, H. Richard. 1984. Deinstitutionalization and the Homeless Mentally Ill. *Hospital and Community Psychiatry* 35: 899–907.

――――, ed. 1984. *The Homeless Mentally Ill*. Washington, D.C.: American Psychiatric Association.

Lamb, H. Richard, and J. A. Talbott. The Homeless Mentally Ill: The Prospective of the American Psychiatric Association. *Journal of the American Medical Association* 256: 496–501.

Layzer, J., B. Gordon, and C. DeLange. 1986. Children in Shelters. *Children Today* (March/April): 6–11.

Lee, Barrett A. 1978. Residential Mobility on Skid Row: Disaffiliation, Powerlessness and Decision Making. *Demography* 15: 285–300.

Levine, Irene S. 1984. Homelessness: Its Implications for Mental Health Policy and Practice. *Psychological Rehabilitation Journal* 13 (1): 6–16.

Levine, Irene S., and C. Kennedy. 1985. The Homeless Mentally Ill: A Consultation Challenge. *Consultation: An International Journal* 4: 52–63.

Levine, Irene S., and James W. Stockdill. 1986. Mentally Ill and Homeless: A National Problem. In *Treating the Homeless: Urban Psychiatry's Challenge*, edited by B. Jones. Washington, D.C.: American Psychiatric Association Press.

Levinson, B. M. 1957. The Socioeconomic Status, Intelligence and Psychiatric Pattern of Native-born White Homeless Men. *Journal of Genetic Psychology* 91: 205–211.

――――. 1963. The Homeless Man: A Psychological Enigma. *Mental Hygiene* 44 (4): 590–601.

Lieutenant Governor's Task Force on Homelessness. *Homelessness in Missouri*. Jefferson City, Mo.: Office of Lieutenant Governor Harriet Woods.

Lipton, Frank, et al. 1983. Down and Out in the City: The Homeless Mentally Ill. *Hospital and Community Psychiatry* 34: 817–821.

Locke, H. J. 1935. Unemployed Men in Chicago Shelters. *Sociology and Social Research* 19: 420–428.

Marcuse, Peter. 1987. Why Are They Homeless? *The Nation* (April 4): 426–429.

Marin, P. 1987. Helping and Hating the Homeless: The Struggle at the Margins of America. *Harpers Magazine* (January): 39–47.

Maurin, J., and L. S. Russell. 1987. *Homelessness in Utah: Utah Homeless Survey Final Report.* Salt Lake City, Utah: The Task Force for Appropriate Treatment of the Homeless Mentally Ill.

Milburn, Norweeta G., and Roderick J. Watts. 1985. Methodological Issues in Research on the Homeless and Homeless Mentally Ill. *International Journal of Mental Health* 14 (4): 42–60.

Momeni, Jamshid A., ed. 1989. *Homelessness in the United States: Volume I, State Surveys.* Westport, Conn.: Greenwood Press.

Morse, Gary, et al. 1985. *Homeless People in St. Louis: A Mental Health Program Evaluation.* Jefferson City: Missouri Department of Mental Health.

Morse, Gary, and Robert J. Calsyn. 1985. Mentally Disturbed Homeless People in St. Louis: Needy, Willing, but Underserved. *International Journal of Mental Health* 14 (4): 74–94.

New York, City of. 1987. *Toward a Comprehensive Policy on Homelessness.* New York: Mayor's Advisory Task Force on the Homeless.

Phillips, M. et al. 1988. Homeless Families: Services Make a Difference. *Social Casework: The Journal of Contemporary Social Work* 69: 48–53.

Piliavin, Irving, Michael Sosin, and Herb Westerfelt. 1987. Tracking the Homeless. *Focus* 10 (4, Winter 1987–1988): 20–25.

Redburn, F. Stevens, and Terry F. Buss. 1986. *Responding to America's Homeless: Public Policy Alternatives.* New York: Praeger Publishers.

Riordan, T. 1987. Housekeeping at HUD: Why the Homeless Problem Could Get Much, Much Worse. *Common Cause Magazine* (March/April): 26–31.

Robertson, M. J., and M. R. Cousineau. 1986. Health Status and Access to Health Services Among the Urban Homeless. *American Journal of Public Health* 76: 561–563.

Robertson, M., and M. Greenblatt, eds. 1987. *Homelessness: The National Perspective.* New York: Plenum.

Rooney, James. 1976. Friendship and Disaffiliation Among the Skid Row Population. *Journal of Gerontology* 31: 82–88.

Ropers, R., and Marjorie Robertson. 1984. *The Inner-City Homeless of Los Angeles: An Empirical Assessment.* Los Angeles: Los Angeles Basic Shelter Project.

Rossi, Peter H., et al. 1987. The Urban Homeless: Estimating Composition and Size. *Science* 235 (March): 1336–1341.

Roth, Dee, and G. J. Bean. 1986. New Perspectives on Homelessness: Findings From a Statewide Epidemiologic Study. *Hospital and Community Psychiatry* 37: 712–719.

Rubington, Earl. 1971. The Changing Skid Row Scene. *Quarterly Journal of Studies on Alcohol* 32: 123–135.

Schwab, Jim. 1986. Sheltering the Homeless. *Planning* (December): 24–27.

Segal, S. P., et al. 1977. Falling Through the Cracks: Mental Disorder and Social Margin in a Young Vagrant Population. *Social Problems* 24: 387–400.

Sexton, Patricia. 1986. Epidemic of Homelessness. *Dissent* (Spring): 137–140.

Siegal, Harvey, and James Inciardi. 1982. The Demise of Skid Row. *Society* (January): 39–45.

Snow, David A., et al. 1986. The Myth of Pervasive Mental Illness Among the Homeless. *Social Problems* 33 (5): 407–423.

Solenberger, Alice. 1911. *One Thousand Homeless Men*. New York: Russell Sage Foundation.

Stark, Louisa R., et al. 1985. Strangers in a Strange Land: The Chronically Mentally Ill Homeless. *International Journal of Mental Health* 14 (4): 95–111.

Stern, Mark J. 1984. The Emergence of the Homeless as a Public Problem. *Social Service Review* 58: 291–296.

Stoner, Madeline. 1984. An Analysis of Public and Private Sector Provisions for Homeless People. *Urban and Social Change Review* 17 (1): 3–8.

Sutherland, E. H., and H. J. Locke. 1936. *Twenty Thousand Homeless Men*. Chicago: J. B. Lippincott.

Tennessee Department of Human Services. 1986. *Problems of Homelessness in 91 Rural Counties*. Nashville, Tenn.: Tennessee Department of Human Services.

Tennessee Legislative Committee on the Homeless. 1987. *Study of Tennessee's Homeless Problem: Report on Findings and Recommendations*. Nashville, Tenn.: Tennessee General Assembly.

U.S. Conference of Mayors. 1985. *Health Care for the Homeless: A 40-City Review*. Washington, D.C.: U.S. Conference of Mayors.

U.S. Department of Housing and Urban Development. 1984. *A Report to the Secretary on the Homeless and Emergency Shelters*. Division of Policy Studies, Office of Policy Development and Research.

U.S. General Accounting Office. 1985. *Homelessness: A Complex Problem and the Federal Response*. Washington, D.C.: Government Printing Office.

Watson, Sophie. 1986. *Housing and Homelessness: A Feminist Perspective*. London: Routledge and Kegan Paul.

Wiegand, R. Bruce. 1985. Counting the Homeless. *American Demographics* 7: 34–37.

Wright, James D., and Julie A. Lam. 1987. Homelessness and the Low Income Housing Supply. *Social Policy* (Spring): 48–53.

Wynne, J. 1984. *Homeless Women in San Diego*. San Diego: County of San Diego, Department of Health Services, Alcohol Program.

Index

About the Contributors

RICHARD P. APPELBAUM is a professor and chair of the Department of Sociology at the University of California at Santa Barbara. He received a Ph.D. in sociology from the University of Chicago in 1971. Dr. Appelbaum has published extensively in the fields of social theory, urban sociology, and public policy, particularly in the areas of housing and homelessness. He is the author of three books and several scholarly journal articles. His work has received a chapter award from the American Planning Association and the Douglas McGregor Award for excellence in behavioral social research. Dr. Appelbaum consults and speaks extensively in the fields of low-income housing, homelessness, and the dynamics of urban growth. He has also testified before the Subcommittee on Housing of the U.S. House of Representatives.

JOAN BRACKMANN is a graduate of California State University, Hayward, and is currently pursuing graduate study in psychology at John F. Kennedy University in Orinda, California. Her areas of specialization are women's issues and homelessness among families.

MARTHA R. BURT is the director of social services research at the Urban Institute, Washington, D.C. She received a Ph.D. in sociology in 1972 from the University of Wisconsin at Madison, and is an expert in issues relative to homelessness and energy assistance, teen pregnancy and parenting, social services policy research, and evaluation. She has authored three books and several scholarly journal articles.

TERRY F. BUSS is director of the Center for Urban Studies at Youngstown State University. He has published seven books and numerous articles on public policy.

BARBARA E. COHEN is a research associate at the Urban Institute, Washington, D.C. She received a Ph.D. in social welfare and social policy from the Heller School of Brandeis University and a master's in public health from the University of North Carolina. As a researcher and nutritionist Dr. Cohen has worked on issues of homelessness, domestic hunger, teen parenting and employment programs, and runaway and homeless youth.

GERALD DALY is an associate professor of environmental studies at York University in Toronto, Canada. He has recently completed a year-long study of homelessness for the Canadian government and has published articles on the subject in several journals, including *Cities, Plan Canada*, and *Urban Geography*. He has also published articles on comparative planning and housing in a number of journals, including *Open House International* and the *Journal of Urban History*.

ELIZABETH D. HUTTMAN is a professor of sociology at California State University at Hayward and has written on housing for 20 years. She has written *Housing and Social Services for the Elderly*, coedited *Housing Needs and Policy Approaches*, and authored "Transitional Housing Policy" in *Home Environments*. She is also the coeditor of the *Handbook on Housing and the Built Environment* (1988), and coorganizer of the International Committee of Housing and the Built Environment.

ANTHONY C. KOUZI is presently a researcher on two federally funded AIDS and IVDU studies dealing with risk factors for HIV among drug users and the heterosexual transmission of AIDS at Narcotic and Drug Research, Inc., a state-affiliated, nonprofit organization in New York City. His interests in addition to the care of the chronically mentally ill in the community include substance abuse epidemiology, political economy, and public policy.

NORWEETA G. MILBURN is a senior research associate at the Institute of Urban Studies and Research, Howard University. She is the author of several articles and monographs on homelessness.

JAMSHID A. MOMENI is a professor at Howard University. He has written or edited nine books, several journal articles, and numerous scholarly book reviews.

SONJIA PARKER REDMOND is an assistant professor of sociology and social services at California State University, Hayward. She has been involved in social work and social work education for 20 years. She has written on the homeless mentally ill and cross-cultural issues affecting social service delivery.

R. BRUCE WIEGAND is on the faculty of the School of Studies of Justice, American University. He is the author of "Counting the Homeless."

JEFFREY C. WILSON is a staff psychiatrist at Mayview State Hospital and an assistant professor of psychiatry at the University of Pittsburgh, Western Psychiatric Institute and Clinic. He has completed a two-year NIMH postdoctoral training program at the University of Pittsburgh where he specialized in public policy and social and community psychiatry. Dr. Wilson's research activities have concentrated on the problems of homelessness and housing and community support for the mentally ill.